BIBLICAL PERSONALITIES
MORE THAN MEETS THE EYE

RABBI JESSE HORN

Published: June 2021

Copyright © Rabbi Jesse Horn
All rights reserved

ISBN 978-1-988022-71-0

AMUD
PUBLICATIONS

Published by **AMUD PUBLICATIONS**
For all your publishing and self-publishing needs in the Jewish market.
www.AmudPublications.com

Printed in Israel

Rabbi Hershel Schachter
24 Bennett Avenue
New York, New York 10033
(212) 795-0630

הרב צבי שכטר
ראש ישיבה ורמ״ כולל
ישיבת רבינו יצחק אלחנן

בס״ד

אלול תשמ״ד

מכתב ברכה –

כב' ידידינו הר״ר וש״ן מוכר הוא
דין הראשונים לפי שיעורו הראשונים,
אשר כבי דורי רלן (– הרבים שמים
כתיבין מסין) ענין רה נהג נהב נאמן
דלוה קמסורא התותח מאיר לפני ולא
עוד דהלגין חיקתי על כמה סוגיות
דגמ' – ע״ם ברב האמות והאמונ
בפשוט המקט וזמן מ״כה - היא
הכינים מאישות רחלוילון סוגיא
של. ולריכתה־שיוב לג לחוה־בהו
לא ברב רב ה רב – למובל תריך וליו איה
דהיה,

בברכ' שכטר

ישיבת הכתל
Yeshivat Hakotel
שע"י מרכז ישיבות בני עקיבא (ע"ר)

בס"ד עוד ...י ...

לעצם הענין

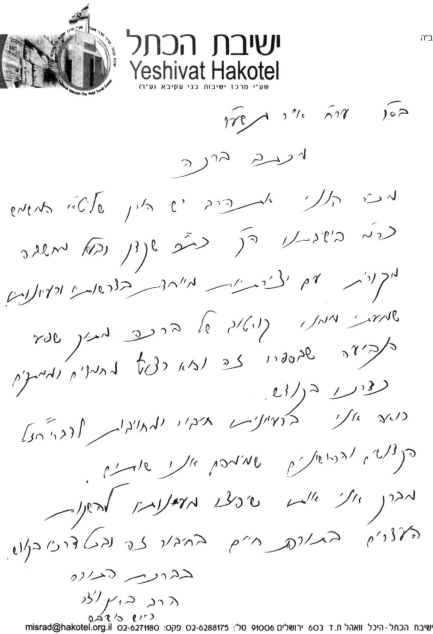

הרב ....
....

ישיבת הכתל - היכל וואהל ת.ד 603 ירושלים 91006 טל': 02-6288175 פקס: 02-6271180 misrad@hakotel.org.il

Yeshivat Hakotel - Hechal Wohl P.O.B 603 Jerusalem 91006 Tel: 02-6288175 Fax: 02-6271180 office@hakotel.org.il

אתר הישיבה: Website: www.hakotel.org.il

It brings me great joy to write Rabbi Jesse Horn a letter for his upcoming book. He is an excellent Rebbi who combines teaching Torah analytically while inspiring talmidim with Yiras Shamayim. He has successfully translated these goals into this sefer.

In additional to excellent analysis of Tanach on a Pshat level, he finds support in the words of Chazal for new ideas rooted in a traditional, Torah outlook. He successfully bridges the gap between Pshat and Drash offering new insights as part of a methodological approach to learning Tanach and Midrash.

I wish him continued success in his teaching of Torah and inspiring Klal Yisrael.

Reuven Taragin

INTRODUCTION

My primary goal in publishing this work is to teach Torah and increase Yiras Shamayim, both to educate and inspire, or simply put להגדיל תורה ולהאדירה — *to greaten Torah and glorify it.* However, these broad objectives can be broken down into several components.

The sefer's primary goal is to strengthen people's understanding of, and respect for Drash, ultimately facilitating greater faith in and deference for Chazal.[1] Every chapter attempts to bridge the gap between Pshat and Drash by offering textual insights and uncovering some of the deeper Pshat layers which support the Drash.

Often, Chazal reveal significantly more information[2] and insight to provide a fuller narrative than the Tanach itself does. This begs the obvious question, namely; from where did Chazal derive this additional information? There are two possible answers. First, that Chazal's statements come strictly from tradition. In other words, either Moshe received extra information at Har Sinai to pass on beyond what the Chumash says, or, after an event occurred, the character involved relayed particular information about it. For example, Avraham, after an incident transpired, shared details with Yitzhak that were not recorded in the Chumash. Yitzhak in turn transmitted them to Yaakov and so on through the tradition until it was ultimately documented by the Midrash. Perhaps this is how Chazal gathered information not communicated by the Tanach. Alternatively, Chazal, with their

---

[1] This too is a central component of Yiras Shamayim. When explaining the Mitzvah of fearing Hashem, the Gemara (Bechoros 6b, Kiddushin 57a, Baba Kamma 41a and Pesachim 22a) comments את לרבות תלמידי חכמים – *'Es' to include Talmiday Chochomim (in the Mitzvah of fearing Hashem).*

[2] Some narratives should be taken literally while others figuratively (Rambam's Introduction to Perek Chelek).

incredibly keen eye and penetrating perspective,[3] were able to read between the lines and derive more than meets the eye. If the latter is correct, my aspiration with this sefer is to begin scratching the surface of what they saw in the text itself. And, even if the first approach is correct and Chazal's statements are strictly based upon tradition, there is much to benefit from this sefer, for it illustrates how the text is not at odds with tradition.

In order to keep the reader's interest, several chapters open with a textual analysis and subsequently find support with Chazal's comments, rather than beginning the chapter with their statements and then attempting to explain them. Either way, the goal remains the same.

A second important goal is to demonstrate some of the depth found in Tanach even when concise texts are provided. By explaining why certain stories and information were recorded while others were omitted, and by uncovering textual clues, thematic[4] and linguistic[5] parallels, chiasms and many other devices the Tanach uses to deliver its message, I hope that readers will see and appreciate more of the Torah's profundity, especially on the Pshat level.

Furthermore, I hope to share insights into several classic Biblical characters' personalities.[6] However, attempting to identify these traits of the Biblical characters is also a means towards a greater end; namely, learning from and inculcating them into our own religious personal growth. It is precisely for this reason that each chapter concludes with a section titled *Applying Text to Life: The Hashkafic Message,* which is

---

[3] Although much of what Chazal say is hinted to in the text itself, much is not. Often their primary goal is teaching morals, values and other wisdom, as opposed to strictly interpreting the text.

[4] Regarding this style, I hope the parallels that I use are convincing enough and that the proof will be in the pudding. However, it should be noted (perhaps for the skeptics) that this type of analysis appears in many classic commentaries (Midrash Shemos Rabbah, Vilna Edition 1:32, Rashi on Bereshis 37:2, Ramban on Bereshis 12:10 to mention a few not used in the book).

[5] Here too (see the previous note) I hope the parallels that I use are convincing enough and the proof will be in the pudding. However, it should be noted again (perhaps again for the skeptics) that this type of analysis appears in many classic commentaries (Rashi on Bereshis 34:1, and 37:8 Rashbam on Bereshis 25:19, 26:5, and 37:8 Baal HaTurim on Bereshis 26:8, to mention a few not used in the book).

[6] Certainly the Biblical characters on which I focus are greater and more nuanced than any summary can capture. However, when writing Tanach, the Author did select certain episodes and information; therefore these observations and conclusions are based on the information chosen and on how Tanach presents the characters.

designed to clearly highlight some of the religious lessons from these episodes and their potential to contribute towards further improvement of Middos and Yiras Shamayim.

In addition to numerous statements by Chazal, there is a great wealth of remarks and thoughts of traditional commentaries included in this work, designed to serve as a resource for information, and answers to questions relating to the text or hashkafah. I tried very hard to satisfy those readers interested in the opinions of these commentaries as well. Often I use the footnotes to accomplish this particular goal.

A lot of work has been put into this book, and many thank yous are in order. Firstly, many thanks to everyone who help fund this book: Nora and Arthur Horn in memory of Chana Esther, Ann Bosnick and Chana Rivka, Anna Horn, Jon and Joyce Bendavid and Family in memory of our siblings Benny Bendavid and Aviva Bendavid, Judy and Barry Goldgrab, Rachel and Jason Cyrulnik, Daniella and Aaron Horn, Rav Eitan and Etta Bendavid, Daniel and Leah Bendavid, Rav Jared and Sarit Anstandig, Avi and Miriam Berman, Benjy Horowitz, Judy and Mordy Dubin, Noah Greenblatt, Ari and Elisheva Schiff, Kaufman family, Tali and Yossi Zimilover, Samara and Ami Younger, Yonasan and Mimi Caller, Avi and Dafna Lent, Elana and Josh Lipman, David and Naomi Bassan, Daniel Ross, David Kramer, Shimon and Etty Cohen, the Kahan family, Ashley Kanarek, Rafi and Tami Cohen and Leora and Harry Salter L'illui Nishmat Sara Rachel bas Asher.

Additionally, a big thank you to all who have made suggestions and helped with the editing: Arthur Horn, Nora Horn, Rachel Cyrulnik, Rabbi Aaron Horn, Jonathan Kazlow, Ben Rabinovitz, Gideon Schwartz, Coby Zwebner and a specific thank you should be given to Ezra Cohen who invested time and effort editing each chapter and offered excellent insights. Your hard work is greatly appreciated.

To my family: siblings and siblings-in-law, Mom and Dad, parents-in-law, my incredible children, Moshe, Eliana, Kayla, Akiva and Elisha, Yakira, Ariella and most importantly my wonderful wife Tara. Thank you so much for everything. Words do not and cannot describe my love and appreciation for you. Thank you for everything.

Contents

Yosef and Yehuda:
The Impact of Mechiras Yosef

The Placement of the Yehuda and Tamar Episode

The Yehuda and Tamar episode is filled with twists and turns, tragedy and serendipity. The story covers the events that occur to Yehuda after he separates from his brothers and starts a family of his own (Bereshis 38). Yet strangely, the entire episode is placed in the middle of another story, Yosef's descent to Egypt. The entire Yehuda and Tamar narrative conspicuously interrupts the Yosef narrative.

If we were to skip from the verse immediately before this interlude to the verse immediately afterward, there would be no gap in the narrative and nothing would seem amiss. To stress that this interruption is intentional, the Torah uses the exact same words both before and after the interval. The verse immediately before describes how Yosef is sold and taken down to Egypt **לְפוֹטִיפַר סְרִיס פַּרְעֹה שַׂר הַטַּבָּחִים** *to Potifar, Paroh's officer, chief executioner* (Bereshis 37:36), and the one immediately after continues right where it left off, with Yosef arriving in Egypt **וַיִּקְנֵהוּ פּוֹטִיפַר סְרִיס פַּרְעֹה שַׂר הַטַּבָּחִים** *and Potifar, Paroh's officer, chief executioner, bought him* (ibid 39:1). The Yehuda episode is deliberately located directly in the middle of the Yosef narrative. The obvious question is why?

The interlude cannot be chronological, as practically no time passes in the Yosef narrative while the story of Yehuda and Tamar spans many years.[7] The only viable explanation for this story's location, then,

---

[7]   Our narrative includes Yehuda getting married, fathering three sons, of whom the oldest,

is a thematic one. Placing the Yehuda and Tamar episode in the middle of Yosef's descent to Egypt must capture an important idea.

The Torah clearly links these stories together, by placing one inside the other, yet, at first glance, they seem completely unrelated. Methodologically, in order to understand the thematic connection, we will outline and then uncover the core theme of the Yehuda and Tamar episode. With that, we will be able to understand how the Torah's placement of these events reinforces this central theme.

SUMMARY OF THE YEHUDA AND TAMAR EPISODE

The story of Yehuda and Tamar begins with Yehuda leaving his brothers, befriending Chira, the Ish Adulami (Bereshis 38:1), and marrying the daughter of Shua (ibid 2). He then fathers three sons with her, first Er and Onan, and then Shelah, who is born while Yehuda is in Kziv (ibid 3-5).[8] Yehuda arranges Er's marriage to Tamar but Er is רַע בְּעֵינֵי יְקֹוָק *wicked in the eyes of Hashem*, and suffers an untimely death (ibid 6-7). Onan then marries Tamar to perform yibum, a mitzvah that requires him to marry the widow and father a child to perpetuate his deceased brother's legacy. However, Onan is unwilling to impregnate Tamar and ultimately suffers the same fate as Er. Fearful for Shelah's life, Yehuda bars Shelah from marrying and performing yibum with Tamar. Meanwhile, she waits faithfully and patiently (ibid 11).

Er, grows up, marries Tamar and then dies. Yehuda's second son, Onan, then marries Tamar and dies as well. After that, as the Torah notes, וַיִּרְבּוּ הַיָּמִים *a long time passed* (ibid 38:12) before Tamar orchestrates her yibum-like act. This entire saga certainly occurs over a time span significantly longer than the brief period during which Yosef is en-route to Egypt. Parenthetically, many of the commentaries (implied by the Ramban 38:7 and stated by the Seforno Bereshis 38:1 and Chizkuni Bereshis 38:1) argue that it occurs after the Mechiras Yosef, as ordered by Torah. The Chizkuni (ibid) even maintains that Yehuda leaves at that point because it is too difficult for him to witness Yaakov's pain. However, according to the Ibn Ezra (Bereshis 38:1), this narrative takes place before Mechiras Yosef yet it is located here to separate the Mechiras Yosef from the event with Eishes Potifar.

8   Seforno (Bereshis 38:5). However, according to the Rashbam (Bereshis 38:5) the whole family was in Kziv, not just Yehuda. The Ramban (Bereshis 38:5) quotes an opinion which clearly agrees with the Seforno. Er, as the first-born, is named by Yehuda, whereas Onan, the second born, is named by Bas Shua, Yehuda's wife. Now it is Yehuda's turn to name the third son; however, because Yehuda is in Kziv, Shelah is named by Yehuda's wife. Clearly, Yehuda alone went to Kziv, while his wife remains at home. Interestingly, the Malbim (Bereshis 38:2) agrees with the Rashbam, and adds that Yehuda takes Bas Shua to Kziv to get her away from her father and convert her.

With the passing of time and the death of Yehuda's wife, Yehuda and Chira return to the area to shear their sheep. Tamar, insistent on ensuring that a proper yibum is fulfilled, disguises herself as a harlot and seduces Yehuda[9] without him aware of who she is (ibid 14-15). As a payment for her services, she is entitled to a goat (ibid 17), yet in the interim, as collateral, Tamar requests and is given Yehuda's ring, cloak and staff (ibid 18). Yehuda subsequently sends Chira to deliver the goat to the harlot (Tamar), but by then she is nowhere to be found and the goat therefore cannot be delivered (ibid 20-22).

Three months later, it becomes evident that Tamar is pregnant and she is sentenced to be burned (ibid 24).[10] Just before her execution she announces that the owner of the ring, cloak and staff is the one with whom she was intimate. Upon recognizing the items, Yehuda confesses to his role in the affair publicly stating צָדְקָה מִמֶּנִּי *She is more righteous than I am* for לֹא נְתַתִּיהָ לְשֵׁלָה בְנִי *I did not give her Shelah, my son* (ibid 26). The sentence is reversed and the narrative concludes with Tamar giving birth to twins, Peretz and Zerach (ibid 29-30).

THE CENTRAL CHARACTER

Although Tamar's heroism features prominently, this story seems to be predominantly about Yehuda. In the first instance, the narrative opens by stating וַיֵּרֶד יְהוּדָה מֵאֵת אֶחָיו *And Yehuda went down from his*

---

[9]   Intimacy with a harlot is sinful (Ohr HaChaim on Bereshis 38:26). The Rabaynu Bachaya (Bereshis 38:26) adds that Yehuda's admission of צָדְקָה מִמֶּנִּי *She is more righteous than I am* (ibid 38:26) means that she intends to perform the mitzvah of yibum while Yehuda intends it לזמות *for harlotry*.

[10] There are several different explanations offered as to why Tamar faced capital punishment. According to the Midrash (Bereshis Rabbah, Vilna Edition 85:10 and quoted by Rashi Bereshis 38:24) she is the daughter of a Kohen, Shem. The Gur Aryeh (Bereshis 38:24) explains that Shem's Beis Din instituted that policy even for a penuyah *single girl* based upon the verse in Vayikra (21:9). The Rashbam (Bereshis 38:24) argues that this is the custom for all women designated for yibum, not just the daughters of Kohanim. Alternatively, according to the Ramban (Bereshis 38:24) the severe punishment is proportional to the immense dishonor she brings due to her status as Yehuda's daughter-in-law, or, the Ramban continues, the sentence is Yehuda's and this is his decision. Others (Rabaynu Yehuda HeChasid quoted by the Baal HaTurim Bereshis 38:24 and Ksav V'Kabbalah Bereshis 38:24) take a significantly different approach arguing that she is never actually sentenced to capital punishment. The burning is only a form of branding her for this sin of harlotry. Parenthetically, according to the Chizkuni (Bereshis 38:24), Yitzhak and Yaakov sit on the Beis Din which sentences her.

brothers (ibid 38:1). Moreover, as a member of the focal family in Sefer Bereshis, it stands to reason that the episode merits inclusion due to Yehuda's role in it. If the story would have happened with Tamar and another man it would have most likely been omitted, yet if it had taken place with Yehuda and another woman, it would have likely been included.

With this in mind, we can refine our study to focus on what the Torah specifically wishes to convey about Yehuda by including this episode.

YEHUDA'S ROLE

In the span of only a few verses, Yehuda suffers the loss of two sons and his wife. This tragedy is accompanied by deep religious shortcomings on Yehuda's part.[11] He withholds Shelah from Tamar for an extended period of time and selfishly ignores her needs and feelings, worrying only about himself.[12] Furthermore, he is in Kziv rather than at his wife's side when she gives birth (ibid 38:5). Yehuda selfishly prioritizes his own needs over his family's. This approach may have influenced Er and Onan (ibid 38:7-10), for they too prioritize themselves over family.

Later, both Yehuda's behavior and his situation improve drastically. Yehuda does teshuva *repents* by publicly exclaiming צָדְקָה מִמֶּנִּי *She is more righteous than I am* (ibid 38:26). Furthermore, Yehuda's family is rebuilt as Tamar gives birth to twins, Peretz and Zerach (ibid 38:29-30). The primary storyline is that of Yehuda's religious and emotional plunge and subsequent recovery.

---

[11] Not only does Yehuda sin, his motives are sinful as well (Meshech Chochoma Bereshis 37:26).

[12] Rashi (Bereshis 38:11 based on Bereshis Rabbah, Vilna Edition 85:5) adds that Yehuda believes that their deaths are somehow linked to marrying Tamar. The Ramban (Bereshis 38:11) disagrees with Rashi, arguing that Yehuda's fear is that Shelah would sin like his brothers, but it has nothing to do with Tamar.

THE MIRROR

There are several fascinating insights woven into this narrative that will help to further develop the Torah's message of Yehuda's fall and recovery.

The literary structure of this incident is particularly noteworthy. The episode is presented in an inverted, chiastic format, meaning that the two halves of the story mirror each other. Whatever occurs in the beginning; the opposite occurs in the end. After detailing this contrast, we will return to understand its significance.

1. In the first half of the chapter, Yehuda takes a wife, בַּת אִישׁ כְּנַעֲנִי וּשְׁמוֹ שׁוּעַ *the daughter of a Canaanite*[13] *man, whose name was Shua* (ibid 38:2) bringing her into his life and family. In the second half the opposite occurs as she dies (ibid 38:12), leaving Yehuda's life and family.

2. Similarly, Yehuda's two sons, Er and Onan, tragically die (ibid 38:7, 10)[14] which is the exact opposite of what occurs later when two new sons are born to him (ibid 38:27). Moreover, the Torah implies that Er and Onan die as a unit by describing Onan's death as וַיָּמֶת גַּם אֹתוֹ *And He (Hashem) put him to death **also*** (ibid 38:10), a perfect contrast with the arrival of two new-born sons who come in the most unitary possible way, twins.[15]

3. Initially, Yehuda cares only about himself, completely ignoring Tamar and her needs. He selfishly withholds his son, שֵׁלָה *Shelah,*

---

13   Informing us that she is a Canaanite is a subtle way of alluding to another one of Yehuda's mistakes, marrying a Canaanite woman (Emes L'Yaakov Bereshis 38:2). This assumes that כְּנַעֲנִי *Canaanite* here means from Canaan, (see Ibn Ezra on Bereshis 38:2 and 46:10), and not that she is a daughter of a merchant, as others (Targum Onkelus and Targum Yonason, Rashi, and Rashbam on Bereshis 38:2) assume.

14   In contrast to those who believe Er and Onan are punished for a particular sin (See Rashi Bereshis 38:7), the Netziv (Bereshis 38:7) argues that the Torah's omission of any specific sin indicates that they die for who they are, not what they do. They die because they are unworthy of having their children inherit kingship. The Torah emphasizes, וַיְהִי עֵר בְּכוֹר יְהוּדָה רַע בְּעֵינֵי יְקֹוָק *And it was that Yehuda's firstborn Er, was bad in the eyes of Hashem* being firstborn entitled him to kingship.

15   Interestingly, according to the Rabaynu Bachaya (Bereshis 38:1) and the Mei Sheloach (Parshas Vayeshev), Peretz and Zerach are reincarnated with Er and Onan's souls. Parenthetically, this follows the Ramchal (Derech Hashem 2:3:10) and Chofetz Chaim (Mishneh Brura 23:5) who subscribe to reincarnation. However, the existence of reincarnation is subject to debate as others reject it (Rav Saadah Gaon in Emunah V'Daos 5:3 and Rav Yosef Albo in Sefer HaIkarim 4:29).

from her even though she is entitled to his yibum, as his name שלה *Shelah,* which means *hers,* clearly conveys.[16] Yet at the end, the opposite occurs as Yehuda selflessly prioritizes Tamar over himself when he announces צָדְקָה מִמֶּנִּי *She is more righteous than I am* (ibid 38:26).[17] In the first section, Yehuda essentially ruins Tamar's life while in the second section, he restores it.

4. Onan, following in his older brother, Er's, ways,[18] acts selfishly[19] and dies as a result. By contrast, Peretz and Zerach survive precisely because of Yehuda's selfless declaration צָדְקָה מִמֶּנִּי *She is more righteous than I am* (ibid 38:26). Whereas selfishness causes Yehuda's first two sons to die, selflessness saves the last two.

5. In the first section, Tamar patiently waits unsuccessfully for yibum because Yehuda does not allow Shelah to perform yibum with her.

---

16   The source of Er's name is subject to debate. Several Midrashim (Bereshis Rabbah, Vilna Edition 85:4, Sechel Tov, Buber, Bereshis 38:3, Yalkut Shemoni Parshas Vayeshev) explain that it is an allusion to שהוער מן העולם *removed from the world.* Alternatively, another Midrash (Sechel Tov, Buber, Bereshis 46:12) points to a different root, ערירי שמת *that he dies without children.* The Ramban (Bereshis 38:3), before offering his own position, insightfully states that names in Tanach יורו על העתיד *predict the future.* At least sometimes, the names given are not what the people are actually called. Instead they are designed to capture something important about them, in this case his future. Then, the Ramban (ibid) suggests that the name Er comes from עוררה את גבורתך *arise your might* (Tehillim 80:3). Onan's name emanates from שהביא אנינה לעצמו *he brought a pre-mourning period on himself* (Bereshis Rabbah 85:4, Yalkut Shemoni on Parshas Vayeshev) or שהביא אנינה לעולם *he brought a pre-mourning period to the world* (Sechel Tov, Buber, Bereshis 38:3). Alternatively, the Ramban (ibid) raises the possibility that Yehuda's wife named him Er based upon the pain she experienced during child-birth.

17   The Ramban (Bereshis 38:26) and Rashbam (Bereshis 38:26) both read Yehuda's statement of צָדְקָה מִמֶּנִּי *She is more righteous than I am* to be one clause. According to the Rashbam, Yehuda confesses for not giving Tamar his son Shelah, and, according to the Ramban, for not doing the yibum himself, for he is obligated to do so after Shelah does not. However, Rashi (Bereshis 38:26) divides Yehuda's statement into two separate parts. צָדְקָה *She is righteous,* and מִמֶּנִּי *the baby is from me.*
Whether Yehuda and Tamar continue their relationship after this episode is subject to an argument that Rashi (Bereshis 38:26) quotes.

18   Rashi (Bereshis 38:7) adds that they sinned in the same fashion, an unnecessary spilling of their seed. The Ibn Ezra (Bereshis 46:10) agrees that in principle that they commit the same sin and are each punished accordingly, but argues that their sin is something else; marrying a Canaanite woman. The Ibn Ezra then adds that Shimon makes the same mistake, as the Torah attests, וְשָׁאוּל בֶּן הַכְּנַעֲנִית *And Shaul son of a Canaanite* (Bereshis 46:10). By contrast, the Gemara (Pesachim 50a) quotes an opinion which reinterprets the verse so Bas Shua is not a Canaanite.
Parenthetically, Rashi (Bereshis 46:10) argues that שָׁאוּל בֶּן הַכְּנַעֲנִית *Shaul son of a Canaanite* is Dina's son, stating בן דינה שנבעלה לכנעני *Dina's son, who (Dina) was intimate with a Canaanite.*

19   Based on the phrase וַיָּמֶת גַּם אֹתוֹ *And He put him to death also* Chazal (Yevamos 34b and Rashi Bereshis 38:7) conclude that Er does the same, intending to retain her beauty.

In the second section, both elements change, Tamar is active and, because of that, achieves her goal.

6. Initially, things look very promising for Tamar; she marries Er and enters into a prestigious, religious family. Things then come crashing down. Her husband Er dies, as does Onan, her second husband. Life quickly transforms from good to bad. However, in the second section the reverse occurs and life quickly transforms back from bad to good. At the outset of the second half of the story she has no family and no opportunity to perform yibum, however, things then improve. She succeeds in performing yibum with Yehuda leading to twins and raising a family.

7. Yehuda is not with his wife when she gives birth to Shelah (ibid 38:5). In other words, Yehuda is absent from the location that he should have been in. Towards the narrative's ending, the state of affairs is reversed when Yehuda searches for the harlot and can not find her. Instead of Yehuda not being where he should be for a woman, now, a woman is not where she should be for him.

8. Even the story's peripheral characters are subject to this kind of reversal. To take a particularly acute example, Yehuda's friend, Chira, the Ish Adulami,[20] is strikingly passive throughout the first half of the narrative, not even meriting a mention after his introduction (ibid 38:1). Yet in the second half of the chapter he emerges from obscurity, accompanies Yehuda to shear the sheep and actively searches for the missing Kedasha *harlot*.

9. Lastly, and perhaps most fascinatingly, in the beginning, Yehuda marries and is intimate with a woman who we, the readers, do not know, but he does. Then in the second half, we know with whom Yehuda is intimate, but he does not.[21]

---

[20] The Midrash (Bereshis Rabbah, Vilna Edition 85:4) quotes a machlokes whether Chida of Dovid's era is Chira, the Ish Adulami or not.

[21] According to the Netziv (Bereshis 38:10) she is unnamed because of her unimportance. By contrast her father, Shua, is presented with a name reflecting his importance. A second answer is offered by the Malbim (Bereshis 38:2) who explains the Torah's omission of her name on the basis that she did not convert. Rav Yaakov Kamenetsky (Emes L'Yaakov Bereshis 38:2) adds that because she never converts, Yehuda is punished. Thirdly, the Bechor Shor (Bereshis 38:12) suggest that her name is actually "Bas Shua". Support for the Bechor Shor can be found by her being labeled as בַּת שׁוּעַ הַכְּנַעֲנִית *The daughter of Shua the Canaanite*, (Dvray Hayamim I 2:3) as if it is her name.

Because this mirror structure is too perfect to be coincidental and therefore unmistakably intended by the Torah, we must ask why it is written that way. Why tell the story in such a format?

This fascinating mirror-structure reinforces the episode's basic storyline; things get reversed. In the beginning Yehuda's life and family plummet as he suffers through an exceedingly difficult period but then things reverse and he rebuilds his life and family. What better way to capture the decline and return of Yehuda than with a chiastic structure?

Yehuda's transformation is also hinted at on a linguistic level. The chapter opens with וַיֵּרֶד יְהוּדָה *And Yehuda **went down*** (ibid 38:1), whereas in the second half, where Yehuda rebounds, the Torah records וַיַּעַל עַל גֹּזְזֵי צֹאנוֹ *And he (Yehuda) **went up** to his sheep shearer* (ibid 38:12) and repeats וַיֻּגַּד לְתָמָר לֵאמֹר הִנֵּה חָמִיךְ **עֹלֶה** *And it was told to Tamar that your father-in-law is **coming up*** (ibid 38:13). The Torah captures more than simply his physical direction with the phrase וַיֵּרֶד יְהוּדָה *And Yehuda went down,* it captures his emotional and spiritual direction as well. Then, in the second section, his direction is reversed, he goes up, as the Torah emphasizes עֹלֶה *up* and וַיַּעַל *and he went up* simultaneously reflecting both Yehuda's physical and emotional-spiritual movement.

Furthermore, the Torah omits the name of Yehuda's destination both when he goes down and when he comes back up. The Torah seems more interested in Yehuda's direction, down and up, than his geographical location. By mentioning the direction Yehuda travels, and that alone, the Torah subtly emphasizes Yehuda's emotional and spiritual journeys.

PARALLELING YEHUDA TO YOSEF

There is another striking observation worth decoding. Numerous things that occur to Yehuda, occur to Yosef as well. In particular, Yehuda's encounter with Tamar parallels Yosef's sale to Mitzrayim and the subsequent occurrences there.[22] There are many identical aspects.

---

22   The Ramban (Bereshis 38:3) contrasts Yehuda to Yaakov. Whereas after Yaakov's wife, Rochel, names her younger son Ben Oni (Bereshis 35:18) due to her birthing difficulties, Yaakov corrects it and renames his son Binyamin (ibid). By contrast, Bas Shua names Onan *grief* and Yehuda leaves it unchanged.

1. Each of the two stories opens with the primary characters, Yehuda and Yosef, descending to a different location, וַיֵּרֶד יְהוּדָה מֵאֵת אֶחָיו *And Yehuda went down from his brothers* (ibid 38:1) and וְיוֹסֵף הוּרַד מִצְרָיְמָה *And Yosef was taken down to Mitzrayim* (ibid 39:1).

2. In this new environment, separated from their brothers and in the outside world, each of their lives crumble,[23] yet both rebound to rebuild their lives.

3. In their new location, Yehuda and Yosef each meet and befriend a new character. Yosef meets Potifar and Yehuda meets Chira, the Ish Adulami.

4. Both Yehuda and Yosef have an intimate encounter with a woman, Yosef with Eishes Potifar, and Yehuda with Tamar. Moreover, both times it is the woman who initiates the encounter and each time does so in a deceitful manner.

5. In each story the intimate encounter results in the transfer of clothing from a man to a woman. Yehuda gives his cloak to Tamar after intimacy, and Yosef leaves his coat with Eishes Potifar when he flees from committing adultery with her.

6. Each story contains a goat. Yehudah uses one as payment for Tamar, while in the Yosef episode, a goat's blood is used to cover Yosef's coat.

7. Yosef, after coming very close to infidelity with Eishes Potifar, corrects himself at the last moment. Yehuda similarly corrects his behavior at the last moment by declaring צָדְקָה מִמֶּנִּי *She is more righteous than I am* and sparing Tamar's life (ibid 38:26).

8. Both stories feature someone who withholds his identity from a family member. Yosef hides his true identity from his brothers when they come to Mitzrayim looking for food, and Tamar hides her face from Yehuda as she dresses up as a harlot.[24]

9. Each story contains a goat which surprisingly plays a central role. It is the blood from a goat which enables Yosef's brothers to hide

---

[23] Bereshis Rabbah, Vilna Edition 85:2

[24] Although the simple understanding is that Tamar covers her face only while attempting to seduce Yehuda, the Midrashic understanding is that Yehuda does not recognize her for she had covered her face the entire time she was at his house. Chazal are critical of this and state, יהא אדם רגיל בקרובותיו *A man should know his relatives well* (Rabaynu Bachaya Bereshis 38:15).

his identity and it is also a goat that Yehuda attempts to send to the harlot with whom he had been (ibid 38:20).[25]

10. The climax in each story occurs when the central character goes to tend sheep and encounters an unexpected event with a family member. Yosef leaves to care for his father's sheep (ibid 37:14) and there he meets his brothers who throw him into a pit and subsequently sell him. Similarly, the climax of Yehuda's story comes after he travels to care for his sheep (ibid 38:12) for that is when Tamar tricks him into intimacy.

11. Interestingly and perhaps most unexpectedly, both stories do not just tell of how Yosef and Yehuda initially descend before rebounding, but also of how each ultimately ascends to royalty. Yosef becomes second to Paroh, and Yehuda ensures his future kingship by saving the future descendants that he will have through Tamar's baby, Peretz, including, Dovid (Rus 4:18-22).

THE PROPS

The collateral that Yehuda gives Tamar, his staff, ring and cloak, contain deep symbolism, for they are all props that a king would have. By giving them away he symbolically reflects giving away his line of royalty. By threatening to kill her, he is unknowingly forfeiting Dovid's birth and therefore his kingship. It is only when Yehuda courageously proclaims צָדְקָה מִמֶּנִּי *She is more righteous than I am* (Bereshis 38:26) that he regains his staff, ring and cloak, thereby regaining the line of kingship.

Physically he retrieves his props and simultaneously, he retrieves his future kingship. Presumably this is what Rebbi Akiva means by מפני שהודה בתמר מה זכה יהודה למלכות מפני *How did Yehuda merit kingship? Because he admitted to (the) Tamar incident* (Tosefta Brachos 4:16). It is precisely by declaring צָדְקָה מִמֶּנִּי *She is more righteous than I am* (Bereshis 38:26) that Yehuda reclaims kingship.

---

[25] The Midrash (Bereshis Rabbah 85:9, Vilna Edition) adds, אמר הקב"ה ליהודה אתה רמית באביך בגדי עזים חייך שתמר מרמה בך בגדי עזים *Hashem said to Yehuda, 'You tricked your father with a goat, by your life, Tamar will trick you with a goat.*

There is a slightly different way of viewing the symbolism of Yehuda giving the props to Tamar. Yehuda does give away his king-like props, still, he never gives away a crown, which represents the kingship itself. He merely gives away props that are associated with kingship. Yehuda might have never given away his kingship, just the strength of it. The kingship itself, represented by his crown, always remains secure.

A different Midrash (Bereshis Rabbah, Vilna Edition, 99:8) supports this nuanced theory: אמר לו הקב"ה אתה הודית במעשה תמר יודוך אחיך להיות מלך עליהם *And Hashem said 'Because you admitted (your sin) concerning the Tamar incident, your brothers will appoint you king'.* Hashem rewards Yehuda's concession with his brothers' recognition of his kingship, not with the kingship itself. Accordingly, Yehuda always remains destined for kingship, but because he admits צָדְקָה מִמֶּנִּי *She is more righteous than I am* (ibid), his brothers acknowledge and accept his kingship.

The Point of the Comparison

On a simple level the Torah weaves so many comparisons into the narrative in order to subtly link these stories. Two brothers are each separated from their family, struggle but ultimately grow into significant leaders. The Torah covers each of their downfalls, challenges and ultimately, their journeys to leadership. The parallel narratives reinforce how each brother plunges and subsequently manages to reverse their descent.

However, there is significantly more to the connection to uncover.

Contrasting Yehuda to the Yosef Story

In addition to the uncanny number of similarities previously listed, there are numerous striking details that exemplify how the stories contrast as well. By listing them, as we did with the similarities, one can appreciate just how many and opposite aspects exist in both stories.

1. Firstly, Eishes Potifar attempts adultery[26] which is the pinnacle of faithlessness. Tamar, by contrast, is exceptionally faithful. She waits loyally for Shelah as long as she can and only after she realizes that she might wait forever does she take action to ensure a proper yibum (Bereshis 38:11-12)[27].

2. In the Yosef story, Eishes Potifar, the female, takes advantage of Yosef, the male. The opposite occurs when Yehuda, the male, takes advantage of Tamar, the female.

3. Yosef and Eishes Potifar do not actually have relations. Yehuda and Tamar do.

4. Yosef is brought down to Egypt against his will, וְיוֹסֵף הוּרַד מִצְרָיְמָה *And Yosef was taken down to Mitzrayim* (ibid 39:1), while Yehuda decides to go down of his own volition, וַיֵּרֶד יְהוּדָה מֵאֵת אֶחָיו *And Yehuda goes down from his brothers* (ibid 38:1).

5. Manipulation occurs in both stories. Yosef oversees the manipulation, acting as an operator. By contrast, Yehuda is duped by Tamar, who acts as the manipulator. Instead of tricking others, Yehuda is tricked.

6. Although both Yosef and Yehuda plummet before ascending, Yehuda does teshuva ascending emotionally and spiritually. Yosef does not sin, so his rebound is physical.

7. Although each story involves a goat, each goat's role is different. In the Yehuda episode, it is the *absent* goat which is critical for it enables Tamar to retain Yehuda's collateral. The goat is not delivered. In the Yosef story, it is the *presence* of the goat which helps the brothers to accomplish their plan of selling Yosef.

8. The transferal of clothing to Tamar and Eishes Potifar is different as well. Yosef leaves his clothing behind *because no* intimacy transpires and Yehuda leaves his clothing behind *because* intimacy has occurred.

---

[26] Rashi (Bereshis 39:1), elaborating, adds that Eishes Potifar saw astrologically that her descendants are to be Yosef's. She therefore mistakenly assumes that Yosef is destined to be intimate with her, as opposed to marrying her daughter. Accordingly, one can add this to the list of comparisons between Eishes Potifar and Tamar, for they each initiate intimacy with good intentions.

[27] וַתָּסַר בִּגְדֵי אַלְמְנוּתָהּ מֵעָלֶיהָ *And she took off her widow's clothing* (ibid 38:14) and after being with Yehuda, וַתִּלְבַּשׁ בִּגְדֵי אַלְמְנוּתָהּ *she gets dresses in her widow's clothing* indicates that she wore her widow's clothing for a long time. Moreover, the Torah, by not using the classic word זונה *harlot* and replacing it with קדשה *harlot (emanating from the root holy)*, presumably attests to her righteousness. The word זונה *harlot* is only mentioned here when she is being seen from Yehuda's mistaken perspective.

Perhaps the clearest visual illustration of the contras between characters is the profound reversal of their roles. Yosef and Yehuda each have a moment where they are both physically and politically on top while the other is at rock bottom, powerless and completely at the other's mercy. Yehuda is at the top of the pit when Yosef is inside below. Later, a reversal occurs as Yosef is elevated on his throne and Yehuda needs his help for food and ultimately, his brother Binyamin.

We are not the first ones to uncover these remarkable parallels and contrasts which are woven into this narrative. This is previously alluded to by the Midrash (Bereshis Rabbah, Vilna Edition 85:9) which clearly links Yehuda's involvement in Mechiras Yosef *sale of Yosef* to the hardship he endures, אמר הקב"ה ליהודה אתה רמית באביך בגדי עזים חייך שתמר מרמה בך בגדי עזים *Hashem said to Yehuda, 'You tricked your father with a goat, in your life, Tamar will trick you with a goat'.*[28]

Another Midrash (ibid 84:19), also building on this parallel, adds אמר הקב"ה ליהודה אתה אמרת הכר נא חייך שתמר אומרת לך הכר נא *Hashem said to Yehuda, 'You said 'Do you recognize this (regarding Yosef's coat)', in your life, Tamar will say 'Do you recognize this (regarding your collateral)'' to you.*[29] Not only does the Midrash link Mechiras Yosef with the Yehuda and Tamar story, but the reason for linking them is to punish Yehuda for Mechiras Yosef.

Lastly, this is echoed by Rashi (Bereshis 38:1) as well who writes, למה נסמכה פרשה זו לכאן והפסיק בפרשתו של יוסף ללמד שהורידוהו אחיו מגדולתו כשראו בצרת אביהם אמרו אתה אמרת למכרו אלו אמרת להשיבו היינו שומעים לך *Why place this episode (of Yehuda and Tamar) here and interrupt Yosef's episode? To teach that his brothers lowered his stature (greatness) when they saw their father's pain. They said, 'you told us to sell him, if you would have said return him (home), we would have listened to you.'*

THE POINT OF THE STORY'S OPPOSITES

The opposites listed above may suggest an additional important message: one of contrast. Yehuda and Yosef play opposite roles. Yosef

---

[28] Rashi (Bereshis 38:23) echoes this and the Seforno (Bereshis 38:1) explicitly links Yehuda's suffering to his role in Yosef's sale.

[29] In addition to internalizing the pain that he causes Yosef, Yehuda also suffers losing children, a feeling that he inflicted on his father.

is the victim placed in a pit, and Yehuda is the one responsible for placing him there (ibid 37:26).[30] By the Torah contrasting the stories, it highlights the two brothers' contrasting roles. Yehuda is the bully and Yosef is the target of bullying.

REVISITING THE STORY'S TEXTUAL LOCATION

The reason that the Torah places the Yehuda and Tamar episode in the middle of the Mechiras Yosef story is to bolster the linkage between the two. Telling the Yehuda narrative without connecting it to Yosef's is incomplete, just as telling the Yosef episode without Yehuda's. Without intertwining them, one may have otherwise missed Yehuda's spiritual fall being a direct result of his central role in selling his brother. These stories are about the direct aftermath of Mechiras Yosef, and specifically how the two main characters, Yehuda and Yosef, are affected by, and respond to it.[31]

However, the placement of the Yehuda and Tamar narrative may capture more than this. By placing this episode in the middle of the Mechiras Yosef account, the Torah figuratively opens up the Mechiras Yosef narrative, and symbolically creates a pit in the middle of it. It is precisely in that pit where the Yehuda and Tamar narrative is placed. Yehuda's emotional and spiritual descent occurs in the exact same pit as Yosef's physical one, and that imagery is precisely what the Torah intends to convey with the placement of the Yehuda and Tamar story.[32]

Support for this theory can be found from the Midrash (Tanchuma, Warsaw Edition, Parshas Vayigash 9) which directly links Yehuda's sons' death to his selling of Yosef,[33] אין לך בנים עד עכשיו ואין אתה יודע צער בנים

---

[30] Yehuda bears the responsibility because the other brothers listen to and follow him (Midrash Tanchuma Buber edition Parshas Vayeshev 8 and Ekev 6, Rashi Bereshis 37:27 and 38:1). The Meshech Chochoma (Bereshis 37:26) writes that Yehuda is the deciding vote because Leah's four sons want to kill Yosef (because Reuven is elsewhere) and the four sons of Bilhah and Zilpah do not. Yehuda votes with Leah's sons.

[31] The Netziv (Bereshis 38:1) and Malbim (Bereshis 38:1) add that Hashem now plants seeds for the Geulah Shelayma *final redemption* by enabling the first Galus, *exile*. The Netziv (ibid) offers textual support, with וַיְהִי בָּעֵת הַהוּא *And it was at that time*, suggesting that precisely at this particular time, before entering into the Galus, Hashem ensures that there will be a Geulah Shelayma.

[32] Meshech Chochoma (Bereshis 37:26)

[33] However, the Midrash focuses on Yehuda causing Yaakov pain, not Yosef.

אתה טגנת את אביך והטעית אותו בטרף טרף יוסף חייך תשא אשה ותקבור את בניך
ותדע צער בנים *You have no children until this point and you do not know
the pain of (losing) children. You fried your father and tricked him (saying)
'(a wild beast) killed him'. By your life, you will marry a woman and bury
your children and you will (then) know the pain of (losing) children.*

Yehuda's suffering is a direct result of his leading role in Mechiras
Yosef.

Our narrative opens with Yehuda's downfall, which is a result
of his selfishness and responsibility in Mechiras Yosef. In order to
unmistakably link his downfall to Mechiras Yosef, the Torah places
one episode inside the other, and couches both parallels and opposites
into the narratives.

WHY YIBUM?

It may not have been by chance that the instrument for Yehuda's
spiritual climb is the mitzvah of yibum. Yibum is designed to facilitate
caring for a brother's legacy and ensuring his legacy is not lost or
forgotten.[34] Therefore yibum is the optimal Mitzvah to use as a medium
for helping Yehuda rise from his spiritual pit. Yibum captures the care a
brother should have for another; precisely the care that Yehuda lacked
by facilitating Mechiras Yosef.[35]

YEHUDA'S OPENNESS TO ADMIT FAULT

Stating צָדְקָה מִמֶּנִּי *She is more righteous than I am* is the turning
point in Yehuda's life. It is when he does sincere teshuva, admits his
shortcomings and gathers the strength needed for successful leadership.
It paves the path for him to continue admitting his mistakes and
rectifying them.

---

[34] Sefer HaChinuch (598)

[35] To reinforce how bad selling a brother is, the Torah repeats the word אח *brother* in the
Mechiras Yosef passage twenty times (Bereshis 37:2, 4, 4, 5, 8, 9, 10, 10, 12, 13, 14, 16,
17, 19, 23, 26, 26, 27, 27, 30).

Later, Yehuda convinces Yaakov to send Binyamin to Egypt to bring back Shimon (ibid 43:8-9). Yehuda is no longer willing to allow any brother to be left behind.

Most dramatically, after Yehuda's mistaken central role in Mechiras Yosef (ibid 37:27), he stands up to Paroh by attempting to prevent Paroh from sending the brothers back while detaining Binyamin, as the Torah powerfully records וַיִּגַּשׁ אֵלָיו יְהוּדָה *And Yehuda approached him* (ibid 44:18).

In addition to the aforementioned Midrashim which praise Yehuda and accredit his kingship to admitting his mistakes with Tamar, Chazal further state that Yehuda convinced Reuven to admit to the mistake made with Bilhah (Sotah 7b). By encouraging others to confess sins, Yehuda illustrates that this is not simply something he does, it is a deeply internalized value; it is who he is.

Additionally, the name יהודה *Yehuda* showcases his predisposition and willingness to confess, for the name יהודה *Yehuda* has the word מודה *admit* at its core.[36]

APPLYING TEXT TO LIFE: THE HASHKAFIC MESSAGE

Comparing and contrasting Yehuda to Yosef highlights how Yehuda struggles and triumphs as a result of Mechiras Yosef, thereby making him more suited for kingship. It is precisely Yehuda's struggles and challenges which prepare him most.[37]

Additionally, one sees the extraordinary power of teshuva, and that a willingness to admit and even welcome mistakes is an essential prerequisite for it.[38] One might avoid admitting mistakes fearing it will reflect negatively. Leaders' mistakes are forgivable, but when covered up, become corruption. Yehuda reattains his previous religious status and regains the kingship because, with a deep sense of integrity, he honestly confronts his flaws as opposed to covering them up in his embarrassment.

---

[36] Tzrur HaMaor (Bereshis 38:1)

[37] On a similar note, Rav Shimshon Rafael Hirsch (Bereshis 12:1) famously comments that we can more easily identify with the Avos, knowing that they are capable of sin and yet still attained greatness.

[38] Drashos HaRan (Drasha 9)

Another important Hashkafic conclusion to draw is the recognition of Hashem's hashgacha pratis *Divine intervention.*[39] This account unmistakably demonstrates how Hashem navigates Yosef to kingship and Yehuda into the terrible situation he finds himself in as a punishment[40] as well as an opportunity to rectify his attitude towards brothers and family and to stand up for Binyamin.[41]

However, there is another often overlooked and powerful point to derive. One may read the Mechiras Yosef story and not realize its profound impact on Yehuda.[42] We are accustomed to looking at the impact that Mechiras Yosef had on Yosef and even Yaakov, but often do not grasp the impact it had on the other brothers as well, most prominently Yehuda. One can easily miss how selfish and mean behavior impacts the one who behaves that way. Sin leaves a stain on our spiritual self even if not noticed at first glance.[43] Sinning as greatly as Yehuda does leaves a dark mark that takes time and great effort to cleanse.

---

[39] Netziv (Bereshis 38:26). The Divine providence is further illustrated by the Midrash (Bereshis Rabbah, Vilna Edition 85:8), which elaborates that an angel causes Yehuda to notice Tamar, for at first, he does not see her (see the Midrash Tanchuma Buber Edition, Parshas Vayeshev 17).

[40] Seforno and Rav Shimshon Rafael Hirsch (Bereshis 38:1)

[41] Complete teshuva is only possible in an identical scenario (Rambam Teshuva 2:1).

[42] According to the Chizkuni (Bereshis 38:1) and Tzrur HaMaor (Bereshis 38:1) Yehuda leaves his brothers because he cannot stand to see Yaakov's sadness having lost Yosef.

[43] By the Torah not explicitly stating how Yehuda's involvement in selling Yosef damages Yehuda, it may be hinting to how the damage is not seen overtly. One has to delve into the story to reveal it just like one has to delve into the Chumash to reveal it.

LOT'S FAILED EXODUS

IT WAS PESACH

The Torah (Bereshis 19:3) describes Lot's hospitality towards the angels who visit him in Sdom by offering them a place to spend the night. Upon arriving at his house, Lot feeds them a meal that includes matzah. Interestingly, Chazal (Bereshis Rabbah 48:12, Vilna Edition and quoted by Rashi Bereshis 19:3) conclude from Lot's feeding the two visiting angels matzah (Bereshis 19:3), that פסח היה *it was Pesach.*

Really?

Is that the only explanation why anyone would eat matzah? Could the Torah not have simply included this detail portraying the general hospitality Lot displays? Additionally, Lot is not Jewish, not committed to observe Mitzvos,[44] and, furthermore, is celebrating a holiday commemorating an event that did not yet occur![45] Why superimpose commemorating Pesach upon him?

---

[44] Even if one argues that the Avos observe all the MItzvos of the Torah (Yoma 28b) it is surprising that Lot does as well.

[45] The Beis HaLevi (Parshas Bo) elaborates adding that both the Torah and its Mitzvos predate creation and therefore these Mitzvos could not have been commanded because of the Exodus. Rather, he continues, the opposite is true. The Exodus happens because of the Mitzvos. טעמי המצוות *Taamay HaMitzvos* do not cause the Mitzvah but, counterintuitively, are caused by the Mitzvah. The Mitzvos predate their Taam. The Beis HaLevi uses this theory to explain the Pesach Hagadah's response to the wicked son, reinforcing to him the message that Hashem redeems us from Mitzrayim to fulfill Mitzvos.

Along these lines, Rabbi Soloveitchik (the Beis HaLevi's great-grandson and name sake) translates טעמי המצוות *Taamay HaMitzvos* as *the taste of Mitzvos* and not *the reasons for Mitzvos*, presumably because the reasons are beyond human comprehension. The best man can do is emotionally connect to the Mitzvah and enjoy its good taste.

The Shem M'Shmuel (Parshas Shamini) disagrees with the Beis HaLevi, stating that the Avos did not keep any Mitzvos commemorating Yitziyas Mitzrayim for it had not yet

One would like to believe that there is more evidence than merely serving the angels matzah that led Chazal to draw their conclusion. What other evidence is there and what prompted this interpretation? And if Chazal are trying to convey something beyond just observing the time of year, what it is?

THE ANGELS' VISITATION AND STRANGE BEHAVIOR

Taking a closer look at this narrative will better enable us to decipher what prompts Chazal's understanding. Initially, the angels meet Lot at the city's gate בָּעֶרֶב *evening time* where Lot greets them (ibid 19:1). Why do the angels not immediately rescue him then or at least inform him that Sdom is bound for destruction? Is that not the reason they come to Sdom? Moreover, strangely, they insist on sleeping outside on the street. If they are coming to save Lot, they should have jumped at the golden opportunity presented. Are these not perfect chances to accomplish their goal? What more are they looking for?

Ultimately the angels change their minds and do accept Lot's invitation (ibid 19:3). That too is strange for, presumably, angels are not fickle. Whatever reason they originally preferred to sleep outside in the street should still exist. Why does their attitude change with Lot's persuasion?

Also, interestingly, just before Sdom's destruction, the angels instruct Lot and his family not to look back at Sdom, lest they perish (ibid 19:17). This instruction is clearly to be taken seriously, for Lot's wife does look back and as a result, she is transformed into a pillar of salt (ibid 19:26). Why do the angels forbid looking back? Is curiosity that bad? And why is looking back punished by death while attempting to send daughters to a lust-hungry mob or tricking one's father into incest, is not?

---

occurred. However, the Avos had the אור המצוות *light of the Mitzvos.*

UNCOVERING OTHER STRANGE DETAILS IN THIS NARRATIVE

Beyond the great difficulty in understanding the motives and actions of the angels, it is hard to understand Lot's behavior and the Torah's presentation of it. Firstly, it is noteworthy that the Torah records both the time of day בָּעֶרֶב *evening time* and Lot's location, יֹשֵׁב בְּשַׁעַר סְדֹם *sitting at the gate of Sdom* (ibid 19:1). Why include these details? Moreover, is dinner time not an appropriate time to be home with his family? Is he expecting someone? If he is waiting for someone else, it is strange that he abandons them by going home once these two strangers arrive.

Seemingly, Lot is waiting for strangers and when they come, he happily welcomes them into his house. Lot is an excellent host, as Chazal maintain, לוט בשביל שהיה מקיים אכילה שתיה לאורחים זכה לנבואה ונמלט מהפיכת סדום *Lot, for he fulfilled feeding and giving drinks to his guests, he merited to prophesy and was saved from the destruction of Sdom* (Otzer Midrashim Alfa Beta D'Ben Sira 37).[46]

It is also worth noting that after Sdom's citizens arrive and the angels warn Lot of the city's imminent destruction,[47] Lot tries to encourage his sons-in-law to leave, yet Lot is rejected and even scorned by them (ibid 19:14). After that, he waits all night long until, הַשַּׁחַר עָלָה *dawn rose* (ibid 19:15), and then still tarries (ibid 19:16), as the Torah records וַיִּתְמַהְמָהּ *and he tarried*. He does not leave Sdom until he is physically pulled out by the angels (ibid 19:16). Why not leave earlier?

---

[46] The Midrash (Bereshis Rabbah 41:6) even adds that Lot resembles Avraham. However, others (Bereshis Rabbah Vilna Edition 50:4, Rashi 18:4 and 19:2) contrast how Avraham welcomed guests significantly better than Lot.

[47] כִּי מַשְׁחִתִים אֲנַחְנוּ אֶת הַמָּקוֹם הַזֶּה *for we are destroying this place* (Bereshis 19:13). Interestingly, they say מַשְׁחִתִים אֲנַחְנוּ *we are destroying*, as if they themselves were responsible for the decision and not merely messengers. Many (Rashi Bereshis 19:13, Rabaynu Bachaya Bereshis 19:13) critique these angels for sinning.

The Meshech Chochma (Bereshis 19:13) agrees that these angels sin, but disagrees how. He believes that their mistake is communicating to the inhabitants of Sdom that Hashem has informed them of Sdom's destruction. The reason for this is based on a controversial philosophical position, Hashem's knowledge of the future does not interfere with free choice until it is explicitly communicated to a man or an angel. Then, what is communicated must happen and all free will that would lead to a different conclusion is restricted. Others (Rav Shimshon Rafael Hirsch Yeshayahu 6:2) would likely argue that angels cannot sin for they are personification of Hashem's will in this world and do not have the individuality to sin. The philosophical ramification of this argument is beyond our prevue.

Why do the angels have to physically force him to leave? Did he not just encourage his family to leave hours earlier?

THE POINT OF THE STORY

Clearly the angels do not come exclusively to rescue Lot, for if they do, they would do so when they first meet him at the city's gate. Even after meeting Lot's family that night, they do not immediately rescue them from Sdom. Instead, they wait until the next morning before grabbing Lot, his wife and daughters. Evidently, the angels come to Sdom with a different agenda. They come to test Lot to see if he deserves to be saved.[48] [49] Is Lot worthy of salvation?

Lot, eagerly waits for guests to arrive and greets them warmly following in Avraham's footsteps, וַיִּשְׁתַּחוּ אַפַּיִם אָרְצָה *And he bowed with his face to the floor* (ibid 19:1). This certainly portrays Lot favorably. Furthermore, this occurring at evening time, a time when he should have been home, demonstrates the importance of hospitality in Lot's eyes.[50] Lot initially appears virtuous.

Instead of immediately rescuing Lot, the angels attempt to determine whether Lot really welcomes guests graciously. They inform Lot of their plans to sleep outside in the city street. Lot, deeply determined to host them, insists upon them sleeping at his house (ibid 19:3). With deep care, Lot is unwilling to allow them to sleep outside in the streets of Sdom. Lot continues by offering them מִשְׁתֶּה וּמַצּוֹת אָפָה *a feast of baked matzah* (ibid 19:3). This further depicts Lot positively and highlights his identity with Avraham. And when Sdom's citizens arrive, Lot makes every effort to protect his guests. He goes outside attempting to negotiate with the mob. He even closes the door behind him (ibid 19:6), to protect the angels and he continues asking for the mob's mercy (ibid 19:7). All of these details are designed to display Lot as exemplary.

---

[48] The word בָּעֶרֶב *erev*, may emanate from the word *mixed* and capture the mixed religious attitude Lot possesses.

[49] Or present him with the opportunity to merit salvation (Ohr Chaim on Bereshis 19:1)

[50] Alternatively, evening is mentioned to inform the reader that the angels left Avraham's house in the morning and travel directly to Sdom arriving evening (Netziv on Bereshis 19:1).

However, things take a turn for the worse. Lot horrifically offers his two daughters to the lust-hungry mob (ibid 19:8).[51] Beyond understanding his unmistakable appalling change in behavior, one must ask: what is he possibly thinking? What conceivable mindset would lead one to care so much for one's guests and so little for one's daughters?

WHO IS LOT?

Lot is a border-line individual, someone who identifies with both Avraham and Sdom. He feels totally comfortable living his life in two separate worlds. Lot has deeply internalized Avraham's values of hospitality,[52] the love for people and desire to care for them.[53] After all, he initially joins Avraham in the לֶךְ לְךָ *go for yourself experience* (ibid 12:1) dream. In addition to that side of Lot, he also identifies with Sdom. Lot moves to Sdom fully aware of what it stands for.[54] He marries a woman from Sdom and raises his family there. There are truly two parts to Lot's personality. Lot genuinely excels at Bein Adam L'Chavaro, like Avraham, yet his moral standard leaves much to be desired, like Sdom.

Lot feels comfortable living in and identifying with Sdom which explains his tolerance for sexual promiscuity.[55] His daughters have grown up in Sdom and, they too, lack the same moral compass that he does. They may have even consented to being sent out to the lust-hungry mob, and after Sdom's destruction, their true colors are seen

---

[51] Astonishingly, the Rabaynu Chananel (Bereshis 19:8) assumes that Lot offers his daughters sarcastically "why don't you just take my daughters?!?", as if to say "I am not giving you these guests like I am not giving you my daughters."

[52] Rashi (Bereshis 19:1). From the Torah itself, Avraham's love of hospitality is abundantly clear. He runs to greet his guests and then runs to prepare them food (Bereshis 18:2,6). The Torah even uncharacteristically records the weather, כְּחֹם הַיּוֹם *heat of the day* (ibid 18:1), illustrating Avraham's conviction and determination to properly serve his guests even during scorching heat, when he has every reason not to.

[53] Zohar (1:105a)

[54] Which may very be why the townsmen respond to Lot, הָאֶחָד בָּא לָגוּר וַיִּשְׁפֹּט שָׁפוֹט *one comes to live with us and now he acts as a judge* (Bereshis 19:9) (translation follows Rav Saadia Gaon Bereshis 19:9), as if to say to Lot "you are fully aware of who we are and came anyway."

[55] Rabaynu Bachaya (Bereshis 19:8)

most clearly. Together they deceive their father, intoxicate him and ultimately violate him engaging in rape and incest.[56]

Lot and his family barely make it out of Sdom, and if not for בְּחֶמְלַת יְקֹוָק *Hashem's grace* (ibid 19:16) they would not have.[57] Moreover, his sons-in-law do not.

Instructing the survivors not to look back is one last test designed to determine whether they can wholeheartedly leave Sdom's ideology behind them. Can they disassociate themselves from Sdom? Lot and his daughters successfully do, while Lot's wife does not. Turning into salt for looking back is not a punishment for Lot's wife. Rather, it is a sign that she cannot properly disassociate herself from Sdom.

Parenthetically, turning into a pillar of salt is the perfect punishment for Lot's wife because salt draws out the real taste of something. Turning into salt uncovers her inner nature, one that she has hidden until this point and one that is unworthy of salvation.

We can now also understand why the command אַל תַּבִּיט אַחֲרֶיךָ *do not look back* (ibid 19:17) is located in between וַיֹּאמֶר הִמָּלֵט עַל נַפְשֶׁךָ *And he said 'Run for your life'* and וְאַל תַּעֲמֹד בְּכָל הַכִּכָּר הָהָרָה הִמָּלֵט פֶּן תִּסָּפֶה *And do not stop in the plain, run to the hills lest you be destroyed*. The entire verse captures one idea, Lot being commanded to physically distance himself from Sdom, symbolizing the need to ideologically distance himself.

---

56 Although the Torah quotes Lot to claim that his daughters have never been with a man (ibid 19:8), it is likely untrue. Nowhere in the story do we see any daughters who are unmarried. The only two daughters mentioned have husbands (ibid 19:12 and 14). Furthermore, if Lot is really offering his married daughters away it could explain why the Torah calls Lot's son-in-laws לֹקְחֵי בְנֹתָיו *(those who) took his daughter (as wives)* (ibid 19:14), an other-wise superfluous description. The Torah is reinforcing that they are in fact married.
This position may even be the opinion of the Midrash (Vilna Edition, Bereshis Rabbah 50:9) which states ארבע בנות היו לו שתים ארוסות ושתים נשואות *Lot had four daughters, two engaged and two married.*
Alternatively they are well experienced in crass activities such as these, yet still virgins (see the Chizkuni Bereshis 19:8 and Perush HaRosh Bereshis 19:8 for greater detail).

57 Ramban (Bereshis 19:16).
Some argue that Lot is saved due to Avraham's merit (Seforno Bereshis 19:16 and see Rambam Bereshis 19:16). The Torah itself hints to this mentioning וַיִּזְכֹּר אֱלֹהִים אֶת אַבְרָהָם *And Hashem remembered Avraham* (Bereshis 19:29) immediately before communicating that Hashem saves Lot, implying that Hashem saves Lot because of Avraham. This may further explain why the Torah only mentions Avraham being Lot's merit at the end of the narrative. Until this point it is unclear if Lot is deserving of salvation. Only after offering his daughters away so horrifically, is there an answer, no. He is saved because of Avraham's merit and Hashem's mercy.

It is very difficult for Lot to physically leave Sdom. He tarries and delays all night long and ultimately needs to be physically removed. This symbolizes his ideological difficulty with leaving Sdom. Clearly, it is not easy for him to let go.

After leaving, Lot gets tired quickly and cannot make it to the hills, the planned destination. Instead, he arrives in Tzoher (ibid 19:22). This struggle to leave Sdom and inability to reach his destination captures his spiritual journey as well. He is incapable of disconnecting. This idea is further reinforced as Lot begs for mercy at one of the local cities (ibid 19:20). He still feels connected.

One can take Lot out of Sdom, but taking Sdom out of Lot is not as easy.[58]

Lot describes why he cannot continue to the hills, and complete the journey, וְאָנֹכִי לֹא אוּכַל לְהִמָּלֵט הָהָרָה פֶּן תִּדְבָּקַנִי הָרָעָה וָמַתִּי *'And I cannot flee to the hills, lest evil attach itself to me and I die.'* Although Lot's statement פֶּן תִּדְבָּקַנִי הָרָעָה וָמַתִּי *lest evil attach itself to me and I die* (ibid 19:19) is cryptic, many argue[59] that Lot here communicates his fears in leaving the comfort of Sdom where he sees himself as religiously successful without having to try hard.

The Torah repeats the word יצא *leaving* nine times (ibid 19:5, 6, 8, 12, 14, 15, 16, 17, and 23) subtly reinforcing the point of this story; how Lot *leaves* Sdom.

THE SETTING

As previously mentioned, the narrative opens with Lot waiting at the border of the city, יֹשֵׁב בְּשַׁעַר סְדֹם *sitting at the gate of Sdom* which may represent more than his simple geographical location. The Torah may be subtly suggesting that Lot is a border-line character. His geographical placement reflects his spiritual placement, half in and half

---

58   The Midrash (Bereshis Rabbah, Vilna Edition 41:8) offers two opinions whether Avraham is correct in separating from Lot. Maybe this debate revolves around whether Lot could have been permanently redirected positively.

59   Rashi (Bereshis 19:19)

out.[60] [61] Moreover, his presence in Sdom indicates Lot's true Sdom-like identity. After all, Lot moves to and lives in Sdom, and is only saved because of בְּחֶמְלַת יְקֹוָק *Hashem's grace* (ibid 19:16).

Lot is located in Sdom, physically and ideologically, barring one exception where he diverges ideologically; his desire to welcome in guests. Lot does briefly leave Sdom to greet his guests (ibid 19:1). This too has great symbolic depth. If Lot's location on the city border reflects his religious nature, then his leaving Sdom to greet and invite in his guests reflects his non-Sdom-like qualities, that of hospitality. It is precisely because Lot leaves physically, symbolizing an ideological disconnect, that he is saved by the angels.

PARALLEL TO THE KARBAN PESACH STORY

This episode of Lot's departure from Sdom, has many elements in common with the Karban Pesach account. We are going to look at how this story and the original Karban Pesach narrative interrelate. After looking at the similarities we will explore the differences and see what we can glean. Here is a list of similarities.

1. In both circumstances the smaller visiting group, Lot and Bnei Yisrael, are saved while the surrounding oppressors perish immediately.

2. Hashem supernaturally destroys both Sdom and Mitzrayim. Sdom is overturned and Mitzrayim is afflicted with ten plagues.

3. Initially each smaller group arrives after separating from one of the Avos. Lot leaves Avraham and Yosef is separated from Yaakov.

4. Both episodes are directly adjacent to the performance of bris milah. Avraham is commanded to perform a bris (Bereshis 17) and Bnei Yisrael are as well (Shemos 12:44). The juxtaposition is even most striking considering how few times the Torah records episodes of bris milah.

---

[60] Rashi (Bereshis 19:1) argues that Lot waits at the gate because that is where the courthouses are located. There are several other recorded examples of elders or judges located at the gate of a city (Devorim 22:15 and 25:7, Yehoshua 20:4 and Rus 4:11). The Bechor Shor (Bereshis 19:1) disagrees, arguing that Lot's house is located at he gate and he is home when the angels arrive.

[61] Rachav as well lives on the border (Yehoshua 2:15). See Double Take *Rachav the Spiritual Zonah* for a further comparison between Lot and Rachav.

5. Lot and his family are forced to remain indoors to stay safe and protected from the lust-hungry mob (Bereshis 19:6). Similarly, Bnei Yisrael place blood on the doorpost and stay inside to remain safe (Shemos 12:13,22).

6. Both episodes stress the central feature of a door. For the Karban Pesach, blood is placed around it (Shemos 12:22), and in Sdom, the door is used to keep the local inhabitants of Sdom outside (Bereshis 19:9-11).[62]

7. Both stories ultimately lead to the birth of a brand new nation. Lot fathers two new nations, Moav and Amon (Bereshis 19:37-38) and the Hebrew slaves are transformed into Am Yisrael.

8. Fireballs hail down as part of the colossal destruction in both stories (Bereshis 19:24 and Shemos 9:23-24).

9. Just before destroying Sdom, angels blind[63] its residents just outside Lot's door (Bereshis 19:11). This undoubtably recalls the ninth plague, Choshech *darkness*, that Hashem brings upon Egypt immediately before the final and tenth plague (Shemos 10:22).

10. Lot feeds his guests matzah (Bereshis 19:3) which unmistakably reminds one of Bnei Yisrael leaving Mitzrayim while eating matzah (Shemos 12:9 and 15-20).

Reinforcing our parallel and adding to our list of similarities, the Midrash (Shemos Rabbah 18:9 Vilna Edition) identifies that both destructions occur at night, as it states כשם שהפך סדום בלילה כך הרג בכורי מצרים בלילה *just like He turned Sdom (upside-down) at night, so too He killed the Egyptian first-born at night.*

Beyond the thematic similarities, there are linguistic ones as well. The word בית *house* appears in each story numerous times. In the Lot episode it occurs five times (Bereshis 19:2, 3, 4, 10, 11) and in the Karban Pesach portion, fourteen (Shemos 12:3, 3, 4, 4, 7, 13, 22, 23, 27, 27, 29, 30, 46, 46). The word משחית *destroy* also appears numerous times in both episodes as well (Bereshis 18:13, 13, 14, 29 and Shemos 12:13, 24). And the word קומו *get up* in Shemos (12:31) echoes קום *get up* in Bereshis (19:15).

---

[62] The Torah mentions twice that the door is closed (Bereshis 19:6, 10).

[63] Rashi (Bereshis 19:11)

The Torah strikingly describes the Egyptians pushing Bnei Yisrael out of Egypt with the same language וַתֶּחֱזַק מִצְרַיִם *And Egypt* **grabbed** (ibid 12:33) as how the angels rescued Lot, וַיַּחֲזִקוּ הָאֲנָשִׁים *And the men* **grabbed** (Bereshis 19:16).

Leaving Sdom is Lot's Exodus story, because Sdom is Lot's Mitzrayim. In fact, that is exactly why he chooses it in the first place. Lot is interested in Sdom precisely because it is כְּאֶרֶץ מִצְרַיִם *like the land of Egypt* (Bereshis 13:10). He actually chooses Sdom immediately after visiting Mitzrayim. However, this is only half of what Lot wants. As the verse records, he desires both כְּגַן יְקֹוָק *Hashem's garden* and כְּאֶרֶץ מִצְרַיִם *like the land of Egypt* (ibid). The Torah testifies to Lot's two different desires. He wants to live in both worlds.

With this parallel in mind, Chazal identify this event as Pesach. Chazal, in their subtle yet deeply insightful manner, highlight the similarity that already exists in the Torah for casual readers who may have missed the parallel.[64]

CONTRASTING SDOM TO THE KARBAN PESACH STORY

However, even more striking than the similarities are the profound differences.

1. Although both narratives include eating matzah, in Bereshis the matzah is eaten immediately when the angels enter, and in Shemos, as they depart. In Bereshis, matzah is eaten as they are welcomed in, and in Shemos, as they are sent out.

2. Bnei Yisrael, the ones saved, eat matzah. By contrast, Lot, who is saved, does not eat matzah, but rather feeds matzah to others.

3. Although both passages focus on door-like entities, in Bereshis the primary prop is the door itself. In Shemos the focus it is on the frame, which is everything besides the door, the mezuzos *side door frame* and mashkof *top door frame*.

---

[64] This answers another question. Assuming that the two angels who visit Lot come from Avraham the same day (Rashi 19:1, also see the Rashbam Bereshis 18:1), one may wonder why Avraham gives the guests bread (Bereshis 18:5) on Pesach. Based on our analysis, it may not have been Pesach according to the calendar; rather claiming that it is Pesach highlights the thematic similarities.

4. Forcefully, the angels physically grab Lot and *pull* him out of Sdom (Bereshis 19:16), saving him from the locals in the process. By contrast, it is the Egyptians, the locals, who force Bnei Yisrael to leave; and they *push* them out and do not do it physically (Shemos 12:33).

5. In Bereshis it is angels who Hashem sends to assist Lot's escape. In Egypt, Hashem goes Himself (Shemos 12:12) as Chazal (Yalkut Shemoni, Parshas Bo) echo אני ולא מלאך *I and not an angel* and אני ולא שרף *I and not a Seraf.*[65]

6. Regarding Sdom, Hashem is the שֹׁפֵט *judge,* as the Torah records הֲשֹׁפֵט כָּל הָאָרֶץ לֹא יַעֲשֶׂה מִשְׁפָּט *Would the judge of the entire world not do justice?* (Bereshis 18:25). However, in Mitzrayim, Hashem does just the opposite, turning others into judges, as the Torah records, אֶעֱשֶׂה שְׁפָטִים אֲנִי יְקֹוָק *I will make them judges, I am Hashem* (Shemos 12:12).[66]

7. Bnei Yisrael leave a בֵּית עֲבָדֶכֶם *the house of your servant* (Shemos 13:3, 14, 20:2 and Devorim 5:6) while Lot, by contrast, welcomes the angels into a בֵּית עֲבָדֶכֶם *the house of your servant* (Bereshis 19:2).

8. In Bereshis (19:16) the Torah describes Lot with the phrase וַיִּתְמַהְמָהּ *and he tarried,* contrasting with Shemos (12:39) where the Torah describes Bnei Yisrael's departure with the same word, yet in a negative context, וְלֹא יָכְלוּ לְהִתְמַהְמֵהַּ *and they could not tarry* (Shemos 12:39).

9. Sdom is destroyed only after Lot and his family leave. In contrast, all ten plagues strike Egypt while Bnei Yisrael are still there.

10. Lot's family leaving Sdom is followed by a repulsive act of incest. By contrast, Bnei Yisrael's Exodus is followed by an incredible change in the world, that of Matan Torah, *the giving of the Torah.* But the contrast is stronger because Lot's family's incest occurs privately in a cave, the most secluded of places, whereas the Gemara (Zevachim 116a) claims that Matan Torah is an event that the entire world is aware of.

Assuming the comparison and contrast is purposeful, which is likely, we must now wonder why.

---

[65] Hagadah Shel Pesach

[66] Meaning the false Gods will recognize that Hashem is true (Ibn Ezra and Rashbam both on Shemos 12:12).

Karban Pesach: A Proclamation of Jewish Identity

The Midrash (Shemos Rabbah 17:3) explains why Hashem specifically chooses blood as the object to place above the doorpost by stating, מה ראה הקב"ה להגן עליהם בדם כדי לזכור להם דם מילת אברהם *Why did Hashem choose to protect them (Bnei Yisrael) with blood? In order to recall the blood of Avraham's bris.* This is strange. What does this have to do with Avraham's bris milah? Is there no more depth to the comparison beyond them each containing blood?

In truth, beyond this midrash, there are other connections from karban pesach to bris milah. Firstly, someone needing a bris milah is disqualified from bringing a karban pesach (Shemos 12:48). Additionally, the karban pesach and bris milah are the only two positive mitzvos where one can get the punishment of kares – *being spiritually cut off* for not performing them.[67] These two mitzvos are rooted in Jewish Identity and therefore command a greater necessity to perform them. By not performing them, one disconnects from Judaism and being cut off, or kares, is the natural result.

The connection between bris milah and Jewish identity is easily understood. Bris milah is the first mitzvah performed on a Jewish baby boy. Additionally, it physically distinguishes Jews from other nations (Sefer HaChinuch, Mitzvah 2). The karban pesach, like bris milah, is a sign of Jewish Identity.[68]

Understanding the Comparison

Why does the Torah write the Sdom story in a way that recalls the karban pesach passage?

---

67 Rishonim debate when the kares is given. According to the Rambam (Milah 1:2) one receives it after one dying without having performed bris. The Raaved (Milah 1:2) disagrees, arguing that kares is giving every single day a man lives without one.
Interestingly, this debate boils down to whether the mitzvah of bris is doing the action of bris milah or living with the status of bris milah. The Rambam understands the mitzvah as the action, therefore dying without having ever done the action warrants kares. The Raaved disagrees arguing that the mitzvah of bris is to live a life with a bris. Every day without one is a violation of that and chayuv kares (Pri Moshe B'inyanay Bris Milah 1:1).

68 Rav Soloveitchik. Others (Sha'arei Teshuva 3:16) argue that these two Mitzvos are the most severe and therefore have punishments of kares for not fulfilling them.

In contrast to how Bnei Yisrael leave Mitzrayim, with conviction, and theological clarity, Lot leaves Sdom with great hesitation. Bnei Yisrael leave projecting a deep sense of Jewish identity, reflected by their slaughtering of the sheep, the Egyptian God,[69] and smearing blood on the doorpost, all designed to distinguish between Bnei Yisrael and Mitzrayim. Lot could not unequivocally create that separation. While Bnei Yisrael completely dissociate themselves from their surroundings, Lot simply can not.

The Exodus from Sdom is not successful like the Exodus from Egypt.

TRACKING THE TIME OF DAY

In the Sdom episode the Torah uncharacteristically labels the time of day more than once. Lot waits by the gate בָּעֶרֶב *evening time* (Bereshis 19:1), and then טֶרֶם יִשְׁכָּבוּ *just before they went to sleep* (ibid 19:4) the lust-hungry mob approaches Lot's house. Then, כְּמוֹ הַשַּׁחַר *about morning* (ibid 19:15) the angels escape with Lot and finally, הַשֶּׁמֶשׁ יָצָא עַל הָאָרֶץ *the sun came out upon the land* (ibid 19:23) and Hashem destroys Sdom. Similarly, and equally unusual, regarding the karban pesach, the Torah records the timing for the events; the obligation to slaughter the karban pesach at בֵּין הָעַרְבָּיִם *evening time* (Shemos 12:6), eat it בַּלַּיְלָה *at night* (ibid 12:8) and then בְּעֶצֶם הַיּוֹם הַזֶּה הוֹצֵאתִי אֶת צִבְאוֹתֵיכֶם מֵאֶרֶץ מִצְרָיִם *in the middle of this day I will take your legions out of Egypt* (ibid 12:17).

The unique use of such a clear timeline for these two episodes, distinct from every other narrative in the Torah, reinforces the aforementioned parallel. There is, however, one main and significant difference; Bnei Yisrael leave Mitzrayim בְּעֶצֶם הַיּוֹם הַזֶּה *in the middle of this day*, whereas Lot leaves Sdom in the early morning and only reaches Tzoher at midday. Leaving Mitzrayim בְּעֶצֶם הַיּוֹם הַזֶּה *in the middle of this day* reflects how Bnei Yisrael leave; with pride[70] and

---

[69] Chazal (Shemos Rabbah, Ville Edition 17:3) further state, אין ישראל יוצאין עד שישחטו את אלהי מצרים לעיניהם שאין להם שאין אלהיהם כלום *Yisrael will not go out from here until the slaughter the Gods of Egypt before them and let them know that their Gods are useless.* (Also see the Ramban Shemos 12:3).

[70] Midrash Taanayim 32:48, Otzer Midrashim p 538

passion. By contrast, Lot fails for he is unable to leave Sdom and what Sdom stands for.

By describing Lot escaping Sdom early in the morning, as opposed to leaving at midday, the Torah buttresses its point; instead of leaving as Bnei Yisrael do, ideologically disconnecting and proud to go serve Hashem, Lot does not. His Exodus is incomplete. Leaving prematurely, in the morning, and not בְּעֶצֶם הַיּוֹם הַזֶּה *in the middle of this day,* is symbolic of his shortcoming; the inability to leave Sdom properly. Lot leaving early represents his shortcomings, the inability leave properly.

THE MEANING OF LOT'S NAME

The word הִמָּלֵט *flee* (Bereshis 19:17, 17, 19, 22) appears four times subtly underscoring how Lot left Sdom; he escapes by fleeing. לוֹט's name emanating from הִמָּלֵט *flee, evade* or *slip out*[71] further reinforces this point. His name represents who he is; someone who is forced to escape, as opposed to someone who can leave proudly, disassociating himself from Sdom. Lot's Exodus from Sdom is a failed version of Yitziyas Mitzrayim.

THE STRUCTURE OF LEAVING SDOM

Interestingly, this episode where the angels come to Lot and take him from Sdom is written in a chiastic structure. Whatever occurs in the beginning of the narrative, the opposite occurs in the end.

1. Whereas in the first half of the episode, the primary theme is entering Sdom, the second half's theme is the opposite, leaving Sdom.

2. The events that occur in the first half of the story capture how Lot welcomes angels into Sdom and into his house. The second half captures the opposite, how the angels take Lot out.

3. Lot initially saves the two guests' lives and in return, the two guests save his.

71 Rashi (Bereshis 19:17)

4. The angels physically pull Lot twice. Initially they pull him into his house (ibid 19:10) and later, they pull him out of it (ibid 19:14).

5. In the beginning, Lot offers his two daughters to the lust-hungry mob to be raped. Later, in contrast to Lot sending his daughters to be raped, they rape him. However, the contrast is actually stronger because for Lot's daughters, in the end, there is no rape, whereas for Lot, there is.

6. The episode's first section occurs at evening time; its second, in the morning.

7. In the first half of the story the citizens of Sdom seem powerful whereas the angels seem weak. The opposite occurs in the second half as the angels appear strong and the people of Sdom are powerless.

8. The Torah describes how initially Lot encourages others with the word וַיִּפְצַר *and he pushes* (ibid 19:3). Later, the reverse happens, as Lot is subject to other וַיִּפְצְרוּ *pushing* him (ibid 19:9).

9. In the first section, the residents of Sdom attack the angels, albeit unsuccessfully, for the angels are not hurt or injured. In the second section it is the angels who attack Sdom and they succeed in destroying the city.

10. While in Sdom, Lot has a big family. After leaving, he no longer does.

11. Whereas in the beginning of the story, Lot waits for the guests all day long. At the end, the opposite occurs, the guests wait for Lot all night long.

Writing the story of Sdom's demise in a chiastic structure may be designed to highlight the point. The chiasm captures how Sdom begins as a strong and powerful city, yet it begins to deteriorate and control is taken from the people. Sdom's role reverses itself. As Sdom gets weaker, the angels become stronger. One might have thought that Lot would have an easier time disconnecting from them, yet, unfortunately, this is not the case. Lot's inability to fully commit is not rooted in a philosophical confusion that is clarified as Sdom is destroyed. Lot is emotionally invested in Sdom. As the city of Sdom shifts from strong to weak and ultimately falls, Lot still cannot ideologically detach himself.

The transition from evening to morning further reinforces that point. Even as morning occurs and it becomes clear, literally and figuratively, that Sdom is on the breach of destruction, Lot cannot disassociate from the city.

APPLYING TEXT TO LIFE: THE HASHKAFIC MESSAGE

This analysis illustrates how Bnei Yisrael leave Mitzrayim ideologically charged. The mitzvah of karban pesach is to further their sense of identity. Defeating Mitzrayim, the world power and nation seen as elite, serves as an excellent way to develop the courage to trust in Hashem[72] and His mission for them.[73]

Additionally, Lot has learned a great deal from Avraham to the point that he sits at the gate of the city hungry to welcome guests. Still he is no Avraham, for Avraham could disconnect completely from the morals and bad culture that surrounded him. It is for that reason Hashem chooses Avraham as our forefather and to start our religion.[74]

Lastly, there is a profound religious message about Pesach to deduce. Pesach challenges us to relive the proper Exodus experience.[75] We disconnect from engaging and worshiping the surrounding value systems, and instead, reiterate that our commitment is to Hashem and His Torah.

The Midrash (Shemos Rabbah, Vilna Edition 16:2) explains that our redemption is dependent on our commitment by stating, אמר לו

---

[72] Beis HaLevi (Bereshis 2:2)

[73] Behind the question of whether Paroh should listen to Hashem and let Bnei Yisrael go lies a theological debate between Paroh and Moshe. Paroh, the polytheist, does not recognize Hashem and more importantly sees His unique role a sole deity (Shemos 5:2). Much of the Exodus narrative is designed to educate Paroh as to who Hashem is.
It is with this aim that Hashem decides to harden Paroh's heart. Hashem is not interested in quickly removing Bnei Yisrael from Mitzrayim. Hashem elongates the process by hardening Paroh's heart to postpone the Exodus and allow for Him to convince Paroh of who He is. Only after the Kreyas Yam Suf *splitting of the Red Sea* does Paroh and Mitzrayim recognize Hashem (Shemos 14:25). One may wonder why after all that effort invested in educating Paroh and Mitzrayim, Hashem kills them. What is the purpose? Perhaps Bnei Yisrael are to see Mitzrayim's defeat and admission to Hashem. This is designed to further strengthen their identity and confidence in themselves and their mission.

[74] See Double Take *Noach, Yonah, Lot and Avraham What it takes to start up a nation* for more on what makes Avraham the ideal forefather.

[75] Rambam (Chometz U'Matzeh 7:6)

הקב"ה למשה כל זמן שישראל עובדין לאלהי מצרים לא יגאלו, לך ואמור להן שיניחו מעשיהן הרעים ולכפור בעבודת כוכבים *Hashem told Moshe 'As long as (Bnei) Yisrael are worshiping Avodah Zara, they will not be redeemed. Go tell them to stop what they are doing and reject Avodah Zara.* This is our challenge, full commitment. The challenge of karban pesach and message of the Exodus, is for Bnei Yisrael to experience[76] the salvation and respond with rededication.

---

[76] Rambam (Chometz UMatzah 7:6)

Achashvarosh's
Important Religious Role in the Megilla

Achashvarosh

Most of the central characters in Megillas Ester have clear, well-defined roles. Mordachi and Ester are heroes and Haman is the villain. Yet, Achashvarosh's role remains ambiguous. Besides being the king, not much else is clear. In fact, the Gemara Megilla (12a) quotes Rav and Shmuel with diametrically opposing opinions as to whether Achashvarosh is a פיקח *wiseman*, or a תיפש *fool*.[77] Through a closer analysis of the Megilla, one can see that Achashvarosh's character is dichotomous and can be viewed with both of these two very different perspectives.

Foolish King

Let us begin with the opinion in the Gemara that Achashvarosh is indeed a foolish king, one steeped in materialism. It is understandable that he throws an enormous and lavish party lasting one hundred and eighty days, designed for one purpose, בְּהַרְאֹתוֹ אֶת עֹשֶׁר כְּבוֹד מַלְכוּתוֹ וְאֶת יְקָר תִּפְאֶרֶת גְּדוּלָּתוֹ *to show off the wealth of his glorious kingdom and the honor of his splendid majesty* (Ester 1:4).[78] This unusually long party

---

[77] The Gemara itself is unsure which opinion is accepted by Rav and Shmuel.

[78] Ra"m Chalev (Ester 1:4).
The Ibn Ezra Nusach Alef (Ester 1:3) and Rabaynu Bachaya (Ester1:7) offer three reasons for the extravagant celebration. First, to celebrate seventy years, the number of years Yirmiyahu prophetically announced would pass before the Jews returned, of Galus that had passed without redemption. The Gemara (Megilla 19a) adds that Achashvarosh uses

reflects a heavily materialistic, shallow, and sexually oriented society. Achashvarosh's desire to show off Vashti's beauty[79] may be the greatest illustration of Achashvarosh's sensualist nature (ibid 1:9-11).[80]

Achashvarosh's character is further depicted this way when he, almost impulsively, orders Vashti's death.[81] He appears to blindly follow the counsel of his advisors (ibid 1:13-15 and 21),[82] only to regret his rash and impulsive decision the next morning (ibid 2:1).[83] In addition to his inability to think for himself, he makes crucial irreversible decisions completely recklessly.

Furthermore, Achashvarosh does not investigate Ester's background. She is able to keep her religion and nationality a total secret (ibid 2:10, 20).[84] By showing no interest in her upbringing and background, he proves to be completely apathetic to developing a deeper relationship with her. He seems to care only about two things: that she be beautiful and a besulah *virgin* (ibid 2:2). And as if that along with his one hundred and eighty day party does not highlight

---

vessels from the Beis Hamikdash and even wears the Kohen Gadol's clothing (Megilla 12a), reveling in the destruction of the Beis Hamikdash. The second, because there is now a time period of quiet after the wars. Last, and the approach they both favor; this is a wedding party for Vashti. The Rabaynu Bachaya (Ester 1:7) adds that Vashti throwing a party for the women reinforces this theory.

[79] Chazal (Vayikra Rabbah Shemini 12:1) add that Achashvarosh wants her to appear unclothed.

[80] According to the R"A Kohen Tzedek (Ester 1:10) having women dance before men is the common practice of the times.

[81] Although the Megilla does not explicitly state that she dies, many (Vayikra Rabbah, Margolis 11:1, Ester Rabbah, Vilna Edition 5:2, Psichta D'Ester Rabbah, Vilna Edition 9, Shachar Tov 22:26, Rashi Ester 1:19, R"A Kohen Tzedek Ester 1:10) assume it to be true. The Ralbag (Ester 1:19) agrees that Achashvarosh kills Vashti, but not as a punishment, rather because of a legal technicality; he is otherwise unable to marry a different queen. Others (Rav Saadah Gaon Ester 1:19, Ibn Ezra Ester Nusach Beis 1:21, Chachmay Tzarfas Ester 1:19, Ra"m Chalev 1:21, Ri"d Ester 1:19) argue that Achashvarosh does not kill Vashti. He divorces or dethrones Vashti. Interestingly the R"I Nachmiash in different comments (Ester 1:19 and 2:1) implies different things.

[82] The advisors are concerned that the women throughout the one hundred and twenty seven countries will rebel. Although it is impossible to determine the likelihood of that revolution, there are grounds for skepticism. Yet, Achashvarosh, almost blindly, accepts this argument.

[83] Achashvarosh's epicurean nature is further emphasized by those (Rashi and Ibn Ezra on Ester 2:1) who claim that Achashvarosh only misses Vashti's beauty.

[84] The Ibn Ezra (Ester 2:10) quotes three opinions as to why Mordachi commands Ester not to reveal her nationality. The first opinion states that Ester is to remain quiet because Achashvarosh would not select someone from the Golah (an outsider). Alternatively, Mordachi had received Navuah that her nationality being kept a secret would be needed for salvation. Last, keeping Mitzvos would be significantly easier for Ester if no one suspected her of being Jewish.

his shallowness enough, after marrying Ester he throws yet another party (ibid 2:18).

Achashvarosh's foolishness and irresponsibility extend to the political arena as well. He carelessly acquiesces to Haman's request to kill the Jews (ibid 3:8). And undoubtably most recklessly, he agrees to genocide without any serious deliberation (ibid 3:11)!

Without hesitation, Achashvarosh removes his ring and gives it to Haman (ibid 3:10). Then, later, when Achashvarosh hands the same ring to Mordachi, the Megilla records, **וַיָּסַר הַמֶּלֶךְ אֶת טַבַּעְתּוֹ אֲשֶׁר הֶעֱבִיר מֵהָמָן** וַיִּתְּנָהּ לְמָרְדֳּכָי *And the king removed his ring, **that he retrieved from Haman**, and gave it to Mordachi* (ibid 8:2). By reiterating אֲשֶׁר הֶעֱבִיר מֵהָמָן *that he retrieved from Haman*, the Megilla illustrates just how fickle Achashvarosh is; he makes contradictory decrees and is willing to offer his ring inconsistently to different people.[85]

With utter simplicity, Achashvarosh has the people bow to Haman. He does not realize how strange it is to have the nation bowing to someone other than the king. Foolishly, Achashvarosh misses the obvious.

Later, Ester invites both Haman and Achashvarosh to a private party. Again, Achashvarosh, too foolish to be suspicious, misses how incriminating it is for Ester to host a party for the king and another man when the party should have been exclusively for the king and queen.

Haman visits Achashvarosh at night intending to request that Achashvarosh kill Mordachi (ibid 6:4). Yet, seemingly, Haman offers no reason to do so. Haman presumably thinks that Achashvarosh would agree to hang Mordachi simply because he requests it. After all, that is what occurred when he asked to annihilate the entire Jewish people. From Haman's perspective, Achashvarosh is his puppet, and incapable of thinking independently.

Achashvarosh forgets that Mordachi has saved his life and that the favor was never repaid (ibid 6:2-3). Being forgetful, especially for something as important as this, further reflects negatively upon him.

---

[85] Moreover, according to the Rid (Ester 4:14), Mordachi challenges Ester with וּמִי יוֹדֵעַ אִם לְעֵת כָּזֹאת הִגַּעַתְּ לַמַּלְכוּת *And who knows if for this moment you became queen* (Ester 4:14) emphasizing כָּזֹאת *this moment*, for Mordachi knows that Achashvarosh is fickle and can change his mind, like he did with Vashti.

Then Achashvarosh, incompetent and incapable of deciding how to reward Mordachi, again looks to his advisors for assistance. Upon hearing Haman's advice, he asks Haman to lead Mordachi through the streets of Shushan, while calling out כָּכָה יֵעָשֶׂה לָאִישׁ אֲשֶׁר הַמֶּלֶךְ חָפֵץ בִּיקָרוֹ *So shall be done to the man that the king wants to honor* (ibid 6:9). Is Achashvarosh unaware of their rivalry, such that he naively tells Haman to do everything that Haman just mentioned for Mordachi? Moreover, Achashvarosh seems completely oblivious to Haman's outrageous self-interest, for he does not see through Haman's transparently greedy motives.[86]

Ester then invites both Haman and Achashvarosh to a second party and again strangely, Achashvarosh remains unconcerned that Haman joins the royal couple, now for a second time.

At the party, when Ester accuses Haman of plotting mass genocide, Achashvarosh is flabbergasted (ibid 7:5-7). Does he not remember his decree? How many mass genocide decrees does he authorize that he cannot keep track of them? Does this decree not take up much mental space? It is almost impossible to imagine someone not taking something like this seriously. Again, the Megilla highlights just how boorish and irresponsible a king Achashvarosh really is.

To put this into perspective, Achashvarosh decides and forgets about the mass genocide almost imminently, yet deeply worries late at night about Mordachi's reward. The lack of ability to allocate mental focus to important issues also reinforces the impression of his foolishness.

After hearing Ester's accusation that Haman has concocted a plan to wipe out the Jews, Achashvarosh leaves for a moment to compose himself. When he returns, he sees Haman begging for Ester's mercy. Seeing this gesture, he mistakenly believes that Haman is intimately interested in Ester (ibid 7:8). Who would have drawn such a wild and incorrect conclusion? Did Ester not just accuse Haman of attempting

---

[86] Haman's arrogance and entitlement is transparent by his entering into the king's palace at night, and even clearer by his remarks, וְהָמָן בָּא ... לֵאמֹר לַמֶּלֶךְ לִתְלוֹת אֶת מָרְדֳּכַי עַל הָעֵץ *And Haman came to tell the king to hang Mordachi on the tree.* Instead of asking, Haman came to לֵאמֹר *tell* the king. However, Rav Saadia (Ester 6:4) translates לֵאמֹר *tell* as לבקש *ask*, minimizing the level of brazenness.
The Ibn Ezra (Ester Nusach Beis 6:4) bothered by this point responds differently arguing that Haman comes in the morning, for no one could have so much temerity as to come at night.

to destroy her entire people? This gross misconstruction of the situation further attests to Achashvarosh's idiocy.

Lastly, upon Charvona's suggestion, Achashvarosh orders Haman to be hanged. Just as easily as he is convinced to kill Vashti and the Jews, he is convinced to kill Haman (ibid 7:9-10). Achashvarosh appears to be mercurial, following whichever direction his counsellors advice.

These facts seem to reinforce the theory that Achashvarosh is imprudent, shallow and does a poor job of connecting the dots. Simply put, Achashvarosh is a תיפש *fool*.

WISE KING

The second opinion quoted by the Gemara argues that Achashvarosh is indeed wise. Accordingly, all of the aforementioned details that paint Achashvarosh foolishly have to be reexamined and reinterpreted in a manner which make Achashvarosh appear intelligent.

Before doing so, it pays to begin with a small introduction. Achashvarosh, according to Chazal (Megilla 11a), is not the biological heir to the throne and thus does not inherit the kingship from his father in the manner that a typical king would. Instead, he rises to power by staging a coup and forcefully conquering the monarchy.[87] Even before returning to the details of the narrative, it should be noted that Achashvarosh demonstrates his skills in rising to power. This already frames Achashvarosh in a significantly more positive light. Additionally, Achashvarosh's quick rise to power is understandably accompanied by a fear of a rebellion from the loyalists to the previous regime.

With this perspective, certain details of the Megilla are now more easily understood. For example, why he insists on rewarding Mordachi and why he loves Haman's idea of a public reward such as parading him around the streets with someone calling out כָּכָה יֵעָשֶׂה לָאִישׁ אֲשֶׁר הַמֶּלֶךְ חָפֵץ בִּיקָרוֹ *So shall be done to the man that the king wants to honor* (Ester 9:6). There is no person Achashvarosh wants to reward more

---

[87] Alternatively, he bribes his way into kingship (Megilla 11a) or marries Vashti, the daughter of the previous king, Belshazar (Megilla 12b), the granddaughter of Nevuchadnetzer (Megilla 7a).

than an informant of a traitor planning to poison him and seize control. It is crucial that his supporters and friends recognize his appreciation.

Beyond Achashvarosh's efforts to inspire the people to identify with the Persian kingdom, he utilizes a second method of disincentives to prevent people from revolting: instilling fear in his citizens. This is why Achashvarosh severely punishes Bigson and Seresh for attempting to assassinate the king. This way a clear public message is sent to anyone considering overthrowing his regime.

Through both direct punishments and public demonstrations of gratitude, the hallmarks of a newly appointed dictator, he clearly sends the message that it is in the best interest of the people to act with loyalty towards Achashvarosh.

This may additionally explain why Achashvarosh encourages others to bow down to Haman. Achashvarosh wants his friends and assistants happy and faithful, and perhaps more importantly, seen publicly that way.

Let us now return to the same narrative with this new perspective. Ruling one hundred and twenty seven countries poses the inherent challenge of unifying them. However, this problem is magnified several-fold since Achashvarosh is not a natural heir to the throne and rises to power by his own exertions. Perhaps as an attempt to unite the masses, Achashvarosh throws an extravagant, six month long, party. If different people from different countries can gather together and internalize a deep sense of national pride and identify with his government, they might be more likely to support him.

With this new perspective, we can explain why Achashvarosh requests that Vashti appear before his guests at the party. By witnessing the queen's beauty, they are to internalize a great sense of Persian pride and return home to their fellow countrymen spreading support for Achashvarosh and his government. Again, Achashvarosh, methodological and calculated, wisely works towards his goal of unifying the one hundred twenty seven nations under his dominion.

When Vashti refuses to appear, Achashvarosh's paranoia surfaces. Fearing that Vashti's disobedience will set a tone that rebelliousness is tolerated, Achashvarosh decides to act quickly. Yet before doing anything impulsive, he seeks guidance from his wise advisors. A quick decision has to be made to quash the potential rebellion. Achashvarosh here displays the same attitude as he did in his sentencing of Bigson and Seresh to death; he unilaterally conveys that disloyalty is not tolerated.

After getting rid of Vashti, the text does not inform us whether Achashvarosh regrets his decision. It only notes that he misses her (ibid 2:1). According to this approach, Achashvarosh is not fickle, but human.

Achashvarosh strategizes that combining pride in the Persian culture, riches, and women, along with inculcating the fear of rebellion in the people, is the glue needed to unite one hundred and twenty seven nations who are unsure of their new self-proclaimed leader.

The criteria Achashvarosh has in selecting a wife, being beautiful and a besulah *virgin,* should be reconsidered as a well. Instead of viewing Achashvarosh as someone interested in beauty for hedonistic and superficial reasons, he chooses Ester because he is looking for a beautiful woman with whom the people can identify.[88] Achashvarosh simply continues attempting to win public support.

Furthermore in this light, Achashvarosh's apathy towards Ester's nationality must also be readdressed. Because Ester is to represent all hundred twenty seven nations, Achashvarosh prefers that people not know that she is Jewish. It is easier for Ester to represent all of Achashvarosh's empire when she is not identified with one specific nation.

Haman successfully convinces Achashvarosh to kill the Jews, arguing יֶשְׁנוֹ עַם אֶחָד מְפֻזָּר וּמְפֹרָד בֵּין הָעַמִּים בְּכֹל מְדִינוֹת מַלְכוּתֶךָ וְדָתֵיהֶם שֹׁנוֹת מִכָּל עָם וְאֶת דָּתֵי הַמֶּלֶךְ אֵינָם עֹשִׂים וְלַמֶּלֶךְ אֵין שֹׁוֶה לְהַנִּיחָם *There is one nation scattered and sprinkled among the nations throughout all of the king's kingdom whose religion is different from all other nations, they do not follow the will of the king and it is not worth it for the king to leave them* (ibid 3:8). Haman speaks directly to Achashvarosh's paranoia, claiming that the Jews will never identify with the grand Persian vision and that undermines his ability to unite the entire kingdom. That is precisely why Haman adds מְפֻזָּר וּמְפֹרָד *scattered and sprinkled* and בְּכֹל מְדִינוֹת מַלְכוּתֶךָ *throughout all of the king's kingdom.* Since the Jews are both unwilling to assimilate and scattered throughout the entire kingdom, the threat is very serious.

---

[88] Many nations identified with Ester (Yalkut Shemoni Ester 1053).

Achashvarosh, being a wise and cautious king, is completely aware and weary of Haman's selfishness and desire for power. He suspects Haman is interested in his own honor and not the king's. Yet patiently and cautiously, Achashvarosh waits to be certain. When Haman visits Achashvarosh at night, a perfect opportunity to test Haman arises. He asks Haman for suggestions regarding how to reward someone. Before even recording Haman's response, the Megilla shares Haman's sinister thoughts, וַיֹּאמֶר הָמָן בְּלִבּוֹ לְמִי יַחְפֹּץ הַמֶּלֶךְ לַעֲשׂוֹת יְקָר יוֹתֵר מִמֶּנִּי *And Haman said to himself 'Who does the king want to honor more than me'* (ibid 6:6) perhaps indicating that Achashvarosh himself is aware of Haman's thoughts; why else would they be mentioned. By asking to have that person dressed in the king's clothing, and crown,[89] paraded around the city with someone calling, כָּכָה יֵעָשֶׂה לָאִישׁ אֲשֶׁר הַמֶּלֶךְ חָפֵץ בִּיקָרוֹ *So shall be done to the man that the king wants to honor* (ibid 6:9), Haman reveals his true colors to Achashvarosh.

Fully aware of Haman's rise to power as well as his greed for more, Achashvarosh commands Haman to publicly lead Mordachi, his nemesis, around the streets of Shushan calling out כָּכָה יֵעָשֶׂה לָאִישׁ אֲשֶׁר הַמֶּלֶךְ חָפֵץ בִּיקָרוֹ *So shall be done to the man that the king wants to honor* (ibid 6:9). The message Achashvarosh sends to Haman is covert but clear, "I am the king and you do what I say. Your job is not to work for your own honor but for mine."[90]

As we previously noted, Achashvarosh sincerely likes the advice of commissioning a public "thank you" to Mordachi because it reiterates to the people something he feels cannot be reiterated enough: rebellion is both dangerous and unwise, and there is substantive reward for anyone who turns in those considering insurrection.

---

[89] Interestingly, Haman originally requests Achashvarosh's crown (Ester 6:8) in his opening remarks, yet omits it in the adjacent verse (ibid 6:9). Rashi (Ester 6:9) explains that after Haman sees Achashvarosh's reaction, he backs down from requesting the crown. This supports our theory that there existed a tension between Haman's desire for power and Achashvarosh's mixed feelings of support and suspicion for Haman.
However, others disagree. The Ralbag (Ester 6:9) downplays the difference, explaining that the second statement is a summary not a retraction. Alternatively the Chachmay Tzarfas (Ester 6:9) explain Haman intentionally left it out because he is now talking, pragmatically, about what is needed for riding.

[90] People bow to Haman. Haman is invited to a special royal meal with the king and queen. If he were also to have been paraded around Shushan, he might have earned the reputation as undisputed second to the king. Perhaps Achashvarosh fears that giving Haman that reputation may incentivize Haman to assassinate him and replace him as king. Haman parading Mordachi throughout the city of Shushan is designed to create political balance.

Ester invites both Haman and Achashvarosh to a party which only makes Achashvarosh more unnerved.[91] Ester, fully aware of Achashvarosh's paranoia, plays to it by inviting Haman to an otherwise intimate dinner between husband and wife. And after a second invitation and second party with just the three of them, Achashvarosh's suspicions are heightened. When Ester senses Achashvarosh's growing distrust towards Haman, she informs Achashvarosh of Haman's evil plan.[92] Achashvarosh is surprised because Haman has never actually articulated his plan for genocide. Haman left his plans vague enough to put all Jews to death without explicit permission and still defend the position that he was given permission by the king.[93] Forgiveness is often more easily attained than permission. Ester's party is designed to foster Achashvarosh's distrust and jealousy of Haman so when this situation arises, it is not Haman's first offense, but rather the straw that breaks the camel's back.

Naturally, Achashvarosh is furious with Haman, yet, responsibly, he wants a chance to think and reflect. Upon Achashvarosh's return, Haman is on the bed with Ester and that along with his previous suspicion pushes Achashvarosh over the limit. Chorvona[94] suggests hanging Haman on the tree designed for Mordachi and Achashvarosh eagerly concurs (ibid 7:9).[95]

---

[91] According to Rashi (Ester 6:1) Achashvarosh struggles with sleeping at night (Ester 6:1) because he is bothered by Haman's possible attraction towards Ester.

[92] Assuming Mimuchan is Haman, as Chazal (Megilla 12b) do, this is not the first time Haman intentionally speaks vaguely. Earlier as well, Haman says יִתֵּן הַמֶּלֶךְ לִרְעוּתָהּ הַטּוֹבָה מִמֶּנָּה the king should give the queenship to a peer, one better than her. Here too, Haman subtly suggests Achashvarosh kill Vashti in a way where he can backtrack.
Alternatively, the Ralbag (Ester 3:8) argues that Haman's case for genocide is falsely based upon the Jews' religious command to kill all others, just as Shaul is instructed regarding Amalek (Shmuel I 13). Still, others (Rashi Ester 1:1) assume Achashvarosh is completely wicked too and therefore it simply does not take much convincing.

[93] Malbim (Ester 3:9-10, 7:4). The Malbim then adds that Achashvarosh assumed that Hamas plan was to cause assimilation not mass-genocide.

[94] Chorvona's name emanates from the root חרבן destruction, for his role in the Megilla is to bring Haman's destruction (quoted by the Ibn Ezra Ester Nusach Alef on Ester 1:10). Perhaps חרבנה Chorvona is שלה חרבן her destruction, meaning that Chorvona is how Ester brought about Haman's destruction. Alternatively, it was a Persian name (Ibn Ezra Ester Nusach Alef 1:10)
Interestingly, the Midrash (Pirkey D'Rebbi Eliezer 3, also quoted by the Ibn Ezra Nusach Alef 7:9) identifies Chorvona as Eliyahu HaNavi.

[95] The Targum Sheni states (Ester 7:9) אמר לו למלך אף לך המלך רצה המן להרוג ולקחת המלכות ממך He (Chorvona) said to the king "Haman wanted to kill you and take the kingdom from you".

APPLYING TEXT TO LIFE: THE HASHKAFIC MESSAGE

After outlining how the details of the Megilla can frame Achashvarosh in two very different manners, the question arises, why is the story written this way? Why portray Achashvarosh in such an ambiguous and unclear fashion?

One may simply suggest that the narrative presents one image of Achashvarosh and Rav and Shmuel dispute what that image is. However, there is an alternative approach. One might suggest that the Megilla intentionally portrays Achashvarosh ambiguously so that the narrative can be understood to depict him as either wise or foolish. If this is correct, we must ask, what is the purpose of this ambivalence?

The theological message is simple. It does not matter whether Achashvarosh is wise or foolish for it does not matter who the local king is, or how he acts; Hashem is in command and can puppeteer as He pleases. No king, no matter how wise or foolish, can intervene with that power. Achashvarosh's abstruse persona only reinforces that idea. Achashvarosh's important religious role in the Megilla is to underscore that Hashem, even when not acting overtly, is the real king.

Chazal (quoted by the Torah Temimah Ester 1:2) claim that in Megillas Ester the word מלך *king* refers to Hashem whereas מלך אחשורוש *King Achashvarosh* refers to Achashvarosh.[96] Using the word מלך *king* to refer to Hashem subtly hints to Hashem quietly being in control. Although it looks like the human king is in control, in truth, Hashem is the real king and He is in control.

Witnessing Hashem operating in a covert and surreptitious manner is a dominant theme in Megillas Ester. After all, the Megilla never mentions Hashem's name. What better way to emphasize the point than by omitting Hashem's name entirely?[97]

---

[96] Therefore בַּלַּיְלָה הַהוּא נָדְדָה שְׁנַת הַמֶּלֶךְ *That night, the king slept*, is referring to Hashem who slept. The Torah Temimah (Ester 1:2 note 32 and 6:1 note 1) explains that Hashem acts as if He is sleeping.

[97] Alternatively, Rav Saadia Gaon (quoted by Ibn Ezra Ester Nusach Beis 4:14, Rabaynu Bachaya Ester 5:4) answers that Mordachi fears that if he is to write Hashem's name the Persian editors would change it to a name of Avodah Zara. Therefore better to leave Hashem's name out entirely. Accordingly, in principle, it would have been better to include Hashem's name.

Support can be found in the name of the Megilla itself, אסתר *Ester* which means "I will hide". The title may not merely be the name of the heroine, but Hashem's role in the Megilla as well. Reinforcing this idea, the Gemara (Chullin 139b) comments, אסתר מן התורה מנין ואנכי הסתר אסתיר פני *Where is Ester found in the Torah? That where it says 'And I will hide (Ester) my face'.* The Ester narrative illustrates how Hashem operates in a covert manner.

The religious lesson is easy to state but more difficult in internalize. One should be able to detect Hashem's fingerprints even when they are not transparent. Seeing Hashem in history may be challenging especially during difficult times, but we should remember that Hashem is in control even when He appears not to be.

HAGAR AND HER INFLUENCE
ON HER SON YISHMAEL

DOES YISHMAEL DO ANYTHING WRONG?

The book of Bereshis is in many ways defined by the division between those children who inherit their parent's spiritual legacy and those who do not. When it comes to Avraham's spiritual bequest, Yitzhak is undoubtably the sole inheritor. He alone continues as Avraham's religious heir. Yishmael, Avraham's first-born and other prominent son, does not. However, Yishmael is blessed and destined to father a great nation (Bereshis 21:13). Additionally, Yishmael undoubtedly stands above the six other less-prominent sons Avraham has with Keturah[98] (ibid 25:2).

Although it is clear that Yishmael is not selected to carry on Avraham's religious mission, surprisingly, the Torah never explicitly records Yishmael's rebelliousness or bad behavior. This stands in strong contrast to Esuv, whose disinterest and wrongdoings are evident on several occasions. Esuv speaks disrespectfully to his father, carelessly trades away his birthright, and even plans to kill Yaakov. Understandably, Esuv is undeserving.[99] This only strengthens our

---

[98] Many assume that Keturah is Hagar (Bereshis Rabbah Vilna Edition 61:4, Midrash Tanchuma Parshas Chaya Sarah 8, Rashi on Bereshis 25:1 and 6). According to the Chizkuni (Bereshis 25:1) and Kli Yakar (Bereshis 25:1) Hagar does teshuva and her new name Keturah reflects her improved actions, like Ketores *(good smelling) incense*. Others argue that they are two distinct people (Ibn Ezra on Bereshis 25:1, Rashbam on Bereshis 25:1,6 and the Ramban on Bereshis 25:6).

[99] For an analysis of Esuv's personality, see the chapter entitled *The Gangster and the Godfather* and footnotes there.

question of what does Yishmael does wrong?[100] Why is he disqualified from receiving the spiritual heritage?

The Torah does not explicitly record what Yishmael's failure is;[101] therefore we must begin by collecting clues. The only critique the Torah alludes to is in labeling him מְצַחֵק *mitzachek* (Bereshis 21:9). But this is only Sarah's point of view, וַתֵּרֶא שָׂרָה אֶת בֶּן הָגָר הַמִּצְרִית אֲשֶׁר יָלְדָה לְאַבְרָהָם מְצַחֵק *And Sarah saw the son of Hagar, the Egyptian, who begat a son to Avraham being mitzachek.* Yishmael being *mitzachek* clearly bothers Sarah, for it leads her to demand that Avraham banish both Hagar and Yishmael.

Interestingly, whatever wrong Yishmael does perpetrate does not seem to bother Avraham, or at least not enough to agree with Sarah's request to banish Yishmael, as the verse records, וַיֵּרַע הַדָּבָר מְאֹד בְּעֵינֵי אַבְרָהָם עַל אוֹדֹת בְּנוֹ *And this was very bad in Avraham's eyes regarding his son* (ibid 21:11). In truth, Sarah is correct, as seen by Hashem siding with her, but if Yishmael really misbehaves so severely, one might have expected Avraham to have cared or at least noticed. How bad could Yishmael have been?

Additionally, the word *mitzachek* does not seem terribly stinging. Although it is not clear exactly what it means, it would seem to come from the word *joke* or *tease*.[102] It seems almost harmless. Why does Sarah see this as worthy of rejection?

---

[100] This question should be asked even according to the Kuzari (1:95), who argues that klepos *peels*, peripheral individuals, are always cast aside, and central elite people are selected to carry on the spiritual legacy continue throughout the generations. One should still ask why both Yishmael and Yitzhak could not have both been chosen; after all, all of Yaakov's sons are.

One potential answer, according to the Kuzari, would be that there is more of a need to continue selecting individuals from klepos until Yaakov's sons. However, we will offer an additional answer.

[101] Rav Yaakov Kamenetsky (Emes L'Yaakov, Bereshis 16:15) argues that Yishmael is born to a Shifcha *maid-servant*. Rashi (Bereshis 21:10) implies that Yishmael is both religiously inferior to Yitzhak and born to a non-Jewish mother.

Arguably, Rochel and Leah have no better lineage than Yishmael and they are considered Jewish (assuming that the concept of being Jewish exists at that time). Perhaps we can uncover something distinctly unfavorable about Yishmael which will explain why he is not selected.

[102] Although it is unclear what מְצַחֵק *mitzachek* (Bereshis 21:9) means (Meshech Chochma Bereshis 21:9), at first glance it does not seem that bad, otherwise Avraham would have agreed to expel Yishmael.

Regarding the translation of *mitzachek*, many understand Yishmael merely teases Yitzhak. The Ramban (Bereshis 21:9), for example, explains that Yishmael teases Yitzhak about a feast that Avraham and Sarah made him (Bereshis 21:8). In a similar fashion, the Seforno

In order to unpack what *mitzachek* contains, we are going to look at how Sarah views Yishmael. Her general perspective of Yishmael should help to explain what she dislikes so greatly when she sees him *mitzachek*.

SARAH'S CONFUSING POSITION: WHO SHE DISLIKES

Sarah's criticism of Yishmael is confusing because it is presented in a contradictory fashion. On the one hand Sarah slates Yishmael for what he does. Her observation of Yishmael as *mitzachek* (ibid 21:9) suggests that her objections to him are personal. As we noted, the word *mitzachek* remains unclear, but it is crystal clear that Sarah detests it when Yishmael does it. Yishmael himself and his behavior is the subject of Sarah's disapproval.

On the other hand, Sarah seems to dislike Hagar and expels Yishmael simply because he is her son. Sarah forcefully commands גָּרֵשׁ הָאָמָה הַזֹּאת וְאֶת בְּנָהּ *expel this maidservant and her son* (ibid). She demands Yishmael's expulsion solely because he is Hagar's son.

This attitude is reinforced when the Torah reiterates Sarah's view of Yishmael, as בֶּן הָגָר הַמִּצְרִית אֲשֶׁר יָלְדָה לְאַבְרָהָם *son of Hagar, the Egyptian, who begat a son to Avraham* (ibid). She does not see him as Yishmael, but rather as Hagar's son, who happens to be biologically related to Avraham. Accordingly, Sarah's distaste towards Yishmael is solely due to his biological relation to Hagar.

(Bereshis 21:9) Ksav V'Kabbalah (Bereshis 21:9) and Malbim (Bereshis 21:9) understand Yishmael to be making fun of Yitzhak for having been conceived from Avimelech. The Ksav V'Kabbalah (Bereshis 21:9) quotes an answer suggesting that Yishmael jokes that Avraham alone birthed Yitzhak, as alluded to אֲשֶׁר יָלְדָה לְאַבְרָהָם *who begat a son to Avraham*. According to the Radak (Bereshis 21:9), Yishmael picks on Yitzhak because he is born to old parents. The Ibn Ezra (Bereshis 21:9) and Chizkuni (Bereshis 21:9) argue that Sarah becomes jealous because Yitzhak could not keep up with Yishmael due to his youth. However, the Chizkuni (ibid 21:10) argues that Sarah demands that Yishmael leave because he requests rights as the firstborn. Similarly, the Rashbam (Bereshis 21:9) argues that Yishmael begins to show signs reflecting his desire to share Avraham's legacy.
However, there are those who do interpret *mitzachek* (ibid 21:9) as something far worse. Rashi (Bereshis 21:9), for example, writes that Yishmael worships idols, commits murder and adultery. Similarly, according to the Baal HaTurim (Bereshis 21:9), Yishmael murders others with his bow and adds that the gematria of *mitzachek* is equal to להרג *to kill* (Bereshis 21:9). According to this school of thought, It is surprising that Avraham is unaware of Yishmael's horrific behavior.
We will offer an additional answer.

Which one is it; does Sarah judge Yishmael based on his actions or his biological connection to Hagar?[103] If Yishmael is banished because he is *mitzachek*, then why does the Torah emphasize that he is Hagar's son? Conversely, if Yishmael is exiled because he is Hagar's son, then why does the Torah recount him being *mitzachek*?[104]

THE DISAGREEMENT REGARDING YISHMAEL

This dispute between Avraham and Sarah is deeper than simply whether or not Yishmael deserves expulsion. Sarah sees Yishmael as בְּנָהּ *her (Hagar's) son,* whereas Avraham sees things differently, as implied by the verse, וַיֵּרַע הַדָּבָר מְאֹד בְּעֵינֵי אַבְרָהָם עַל אוֹדֹת בְּנוֹ *And this was very bad in Avraham's eyes regarding his son* (ibid 21:11). The Torah hints to their different perspectives on Yishmael. Sarah sees Yishmael as בְּנָהּ *her (Hagar's) son,* whereas Avraham looks at Yishmael as בְּנוֹ *his son.*[105]

---

[103] The Torah does not indicate whether Sarah acts correctly. The Ksav V'Kabbalah (ibid 21:10) defends her, explaining that she does not act jealously, rather protective. As proof, he quotes the Shadal, who distinguishes between Nachalah *endowment* and Yerushah *inheritance.* A Nachalah is divided whereas a Yerushah is taken entirely by one person, and that is precisely what Yishmael wants, the sole inheritance. This is what Sarah testifies to, כִּי לֹא יִירַשׁ *for he should not inherit (Bereshis 21:10).* Rav Yaakov Kamenetsky (Emes L'Yaakov Bereshis 21:8) support this further arguing that until now Sarah does not want to expel Yishmael. She only requests it once she sees that Yishmael is *mitzachek.*
However, the Ibn Ezra (Bereshis 21:9) argues that Sarah does act jealously. The Ramban (Bereshis 16:6) and the Radak (Bereshis 16:6) are critical of Sarah for her harshness towards Hagar (Bereshis 16:6). The Ramban (ibid) adds that Avraham too is mistaken for allowing this to happen.

[104] According to the Ramban (Bereshis 21:9), Sarah only dislikes Yishmael. Hagar is asked to leave to care for her son.

[105] According to Rav Yaakov Kamenetsky (Emes L'Yaakov Bereshis 16:15 and 21:8), Sarah reasons that Yishmael is not Jewish, following his mother. Avraham disagrees, arguing that matrilineal descent has not begun yet and Yishmael is Jewish, following his father's status. Rav Yaakov Kamenetsky (ibid) continues (based on the Ramban Bereshis 17:4) that Avraham attains his Jewish status with his bris milah. Accordingly, Hashem commands Avraham to have his bris before giving birth to Yitzhak ensuring that is he born Jewish.
It pays to note that many (Ramban Vayikra 24:10 quotes French Rabbis, the Perush HaRosh 24:10 quotes the R"I, and the Chizkuni on Vayikra 24:10 in his first interpretation) argue that before Har Sinai, one's status as a Jew follows patrilineal descent. However, others argue that one's status as a Jew follows matrilineal descent even before Matan Torah. The Ramban (Vayikra 24:10), Rabaynu Tam (quoted by the Perush HaRosh on Vayikra 24:10), and the Chizkuni (Vayikra 24:10 in his second interpretation) argue that the M'Kalel (Vayikra 24:10-12) is born Jewish because his mother is.

There is a clear disagreement between Avraham and Sarah regarding how to look at Yishmael.[106]

HASHEM'S PERSPECTIVE

Hashem unquestionably sides with Sarah by commanding Avraham, כֹּל אֲשֶׁר תֹּאמַר אֵלֶיךָ שָׂרָה שְׁמַע בְּקֹלָהּ *all that Sarah told you, listen to her.* Hashem, not only agrees with Sarah's position; He agrees with her reasoning too, as He reiterates, כִּי בְיִצְחָק יִקָּרֵא לְךָ זָרַע *for through Yitzhak will your descendants be called* (ibid 21:12).[107]

WHAT SARAH DISLIKES

In order to decipher Sarah's motivations, we can suggest that the Torah indicates both that Sarah dislikes Yishmael for who he is, and for being Hagar's son. Sarah does not like Yishmael, but it stems from her view of Hagar's influence on him.[108] Sarah despises Hagar and what she stands for, and because of her influence on Yishmael, she has grown to dislike him as well. This perspective explains Sarah's hostility towards Yishmael both for being *mitzachek* and simultaneously for being Hagar's son. Yishmael's being *mitzachek* is precisely because of Hagar's negative influence.

Moreover, if Yishmael's being *mitzachek* is because of Hagar's influence, then we can better understand Sarah's vantage-point: בֶּן הָגָר הַמִּצְרִית אֲשֶׁר יָלְדָה לְאַבְרָהָם מְצַחֵק *son of Hagar, the Egyptian, who begat a son to Avraham being mitzachek* (ibid 21:9). The verse's connection between Sarah seeing Yishmael as בֶּן הָגָר הַמִּצְרִית אֲשֶׁר יָלְדָה לְאַבְרָהָם *son*

---

[106] This is also seen when Sarah commands Avraham גָּרֵשׁ הָאָמָה הַזֹּאת וְאֶת בְּנָהּ *expel this maidservant and her son* (Bereshis 21:10). Although Avraham disapproves (ibid 21:11), Hashem commands Avraham to obey Sarah (ibid 21:12). Some (Maharshal quoted by the Sifsi Chochomim and Baer Hativ both on Bereshis 21:14) argue that Avraham conforms on some level, but not completely, as insinuated by וַיְשַׁלְּחֶהָ *and he sent her* (ibid 21:14) as opposed to expelling her. Avraham intends for Hagar and Yishmael to leave temporary, just until things cool down. This explains why the Torah records, וַתֵּתַע *and she got lost* (ibid 21:14), an otherwise irrelevant detail; it answers why they do not immediately return.

[107] From here Chazal (Shemos Rabbah 1:1 Vilna Edition) conclude that Avraham is inferior to Sarah in prophecy.

[108] See Malbim (Bereshis 21:9)

of Hagar, the Egyptian, who begat a son to Avraham and Yishmael *being mitzachek* reflects the connection that Sarah sees. This is precisely what prompts Sarah's strong response גָּרֵשׁ הָאָמָה הַזֹּאת וְאֶת בְּנָהּ *expel this maidservant and her son* (ibid 21:10).[109]

What still has to be uncovered is how exactly Hagar influences Yishmael and why Sarah so greatly detests it. In other words, if it is indeed Hagar's influence on Yishmael that upsets Sarah, we must then ask, how she influences him? A better understanding of Hagar and her influence on Yishmael can be derived from a look at their interactions.

GERUSH YISHMAEL

The only account in the Torah which captures any serious interaction between Hagar and Yishmael is the aftermath of Gerush Yishmael, *the expulsion of Yishmael.* After being sent away, Hagar and Yishmael get lost in the desert, run out of food, and Yishmael takes ill to the point that Hagar fears for his life. Hagar cannot bear to witness her son's pain, and in order to avoid this dreadful situation, leaves her son's side (Bereshis 21:15). She watches him from a distance of הַרְחֵק כִּמְטַחֲוֵי קֶשֶׁת *a bow's shot away* (ibid 21:16) explaining אַל אֶרְאֶה בְּמוֹת הַיָּלֶד *I cannot watch the boy die* (ibid 21:16). Then at the last minute, an angel unexpectedly appears, saves Yishmael and remarks, אַל תִּירְאִי כִּי שָׁמַע אֱלֹהִים אֶל קוֹל הַנַּעַר בַּאֲשֶׁר הוּא שָׁם *Do not be afraid for Hashem heard the voice of the lad where he is now* (ibid 21:17).

The description of the distance that Hagar stands from Yishmael, הַרְחֵק כִּמְטַחֲוֵי קֶשֶׁת *a bow's shot away* (ibid 21:16) is extremely unusual. It is uncommon for the Torah to inform us how far people stand from one another and moreover, this measurement, *a bow's shot away*, is unprecedented. Why does the Torah specify this distance and indeed, why does the Torah recount this entire story?

Although Hagar's pain is unimaginable and her inability to stand next to Yishmael is understandable, it is not justifiable. Hagar should

---

[109] This aligns with the Rabaynu Yonah (Avos 5:3) who counts expelling both Hagar and Yishmael as only one of the ten tests. This stands in contrast to the Rambam (Avos 5:3) who counts Gerush Hagar and Gerush Yishmael as two of the separate tests and uses different verbs to describe each expulsion; Hagar's expulsion is called gerush *expulsion*, whereas Yishmael's is harchakas *distance*.

not be thinking of herself and her pain, but Yishmael and his dreadful predicament. He is lying in the heat of the desert facing death, and in immense need of his mother; yet she is selfishly tending to her own emotional needs over his.

With this new perspective, we can now understand why Yishmael becomes a רֹבֶה קַשָּׁת *an archer*, why the Torah records it (ibid 21:20) as part of the Gerush Yishmael story as well as the significant impact for Hagar standing הַרְחֵק כִּמְטַחֲוֵי קֶשֶׁת *a bow's shot away*. Psychologically, Yishmael is damaged by his mother's self-interest and that tremendous pain leads to his career of violence.[110] The Torah may showcase this story to represent Hagar's relationship with and profound impact upon Yishmael. Yishmael feels the pain of his mother's selfishness.

THE FIRST TRACES OF HAGAR'S SELFISHNESS

The first traces of Hagar's selfish and competitive nature are found significantly earlier. After ten years of unsuccessfully attempting to get pregnant, Sarah selflessly allows Hagar to bear a child for Avraham (ibid 16:2). Immediately upon becoming pregnant, Hagar arrogantly begins to look down at Sarah (ibid 16:4).[111] Becoming pregnant, in Hagar's eyes, elevates her above Sarah, for not only is she pregnant whereas Sarah is not, but her pregnancy means that she is destined to deliver Avraham's first child. Hagar begins to see herself as the central wife and her son, Yishmael, as Avraham's central son, and therefore, his sole heir.

YISHMAEL'S WIFE

There may be no clearer evidence of Hagar's profound impact on Yishmael than his marriage to an Egyptian wife (ibid 21:21). It is not coincidental that she comes from Egypt, Hagar homeland (ibid 16:1). Moreover, the Torah writes that Hagar actually chooses this wife for

---

[110] In contrast to a peaceful career, for example as a shepherd, a line of work pursued by the Avos and one which cultivates generosity towards animals by caring for them, Yishmael is an archer. He hunts and kills animals.

[111] Hagar even sees herself as spiritually superior on the grounds that she becomes pregnant on the first night, whereas Sarah is unsuccessful after years of trying (Bereshis Rabbah 45:4, Vilna Edition, and quoted by Rashi Bereshis 16:4).

him, וַתִּקַּח לוֹ אִמּוֹ אִשָּׁה מֵאֶרֶץ מִצְרָיִם *and his mother took for him a wife from Egypt* (ibid 21:21).

HOW HAGAR'S SELFISHNESS IMPACTS YISHMAEL

Hagar's profound impact on Yishmael extends beyond influencing his choice of career and wife. She indoctrinates Yishmael to believe he is entitled to be Avraham's sole heir, as seen from Yishmael's reaction to Yitzhak's birth according to Chazal (Bereshis Rabbah, Vilna Edition 53:11), שבשעה שנולד אבינו יצחק היו הכל שמחים אמר להם ישמעאל שוטים אתם אני בכור ואני נוטל פי שנים *At the time when Yitzhak, our father, was born, all were happy. Yishmael said to them 'You are all foolish. I am the firstborn and I will take double (the portion allocated for the firstborn).'*[112]

Just as Hagar sees herself as a replacement for Sarah as Avraham's primary wife, she sees Yishmael as Avraham's primary son.

Hagar's influence on Yishmael can be further developed by uncovering a fascinating parallel between this episode and Avraham at the Akeida.

PARALLEL TO THE AKEIDA

Beyond the juxtaposition between Gerush Yishmael and the Akeida, there are remarkable parallels between the two, both in language and theme. We will list the similarities and then differences and uncover something fascinating in the process.

1. The Gerush Yishmael story reports וַיַּשְׁכֵּם אַבְרָהָם בַּבֹּקֶר *And Avraham woke up early in the morning* (ibid 21:14) a hallmark of the Akeida narrative (ibid 22:3).

2. Both stories occur elsewhere, but mention בְּאֵר שָׁבַע *Baer Sheva* parenthetically, (ibid 21:14, 22:19).

---

[112] Similarly, the Midrash (Bereshis Rabbah, Vilna Edition 55:4 and quoted by Rashi Bereshis 22:1) records a debate where Yishmael brags to Yitzhak, claiming higher spiritual status for he has his bris at age thirteen without objecting. Yitzhak responds that he is willing to sacrifice his entire body if requested to do so. The Midrash adds that Yitzhak's comments prompt Akeidas Yitzhak.

3. In each story, Hashem commands Avraham to do something greatly damaging to a son. In one instance, Avraham is commanded to kill a son and on the other occasion to expel one.

4. The Gerush Yishmael incident features one of Avraham's sons and one parent, Hagar, facing death under branches (ibid 21:15). The Akeida also captures one of Avraham's sons alone with one parent, and again, the son, faces death as he is put under branches (ibid 22:9).

5. Facing imminent death, an angel calls out from the heavens (ibid 21:17, 22:11) instructing the respective parent (Hagar and Avraham) to relocate their hand and informs the parent that their son will live (ibid 21:18, 22:12).

6. The angel, in both episodes, proceeds to save the child with something which has been present the entire time, yet previously went unnoticed (ibid 21:19, 22:13). The angel reveals to Hagar that there is water nearby, and to Avraham that there is a ram to replace Yitzhak.

7. Both stories conclude with a blessing for the boys that they will have numerous children (ibid 21:18, 22:17).

8. Immediately after these near-death experiences, both Yishmael and Yitzhak take a wife (ibid 21:21, 24:1). However, the parallel is deeper, for each child, Yishmael and Yitzhak, immediately marry a spouse from their respective parent's birthplace. Yishmael takes a wife who is Egyptian like Hagar (ibid 16:1). Yitzhak takes, Rivka, who derives from the exact same house from which Avraham originated.

Naturally, one might wonder why the Torah subtly hints to a connection between these two stories. Before answering that, let us list the opposites between the two episodes.

Contrast to the Akeida

In addition to the similarities between these two episodes there are many significant differences as well.

1. The angel, after stopping Avraham, proceeds to communicate to Avraham that he *is* a God-fearing man, עַתָּה יָדַעְתִּי כִּי יְרֵא אֱלֹהִים אַתָּה

now I know that you are a God-fearing man (ibid 22:12). By contrast, Hagar is commanded by the angel *not* to fear אַל תִּירְאִי *Do not be afraid* (ibid 21:17). Avraham is complimented because of how he acted in the past and Hagar receives instructions for the future and Avraham is told is does fear Hashem, and Hagar, the opposite, not to fear.

2. While the angel commands Avraham to move his hand away from his son, instructing him not to lay a hand upon his son (ibid 22:12), the angel instructs Hagar to do the exact opposite וְהַחֲזִיקִי אֶת יָדֵךְ בּוֹ *and grab him with your hand* (ibid 21:18).

3. Yishmael is saved because he is judged בַּאֲשֶׁר הוּא שָׁם *where he is now* (ibid 21:17), and is answered despite the fact that it is Hagar who prayed (ibid 22:16-17). Yitzhak, however, is saved because of his father.[113]

4. The Torah stresses that Avraham and Yitzhak engage in conversation with the word וַיֹּאמֶר *And he said* (Bereshis 22:7-8) which appears five times in just two verses.[114] By contrast, Hagar says nothing to Yishmael.

5. Avraham responds הִנֵּנִי *here I am* (ibid 22:7) to Yitzhak and remains alongside him during an incredibly trying time. Hagar separates herself from Yishmael when he needs her most.

6. Avraham and Yitzhak consistently address each other with the relationship title אָבִי *my father* and בְּנִי *my son* (22:7, 7, 7, 8) whereas Hagar and Yishmael do not.

There are too many parallels for these stories not to be linked. And the opposites too, are far too striking for this to be explained as coincidence. Therefore, we must ask, what is the Torah's reason for hinting to these comparisons and contrasts?

---

[113] The entire test was for Avraham (Bereshis 22:1)

[114] Interestingly, and perhaps to stress our point, this is the only time that the Torah records direct communication between Avraham and Yitzhak.

Two Distinct Styles of Parenting

Contrasting the Gerush Yishmael with the Akeidas Yitzhak episode illustrates the different parenting techniques Hagar and Avraham use. Hagar distances herself from Yishmael in this exceedingly difficult situation, while Avraham, by contrast, finds himself in a significantly more difficult situation. He is commanded to sacrifice his son, yet still miraculously manages to remain close with Yitzhak. Avraham, almost unfathomably, inspires trust in Yitzhak by stating, הִנֵּנִי *here I am* (ibid 22:7).

Avraham ambiguously communicates to Yitzhak, אֱלֹהִים יִרְאֶה לּוֹ הַשֶּׂה לְעֹלָה בְּנִי *Hashem will show us the sheep for the (karban) Olah, my son.* It is unclear whether by adding בְּנִי *my son* Avraham means to address Yitzhak, or imply that he is the sacrifice. In that way, Avraham subtly informs Yitzhak that he genuinely does not know the outcome of the endeavor.[115] Remarkably, they continue together, united, with complete faith in Hashem. To emphasize this, the Torah uses the exact same language, וַיֵּלְכוּ שְׁנֵיהֶם יַחְדָּו *and they walked together* (Bereshis 22:7) that it does earlier in the narrative (ibid 22:6). Yitzhak now knows, and is equally committed.[116]

The point is clear. Avraham creates a deep feeling of safety in an uncertain environment. In contrast to Avraham who selflessly cares for Yitzhak in an unimaginably difficult situation, Hagar acts selfishly when one would have expected otherwise from a mother. Whereas Avraham is there for Yitzhak when he has every excuse not to be, Hagar is not there for Yishmael, when she has every reason to be.

Sarah's Correct and Realistic Viewpoint

Sarah demands from Avraham, גָּרֵשׁ הָאָמָה הַזֹּאת וְאֶת בְּנָהּ *expel this maidservant and her son* (ibid 21:10) because כִּי לֹא יִירַשׁ בֶּן הָאָמָה הַזֹּאת

---

[115] Alternatively, Avraham informs Yitzhak unambiguously that אמר יצחק לאביו אבא הרי האש והעצים היכן הוא הכבש לעולה אמר לו בני אתה הוא הכבש לעולה *Yitzhak said to his father 'here is the fire and the wood. Where is the sheep for the Olah?' He (Avraham) responded 'my son, you are the sheep for the Olah'* (Pirkey D'Rebbi Eliezer 30).

[116] Rashi (Bereshis 22:8). וַיֵּלְכוּ שְׁנֵיהֶם יַחְדָּו *and they walked together* is stated both before and after their conversation, indicating that Yitzhak is completely informed and as equally committed now as he was beforehand.

עִם בְּנִי עִם יִצְחָק *for he should not inherit with my son, with Yitzhak* (ibid 21:10). Moreover, when Sarah describes Yishmael as אֲשֶׁר בֶּן הָגָר הַמִּצְרִית יָלְדָה לְאַבְרָהָם מְצַחֵק *son of Hagar, the Egyptian, who begat a son to Avraham being mitzachek* (ibid 21:9) she could be communicating something more subtle.

The word מְצַחֵק *mitzachek* comes from the name יצחק *Yitzhak*. Sarah understands that Yishmael is attempting to become Yitzhak. Aware of the enormous danger this poses, she demands his expulsion.

Hashem agrees with Sarah and commands Avraham, כֹּל אֲשֶׁר תֹּאמַר אֵלֶיךָ שָׂרָה שְׁמַע בְּקֹלָהּ *all that Sarah told you, listen to her* (ibid 21:12). Hashem further reinforces her reasoning, reaffirming, כִּי בְיִצְחָק יִקָּרֵא לְךָ זָרַע *for through Yitzhak will your descendants be called* (ibid 21:12). Sarah instructs Avraham that Yitzhak will be the only son carrying on Avraham's spiritual legacy.

AVRAHAM'S OPTIMISTIC VIEWPOINT

Avraham, an incredible optimist, lover of all people, and believer in all mankind,[117] deeply believes in Yishmael as well as Yitzhak. Even after hearing Sarah's concerns, Avraham still wants to include Yishmael in his future vision for the world (ibid 21:11).[118] That is precisely why Hashem has to intercede and validate Sarah's concerns (ibid 21:12).

It is precisely this optimism and belief in Yishmael that leads Hashem to slowly and gradually communicate to Avraham that it is only Sarah and her son, Yitzhak, who will carry the legacy alongside Avraham, as we will now explain.

---

[117] Avraham became an אב המון גוים *father to many nations* because he saw himself as an אב המון גוים *father to many nations* (Rabbi Reuven Taragin).

[118] According to Rashi (Bereshis 18:7) Avraham invests in Yishmael's religious education raising him to hosts guests properly. The Meshech Chochma (Bereshis 33:18) disagrees arguing that Avraham does not currently see Yishmael as successful and therefore travels specifically to Mitzrayim to educate him there, for Mitzrayim is the epicenter of philosophy. Yaakov, by contrast to Avraham, has committed children and therefore adopts an insular approach. Yaakov's strong religious introversion leads him to be upset at Rochel for taking Lavan's Avodah Zara and trying to prevent him from sinning further. Similarly, Yaakov and his sons remaining in Goshen, separate from the Egyptians.

SARAH'S STRANGE NAME CHANGE

Hashem changes Sarah's name from Sari to Sarah but does so in a very unusual manner. First of all, He informs only Avraham of the name change, not Sarah, **וַיֹּאמֶר אֱלֹהִים אֶל אַבְרָהָם** שָׂרַי אִשְׁתְּךָ לֹא תִקְרָא אֶת שְׁמָהּ שָׂרָי כִּי שָׂרָה שְׁמָהּ *And Hashem said to Avraham, 'Sari your wife, do not call her Sari, because Sarah is her name'* (ibid 17:15). Presumably Avraham informs Sarah but one certainly would have expected Hashem to communicate Sarah's name change to her directly.

Equally strange is how Hashem does it. Hashem corrects Avraham for calling her Sari; שָׂרַי אִשְׁתְּךָ לֹא תִקְרָא אֶת שְׁמָהּ שָׂרַי כִּי שָׂרָה שְׁמָהּ *Sari your wife, do not call her Sari, because Sarah is her name* (ibid 17:15), implying that Avraham has been calling her by the wrong name all this time.

This bizarre manner of how Hashem changes Sarah's name is highlighted by contrasting it with how Hashem changes Avraham's name. In Avraham's case, Hashem explains **וְלֹא יִקָּרֵא עוֹד אֶת שִׁמְךָ** אַבְרָם וְהָיָה שִׁמְךָ אַבְרָהָם *And **no longer should you call** your name Avram, it should be Avraham* (ibid 17:5). Hashem clearly states that until this point, Avraham was Avram and going forward he will be known as Avraham; the word עוֹד *no longer* leaves no doubt.

Yet Sarah's original name until this point, undeniably, was Sari. This is explicit numerous times before (ibid 11:29, 30, 31 12:5, 10, 15, 16:2, 2, 3, 5, 6, 6, 8, 8) and is even evident when Avraham is informed by Hashem of her name change, וַיֹּאמֶר אֱלֹהִים אֶל אַבְרָהָם שָׂרַי אִשְׁתְּךָ *And Hashem said to Avraham, Sari, your wife* (ibid 17:15). When then, does Sari become Sarah? The Torah never records it.

UNDERSTANDING SARAH'S NAME CHANGE

When Avram becomes Avraham (ibid 17:5), there is a transformation in more than merely his name. There is one in his religious role as well. He is now destined to have children, as Hashem promises him in the adjacent verse, וְהִפְרֵתִי אֹתְךָ בִּמְאֹד מְאֹד וּנְתַתִּיךָ לְגוֹיִם וּמְלָכִים מִמְּךָ יֵצֵאוּ *And I will multiply you greatly, and make nations come from you and kings will descend from you* (ibid 17:6).

However, couched in Avraham's name change may be more. When Avram becomes Avraham, his entire family dynamic transforms, as implied by the next verse, וַהֲקִמֹתִי אֶת בְּרִיתִי בֵּינִי וּבֵינֶךָ וּבֵין זַרְעֲךָ אַחֲרֶיךָ לְדֹרֹתָם לִבְרִית עוֹלָם לִהְיוֹת לְךָ לֵאלֹהִים וּלְזַרְעֲךָ אַחֲרֶיךָ *And I will establish my bris with you and your son and descendants who come after you for generations as an eternal bris so that I will be a God to you and your descendants afterwards* (ibid 17:7).

Beyond Avraham being blessed with children who will continue Avraham's spiritual future,[119] there still is more. As Sari becomes Sarah, she goes through a transformation as well. When Avraham's role transforms, the role of Sarah, his life partner, does as well. Automatically, she becomes Sarah and is no longer Sari. Hence, it is accurate for Hashem to correct Avraham. Sarah's name has been switched ever since Avraham's name has been, Avraham just needs to be informed.[120]

Still, why does Hashem not communicate to Sarah directly?

WHAT ABOUT YISHMAEL?

After hearing about his son to be born to Sarah, Avraham initially celebrates, but then curiously remarks, לוּ יִשְׁמָעֵאל יִחְיֶה לְפָנֶיךָ *O that Yishmael might live before you* (ibid 17:18). Again, Avraham's optimism (and maybe Hagar's influence) causes him to believe that Yishmael will, indeed, be part of Avraham's future legacy. Hashem corrects Avraham by informing him that Sarah and Yitzhak alone are part of this covenant, **אֲבָל** שָׂרָה אִשְׁתְּךָ יֹלֶדֶת לְךָ בֵּן וְקָרָאתָ אֶת שְׁמוֹ יִצְחָק **וַהֲקִמֹתִי אֶת בְּרִיתִי אִתּוֹ** לִבְרִית עוֹלָם לְזַרְעוֹ אַחֲרָיו *but Sarah, your wife, will have a son and you will call him Yitzhak and **I will establish my bris with him**, the eternal bris for his descendants afterwards* (ibid 17:19).

Hashem now informs Avraham that his name change, reflecting a spiritual transformation, is for Sarah and her future children only. Sarah, fully aware of who Yishmael is, realizes that he is excluded. Immediately she understands what Avraham does not yet comprehend.[121]

---

[119] Netziv (Bereshis 17:4 and Devorim 29:1)

[120] Rav Soloveitchik (Dvrei HaRav 245).

[121] Chazal (Shemos Rabbah, Vilna Edition 1:1 and quoted Rashi Bereshis 21:12) state that Sarah has greater prophecy than Avraham.

Therefore Hashem only has to communicate her name change to Avraham.

In addition to Avram becoming Avraham and this representing his new mission of becoming the אב המון גוים *father to many nations*, Sari becoming Sarah captures a parallel ideological shift, as Chazal (Tosefta Brachos 1:13)[122] remark כיוצא בו שרי אשתך לא תקרא את שמה שרי כי שרה שמה בתחלה הרי היא שרי על עמה עכשיו הרי היא שרה על כל באי עולם *Similarly (to Avraham) 'Sari your wife, do not call her Sari, because Sarah is her name'. At first she was a princess (Sari) for her nation, now she is a princess (Sarah) for the whole world.*

Understanding Hagar's Name

Hagar is a second wife who tries to use her son to elevate herself into the position of the primary wife's role. Hashem responds by protecting Sarah and the future of the bris by ensuring that Hagar remains an outsider and stranger.

This outside nature is reflected by her name הגר *the stranger*, or *the outsider*. Her name represents who she is: an outsider.

Yishmael's Teshuva

Chazal (Bereshis Rabbah 38:12, Vilna Edition, Baba Basra 16b and quoted by Rashi Bereshis 25:9), state that at the end of Yishmael's life, he does teshuva *repentance*.[123] By giving Yitzhak primacy at Avraham's funeral (Bereshis 25:9), Yishmael corrects his behavior.[124]

---

[122] A similar version appears in Rashi (Bereshis 17:15).

[123] The Meshech Chochma (Bereshis 15:15) notes that Yishmael's decedents will follow in his path by repenting at the end of days as well.

[124] Rashi (ibid 25:9). Because the Torah states וַיִּקְבְּרוּ אֹתוֹ יִצְחָק וְיִשְׁמָעֵאל בָּנָיו *and Yitzhak and Yishmael, his sons, buried him (Avraham)*, the Midrash (Midrash Agada, Buber edition, Parshas Chaya Sarah 25) concludes היה ישמעאל בכור והנהיג יצחק לפניו, לפי שהיה יודע בו שהוא צדיק ממנו *Yishmael was the firstborn, yet he allowed Yitzhak to go first for he knew that he (Yitzhak) was more righteous.*
From the Midrash's perspective on Esuv, אבל עשו לא עשה תשובה, שהרי לא נאמר ויקברו אותו עשו ויעקב בניו *But Esuv did not do teshuva, for it (the Torah) never says 'and Yaakov and Esuv, his sons, buried him'* one can assume Yishmael's teshuva is an attitude which allows Yitzhak to proceed in burying Avraham.

The implication is that, if prioritizing Yitzhak is Yishmael's teshuva, his sin must have been failure to give precedence to Yitzhak.[125] Until this point, Yishmael erroneously has seen himself as the primary offspring, an attitude that he undoubtedly inherited from his mother.

Now, instead of trying to become Yitzhak, Yishmael accepts his role happily. Once he does this, the Torah communicates its approval by recording Yishmael's lineage (Bereshis 25:12-16) and death (ibid 25:17), both out of respect.[126]

AVRAHAM'S SON YITZHAK

Yitzhak, unlike Yishmael, is raised to be comfortable with himself. It may be precisely that comfort and confidence that enables him to follow in Avraham's path and not insist on blazing his own personal trail.

Perhaps more than anything else, Yitzhak displays an ability to solidify what Avraham has forged. There are numerous ways in which Yitzhak appears to mimic Avraham.[127]

1. Yitzhak, just like Avraham, plans to leave Eretz Yisrael during a time of famine.

2. Both Avraham and Yitzhak's wives are threatened by a king named Avimelech in Grar (Bereshis 20:2 and 26:1, 9). And when fearful of his neighbors in Grar possibly taking his wife, Yitzhak, follows Avraham's lead (ibid 20:2) in claiming his wife is really his sister (ibid 26:7).

However, some (Shem M'Shmuel, Parshas Shemos) argue that Yishmael never does full teshuva, and allowing Yitzhak to go first does not reflect and internal religious transformation.

[125] Lubavitcher Rebbe (also see Meshech Chochoma Bereshis 25:9)

[126] It is uncommon for the Torah to record irreligious people's linage and death. By the Torah recording Yishmael's, the Torah hints again to Yishmael's righteousness and teshuva. Alternatively, the Torah includes Esuv's death and lineage for a technical reason, to show respect for Avraham (Rashbam on Bereshis 25:17) or for other calculations, namely details about Yaakov (Megilla 17a and Rashi on Bereshis 25:17).

[127] See Double Take the chapter entitled *Shimshon's Leadership, Individuality, and Central Role in Sefer Shoftim* for the greater significance of these similarities.

3. Avimelech rebukes both Avraham and Yitzhak for misleading the local people by claiming that their wives are their sisters (ibid 20:9, 26:9).

4. Both Avraham and Yitzhak ultimately make peace with Avimelech (ibid 20:14-18, and ibid 26:31).

5. Avraham and Yitzhak are both blessed with similar brachos *blessings* (land, numerous descendants, a blessing).

6. Just as Avraham debates his wife about his older son Yishmael's role, Yitzhak debates Rivka, his wife, about their older son Esav's role (Bereshis 20:1). Furthermore, Yitzhak, like Avraham, takes a more accepting, loving and welcoming approach regarding his elder son.

7. Yitzhak digs the exact same wells that Avraham has previously dug (Bereshis 26:18). Moreover, and in an unmistakably similar fashion, Yitzhak names them with the same exact names that Avraham has chosen (Bereshis 26:18).

8. Both of their younger sons, Yitzhak and Yaakov, meet their wives, Rivka and Rachel, at wells. Additionally, each of the wives met at the wells is a cousin.

After trailblazing, innovating, discovering and creating the way Avraham has, there is a need for the concretization. Yitzhak represents the concretizing and solidifying of these values. Who better than someone as humble, and comfortable in his own skin as Yitzhak to accomplish this goal? Yitzhak has developed the ideal personality traits for the task at hand.

Whereas for Avraham's generation, the goal is to create, for Yitzhak's, it is to solidify.[128] Chazal (Bereshis Rabbah, Vilna Edition 1:15) reinforce how Avraham and Yitzhak work together accomplishing this goal by stating that שקולין זה כזה *they are equal to each other.*[129]

---

[128] The Malbim (Bereshis 26:1) contrasts Avraham who initiates this revolutionary movement, discovers Hashem through philosophy and requires ten tests to stabilize himself with Yitzhak, who is the second generation. Yitzhak inherits his belief from his father and does not need these tests to fortify his faith. Based on this one can further understand the difference between Avraham's creative role and Yitzhak's concretizing role.

[129] The Midrash adds Yaakov as being equal to Avraham and Yitzhak.

NOT A BEN SORRER U'MOREH

In contrast to Yishmael who is judged בַּאֲשֶׁר הוּא שָׁם *where he was at the time* (Bereshis 21:17), the Ben Sorrer U'Moreh, *wayward son*, is נדון על שם סופו *judged based upon his future* (Sanhedrin 71b).[130] Naturally, one should consider why this difference exists. When is one judged בַּאֲשֶׁר הוּא שָׁם *where he was at the time* and when is one נדון על שם סופו *judged based upon his future?*

The Ben Sorrer U'Moreh is נדון על שם סופו *judged based upon his future* because it can be assumed that there is no chance of him repenting. Better to eliminate the evil before it begins. By contrast, Yishmael does teshuva. Even at a young age, there is hope for Yishmael. Yishmael's hope is Avraham's optimism and ability to inspire him.

Chazal (Sanhedrin 71a) state that to be a Ben Sorrer U'Moreh, one must parents who have are identical to the degree that they have indistinguishable voices.[131] By contrast, Yishmael has two completely different parents with completely different ideologies.[132] Although Hagar heavily influences Yishmael's life, Avraham does so too.

When presenting the laws of the Ben Sorrer U'Moreh, the Torah describes his actions as וְלֹא יִשְׁמַע אֲלֵיהֶם *and he does not listen to them* (Devorim 21:18), which may have a hint couched in it. One can move the space between the words and read וְלֹא יִשְׁמַע אֲלֵיהֶם *and he does not listen to them* as ולא ישמעאים הם *these are not Yishmaels*. The Torah here hints to the Ben Sorrer U'Moreh not being like Yishmael's situation.

However, there may be more to this hint, for what better words are there to weave this idea into than וְלֹא יִשְׁמַע אֲלֵיהֶם *and he does not listen to them*, the exact phrase that captures why the Ben Sorrer U'Moreh is different from Yishmael namely that his parents are identical. Consequently, the Ben Sorrer U'Moreh lacks the fresh voice, the voice of Avraham that inspires Yishmael.

---

[130] And sentenced to death. It should be noted that this situation never occurred nor will it, it is strictly designed for theoretical academic purposes (Sanhedrin 71a).

[131] As hinted to by the Torah, אֵינֶנּוּ שֹׁמֵעַ בְּקוֹל אָבִיו וּבְקוֹל אִמּוֹ *He does not listen to the voice of his father or the voice of his mother* (Devorim 21:18).

[132] The Torah omits almost all interaction between Avraham and Hagar. By contrast, Avraham has a remarkably positive relationship with Sarah (Bereshis 19). For more, see Double Take, the chapter entitled *Shimshon's Leadership, Individually and Central Role in Sefer Shoftim.*

TOLDOS

After Yishmael's teshuva, the Torah states, וְאֵלֶּה תֹּלְדֹת יִשְׁמָעֵאל
בֶּן אַבְרָהָם אֲשֶׁר יָלְדָה הָגָר הַמִּצְרִית שִׁפְחַת שָׂרָה לְאַבְרָהָם *And these are the
generations of Yishmael, the son of Avraham, that Hagar, the Egyptian,
the maidservant of Sarah, bore to Avraham* (ibid 25:12) in an almost
identical fashion to the description of Yitzhak as וְאֵלֶּה תֹּולְדֹת יִצְחָק בֶּן
אַבְרָהָם אַבְרָהָם הוֹלִיד אֶת יִצְחָק *And these are the generations of Yitzhak, the
son of Avraham; Avraham gave birth to Yitzhak* (ibid 25:19).[133]

The unmistakable parallel language the Torah used between the
beginnings of each of the תֹּלְדֹת *generation* highlights that each son is a
son to Avraham. However, the end of each verse underscores the exact
opposite. While Yishmael is the child אֲשֶׁר יָלְדָה הָגָר הַמִּצְרִית שִׁפְחַת שָׂרָה
לְאַבְרָהָם *that Hagar, the Egyptian, the maidservant of Sarah to Avraham
gave birth to*, Yitzhak is deeply influenced by Avraham, as the Torah
reiterates, אַבְרָהָם הוֹלִיד אֶת יִצְחָק *Avraham gave birth to Yitzhak*. Avraham
has a profound impact on Yitzhak, whereas Yishmael's influence comes
from both Hagar and Avraham. His desire to jealously look at Yitzhak
attempting to take his role comes from Hagar, whereas the teshuva he
does is inspired by Avraham.

APPLYING TEXT TO LIFE: THE HASHKAFIC MESSAGE

Hagar is an outsider attempting to become an insider. This alone
is not inherently bad. Hagar's mistake is how she goes about doing it.
Instead of trying to replace Sarah with jealous motivations, she should
have been content excelling at her own role. Success in life is when
one happily plays one's hand as best as possible, not steal someone
else's cards. The secret to feeling like an insider is feeling comfortable
as oneself or as Chazal summarize, איזהו עשיר השמח בחלקו *Who is rich?
One who is happy with what one has* (Avos 4:1).

Yishmael's insecure and overly competitive nature results directly
from the influence Hagar has on him. This manifests itself in Yishmael's
desire to replace Yitzhak, his marriage to an Egyptian wife, and his
career choice as an archer. The Torah covertly stresses the power of the

---

[133] Rashbam (Bereshis 25:19)

influence parents have on their children. Moreover, the Torah may have even intentionally communicated this message covertly, because that is precisely how the influence on one's children is done, surreptitiously.

Yet, there is another important lesson to learn. Yishmael does teshuva at the end of his life, and the Torah respects that. Simply put, it is never too late to repent.

Additionally, there is much to learn from Avraham's optimism and belief in mankind. Because of Avraham's belief in Yishmael, Yishmael ultimately comes around, which is what Rav Yochanan (Baba Basra 16b) means when he comments, ישמעאל עשה תשובה בחיי אביו *Yishmael did teshuva in his father's lifetime.* Rather than merely representing a historical demarcation, Rav Yochanan conveys that Avraham is the root of Yishmael's transformation.[134] One can never know when the seeds of belief in others will sprout.

---

[134] Interestingly, it is debated (Bereshis Rabbah Vilna Edition 41:8) whether Avraham is right or wrong for allowing Lot to leave him.

Aharon's Surprising Involvement in the Chet HaEgel

Moshe and Aharon

If empowered with the extraordinary task of assigning leadership roles to Moshe and Aharon, one would most likely do the exact opposite of what Hashem does. Moshe seems appropriate for the position of Kohen Gadol, and Aharon, the position of religious and political leader. After all, Aharon personifies אוהב שלום ורודף שלום *love peace and pursue peace* (Avos 1:12); a paradigmatic man of the people. What trait would be a better barometer for leadership? By contrast, Moshe's strength lies in his unique humility, as the Torah itself attests, he is עָנָיו מְאֹד מִכֹּל הָאָדָם *the humblest of all people* (Bamidbar 12:3). Moreover, his ability to converse with Hashem is unparalleled as the Torah records, פָּנִים אֶל פָּנִים כַּאֲשֶׁר יְדַבֵּר אִישׁ אֶל רֵעֵהוּ *face to face, like a man speaks with his friend* (Shemos 33:11). Should their jobs not be switched? Since Hashem does not err, we must understand what logic lies behind appointing Moshe as the national leader and Aharon as the Kohen Gadol.

What the Alternative Would Have Looked Like

Would it not be wonderful to see what that would look like? There is one small glimpse of Moshe engrossed in pure spirituality, while Aharon oversees the people; the story of Chet HaEgel *sin of the (Golden) Calf*. Yet, instead of the expected success, there is utter catastrophe.

One must therefore wonder why there is such colossal failure in the only situation where Aharon leads the people and Moshe plays the role of the kohen? An in-depth look at the Chet HaEgel episode, and specifically the roles of Moshe and Aharon, should offer the perspective needed to answer this question.

CHET HAEGEL, NOT SUCH A SIMPLE STORY

With a casual read, the account of the Chet HaEgel seems to be an easily understood story: it is straight-forward and unambiguous. However, in truth, there is a lot to uncover.

A central issue that requires explanation is how could this happen? How could Bnei Yisrael worship an idol so soon after the Exodus and Har Sinai?[135] How short is their memory?[136] However, a far more penetrating question is; whether they honestly believe that this egel HaZahav *Golden Calf* orchestrated the Exodus. It is almost impossible to imagine any intelligent human being attributing the Exodus to an idol, specifically one that they themselves fashioned. This difficulty is compounded because Bnei Yisrael created it after the Exodus.[137]

In addition to Bnei Yisrael's baffling actions of worshiping an egel, one should wonder why they even choose an egel in the first place. Of all animals, and really anything, why choose a cow and more specifically a calf? If anything, one might expect a bull, symbolizing strength, or a sheep, for that is what the Egyptians worshiped.[138] What does a calf represent?

---

[135] According to the Ramban (Shemos 13:16) the greatest miracles occur during the Exodus, whereas according to the Rambam (Yesodei HaTorah 8:1) and Sefer HaIkarim (1:18-20) they take place at Har Sinai.

[136] Many offer insight to the yetzer hara to worship idols. The Kuzari (quoted by the Malbim on Shemos 32:1) attributes it to the heavy influence the Egyptians have on Bnei Yisrael, and points to the worshiping of the egel as a proof of that influence. The Meiri (Introduction to Avos) explains that people yearn to worship something tangible over something abstract. Additionally, creating one's own divinity enables one to create the rules, as Chazal state, יודעין היו ישראל בעבודה זרה שאין בה ממש, ולא עבדו עבודה זרה אלא להתיר להם עריות בפרהסיא *Yisrael knew that idolatry is empty; they did not worship idols for another reason than to justify public sexual promiscuity* (Sanhedrin 63b).

[137] These questions are even more difficult according to the Yerushalmi (Sanhedrin 10:2) which states that Bnei Yisrael construct twelve calves.

[138] Ramban (Shemos 12:3)

What is also astonishing is why Aharon joins this rebellious movement. Aharon certainly should know better, yet he seems to play a central role in both, the construction of and worshipping of the egel. How do we understand that?

Remarkably, no one is punished for this sin; not the instigators, not Aharon, nor the bystanders. True, some people are subsequently punished, but only for not joining Moshe after he calls, מִי לַיקֹוָק אֵלָי *Who is for Hashem, with me* (Shemos 32:26). They are not punished for participating in the Chet HaEgel itself. Is idolatry not a greater sin? Why does Hashem not punish anyone for the creating and worshiping the egel yet He severely punishes them for not heeding Moshe's call מִי לַיקֹוָק אֵלָי? *Who is for Hashem, with me*? Is the former not significantly worse?

The absence of any punishment is particularly strange considering Hashem's initial reaction, desiring to destroy all of Bnei Yisrael (ibid 32:7-10). Is Hashem fickle? How can His initial response to obliterate the entire nation change so drastically to the point where no one faces any punishment at all?

Lastly, Moshe's response to the Egel HaZahav is once again confounding. He burns and minces the egel, pours it into water and has Bnei Yisrael drink it (ibid 32:20). Not only is this unprecedented, it is extremely strange. What does it accomplish?[139] Why drink wet particles of the idol?

Aharon's Unusual Behavior

While attempting to understanding Aharon's involvement, we should also try to understand why Bnei Yisrael approach specifically him in the first place. He should have been the last person they turn to! If anyone is to stop this rebellious uprising while is gone, it is surely Aharon.

In trying to understand Aharon's involvement, there are two basic theories. There are those who explain that although Aharon does not condone the idolatry, he fears that without his involvement, the situation will be that much worse. Aharon is not even partially on

---

[139] According to the Chizkuni (Shemos 32:20), it merely appears as if Bnei Yisrael drink it.

board, yet he rationalizes that redirecting their motives and navigating them towards Hashem is tactically wise. This attitude may have come across more clearly in his declaration, חַג לַיקֹוָק מָחָר *there is a holiday for Hashem tomorrow* (ibid 32:5) redirecting the group to act לַיקֹוָק *for Hashem.*[140]

Others[141] respond that Aharon is simply stalling, hopeful that Moshe will quickly return.[142] Textual support can be found for this position as well. Firstly, Aharon calls for the holiday מָחָר *tomorrow* (ibid 32:5) and not today. Additionally, Aharon requests that the men take jewelry directly from their wives' and children's ears פָּרְקוּ נִזְמֵי הַזָּהָב אֲשֶׁר בְּאָזְנֵי נְשֵׁיכֶם בְּנֵיכֶם וּבְנֹתֵיכֶם *remove the golden rings from the ears of your wives, sons and daughters* (ibid 32:2).[143] Perhaps pulling the jewelry, literally, off their faces would cause the women to refuse and therefore slow things down.[144]

---

[140] Rashi (Shemos 32:5), Ibn Ezra (Shemos 32:1), Ramban (Shemos 32:5), Bechor Shor (Shemos 32:5), Chizkuni (Shemos 32:5), Daas Zekanim M'Baalay HaTosfos (Shemos 32:5) Perush HaRosh (32:1), Rav Shimshon Rafael Hirsch (Shemos 32:1) and Malbim (Shemos 32:5)

[141] Midrash Tanchuma (Parshas Ki Sisa 19), Rashi (Shemos 32:5), Ramban (Shemos 32:5), Bechor Shor (Shemos 32:5), Chizkuni (Shemos 32:5), Daas Zekanim M'Baalay HaTosfos (Shemos 32:5), Malbim (Shemos 32:5), the Ohr HaChaim (Shemos 32:2). Perhaps even the building of the mizbayach is a delay tactic (Rashi Shemos 32:5 and Chizkuni Shemos 32:5).
Furthermore Chazal (Shemos Rabbah, Vilna Edition 37:2) echo this theory stating, והוא לא נתכוין אלא לעכבם עד שירד משה *and he only intends to delay them until Moshe descends* and אמר להם פרקו נזמי הזהב אמר להם אני כהן אני אעשה אותו ומקריב לפניו, והוא לא נתעסק אלא לעכבן עד שיבא משה, *and he (Aharon) said to them 'remove the golden' and he (Aharon) said to them 'I am a Kohen. I will do it and sacrifice before him' and he (Aharon) was only involved to delay until Moshe comes.*
Aharon even specifically requests the gold אֲשֶׁר בְּאָזְנֵי נְשֵׁיכֶם בְּנֵיכֶם *from the ears of your wives, sons and daughters* as opposed to other gold to cause for a delay (Zohar 2:192).

[142] According to some (Shabbos 89a and Rashi Shemos 32:1) this event takes place on the sixteenth of Tamuz, one day before Moshe's scheduled return. According to the Ibn Ezra (Shemos 32:1) the date of Moshe's descent is unknown.

[143] The Midrash (Tanchuma Parshas Ki Sisa 19) elaborates that the women reject this request from the men yet the men proceed to take the jewelry while it is still being worn.

[144] There are several other answers offered regarding Aharon's behavior. Chazal (Vayikra Rabbah, Vilna Edition and quoted by Rashi Shemos 32:5, Sanhedrin 6b-7a) elaborate stating that the worshipers have already murdered Chor who has refused to partake in their idolatrous assembly. Aharon, justifiably, fears for his life. The Ohr HaChaim (Shemos 32:1) adds that the Torah does not explicitly mention Chor's murder in order not to further disgrace Bnei Yisrael. Parenthetically, this raises a central methodological question, beyond our scope, of what information the Torah chooses to include and exclude.
Many (Ibn Ezra Shemos 32:1) wonder how Aharon could have engaged in avodah zara ignoring the law of yaharog v'al yavore *better to die* than *violate the sin*? Some (Rav SaadiaSaadia Gaon quoted by the Ibn Ezra Shemos 32:1, Kuzari 1:97) suggest that this is

These two theories also explain Moshe's ensuing conversation with Aharon where Moshe asks Aharon מֶה עָשָׂה לְךָ הָעָם הַזֶּה כִּי הֵבֵאתָ עָלָיו חֲטָאָה גְדֹלָה *What did the nation do to you that you committed such a great sin* (ibid 32:21). The question presupposes that Aharon has no interest in being involved. The people must have somehow convinced him. Moreover, Aharon subsequently responds to Moshe that, in fact, the people did misbehave, אַתָּה יָדַעְתָּ אֶת הָעָם כִּי בְרָע הוּא *You know that the nation is bad* (ibid 32:22). From Aharon's response, one can see his virtuous motives.

Building off of both positions,[145] we can posit that Aharon has completely noble intentions.[146] His shortcoming, sadly, lies in is his execution, and his strategy. Instead of confronting this mistaken ideology head on, Aharon tries to navigate the situation diplomatically. Aharon's mistake is avoiding confrontation and choosing flexibility when he should have taken a firm line.

This may further answer why Aharon is never criticized or punished.[147] True, he wrongly sins, but his motives are totally pure, mitigating his guilt considerably. Hashem completely faults Bnei Yisrael without placing any blame on Aharon (ibid 31:7-10).

With this background, we can now return and answer the question of why the people come directly to Aharon. Mindful of Aharon's sensitivity and flexibility, they trust him to not quash their rebellion. Once that fear is alleviated, strategically it is great to have Aharon on

---

Aharon's attempt to oust those who are guilty, like Yayhu does (Melachim 2 10:19). The Malbim (Devorim 9:20-21) responds that this episode precedes the principle of yaharog v'al yavore. The Ibn Ezra quotes several additional approaches regarding Aharon's motivates. One argues that Aharon is tricked. Another shocking suggestion is that it is actually a different person with the same name Aharon, for Aharon HaKohen would never engaged in such sinful activity.

[145] As the Midrash (Vayikra Rabbah, Vilna Edition 10:3) does stating חג לעגל מחר אין כתיב כאן אלא חג לה' מחר *It does not say "a Holiday for the egel", rather a holiday for Hashem tomorrow.* By stressing both *for Hashem* and *tomorrow*, Aharon, is both redirection their worship and delaying.

[146] The Meshech Chochoma (Bereshis 37:26) calls this an Avara Lishma *sin with good intensions* based on the Gemara (Nazir 23b).

[147] The Torah does not record any punishment as a direct result of this sin, yet there are those who argue that Aharon does receive punishment. Rashi (Bamidbar 19:22), for example, explains that Eliezar, his son, is appointed responsible for the Parah Adumah. Because of Aharon's involvement in the Chet HaEgel he is unbefitting to deal with the Parah Adumah, which serves as a kaparah *forgiveness* for the Chet HaEgel.

board. Having Aharon on board makes it very difficult for any other opposition to arise.

This may also shed light on why the masses, who are not directly involved, are not punished for the Chet HaEgel episode. Who can blame them for not opposing a movement that is led by Aharon and openly sold as a project designed to serve Hashem?

A LOOK AT AHARON THROUGHOUT THE TORAH

Throughout the Torah, Aharon is depicted as peace-loving, flexible and beloved. Chazal understand that to be the reason why the people mourned Aharon for thirty days, as the Midrash (Tanchuma, Buber Edition, Bamidbar) records,

And all of Yisrael loved Aharon, men and women, therefore our Rabbis, said 'One should be like the students of Aharon, love peace, pursuit peace, love people and bring them closer to Torah' therefore (it states)' and all of the house of Israel cried for Aharon for thirty days'	והיו כל ישראל אוהבים את אהרן אנשים ונשים, ולכך אמרו רבותינו ז"ל הוי מתלמידיו של אהרן אוהב שלום ורודף שלום, אוהב את הבריות ומקרבן לתורה, ועל כך ויבכו את אהרן שלשים יום כל בית ישראל

Identifying with people and steering them towards Hashem are Aharon's core strengths. Chazal (Avos D'Rebbi Nassan 12:3) add that people close to Aharon act virtuously because they see themselves associated with him. Additionally, when people would fight, Aharon would interfere and make peace (ibid).

This quality of Aharon may shed light on his willingness to listen to Miriam's lashon hara, *slander*, about Moshe as well. He does not initiate or even add to what is said, yet he also does not correct Miriam. Here too, Aharon avoids confrontation.[148]

Aharon's strength and weakness are the same. He has a unique ability to understand others which allows him to help them avoid conflict. However, that also creates a softness that prevents him from putting his foot down when the situation requires it.

---

[148] According to Chazal (Shabbos 97a), Aharon is punished with Tzaraas as well as Miriam.

Understanding Moshe and Aharon's Different Roles

In contrast to Aharon, Moshe's personality is rooted in truth and earnestness. If Moshe were with the people, he would have openly opposed the egel. Moshe does not aim to avoid confrontation. Whereas Aharon evades reprimanding Bnei Yisrael with a firm "no", Moshe, upon descending, reacts by breaking the luchos, וַיִּחַר אַף מֹשֶׁה וַיַּשְׁלֵךְ מִיָּדָיו אֶת הַלֻּחֹת וַיְשַׁבֵּר אֹתָם תַּחַת הָהָר *And Moshe gets angry and sends the luchos (tablets) from his hands, and breaks them at the foot of the mountain.*[149] Taking this drastic action (Devorim 9:17) unequivocally conveys Moshe's deep disapproval.

The contrast between their personalities is encapsulated in this episode. While both Moshe and Aharon disapprove, Moshe's response is *breaking* the luchos, a physical object designed by *Hashem*, whereas Aharon does the exact opposite. He assists by *creating* a physical object designed by *the people*. These different actions underscore their different attitudes. Moshe stands primarily for truth whereas Aharon, peace and tolerance.

The sin of the Chet HaEgel is an outgrowth of the nation's confusion resulting in a lack of balance in leadership. Moshe is engrossed in spirituality when the people need a stern reproach, while Aharon cushions Bnei Yisrael by showing tolerance when reprimanding them is the required response.

In order to reinforce this idea, the Torah begins the episode with Bnei Yisrael's response to Moshe tarrying on Har Sinai. The opening verse is וַיִּתֵּן אֶל מֹשֶׁה כְּכַלֹּתוֹ לְדַבֵּר אִתּוֹ בְּהַר סִינַי שְׁנֵי לֻחֹת הָעֵדֻת לֻחֹת אֶבֶן כְּתֻבִים בְּאֶצְבַּע אֱלֹהִים *And He gave the two luchos ha-edus, luchos of stone written with the finger of Hashem* (Shemos 31:18). Moshe receiving the Torah on Har Sinai is not the part of the previous episode but the beginning of this one. The Torah then records Moshe's delay, כִּי בֹשֵׁשׁ מֹשֶׁה *that Moshe tarried,* and that the nation see it, וַיַּרְא הָעָם *And the nation saw* (ibid 32:1). The combination of Moshe's extended time with Hashem, along with Aharon's soft style of discipline, together, causes panic and

---

[149] The Gemara (Shabbos 17a) compares Hillel allowing Shamai to rule on many Halachos to the Chet HaEgel. The Chasam Sofer (Shabbos 17a) explains that Hillel, the paramount symbol of humility, like Aharon, prefers avoiding conflict over correcting others.

confusion. Confusion leads to unrest and ultimately the construction of an egel.

The combination of Moshe as the national leader and Aharon as Kohen Gadol, is designed precisely to avoid situations like this. Moshe's unflinching commitment to truth is complemented by Aharon's soft touch. Conversely, Moshe's absence produces not just imbalance, but insecurity; just as Bnei Yisrael take comfort in his presence, they resort to panic when he is gone.

WHAT BNEI YISRAEL WANT

Bnei Yisrael do not actually believe that the Egel HaZahav miraculously redeemed them from Mitzrayim.[150] Rather, in the wake of Moshe's unaccounted absence, they desire a middleman. Interacting with Hashem directly is too much for them. The Egel HaZahav is the middleman they yearn for.[151] [152]

Still, why an idol? Why not replace Moshe with a different leader, most obviously Aharon? Given the choice between Aharon replacing Moshe and an egel replacing him, is Aharon not a more logical substitute?

Bnei Yisrael do not accidentally replace a man with an idol. They are certain about what they want, כִּי זֶה מֹשֶׁה הָאִישׁ אֲשֶׁר הֶעֱלָנוּ מֵאֶרֶץ מִצְרַיִם, לֹא יָדַעְנוּ מֶה הָיָה לוֹ *because Moshe, a man, who brought us out of the land of Egypt, we do not know what has happened to him* (ibid 32:1). Focusing

---

[150] Rashbam (Shemos 32:4). However, he adds that Bnei Yisrael confuse the egel's ability to speak as Ruach HaKodesh and not Ruach HaTumah.

[151] Ramban (Shemos 32:1), Rabaynu Bachaya (Shemos 32:1), Chizkuni (Shemos 32:1), Ohr HaChaim (Shemos 32:1), Malbim (Shemos 32:1) and others.

[152] Yet they lack integrity for they know that this is not Hashem's choice. Perhaps this also expresses itself in how Bnei Yisrael initially explain the role of the egel, אֵלֶּה אֱלֹהֶיךָ יִשְׂרָאֵל אֲשֶׁר הֶעֱלוּךָ מֵאֶרֶץ מִצְרַיִם *These are the Gods, Yisrael, who took you out of Egypt* (ibid 32:2). Bnei Yisrael open with אֵלֶּה אֱלֹהֶיךָ יִשְׂרָאֵל *These are the Gods, Yisrael*, addressing themselves, as if they are trying to convince themselves of the legitimacy of the egel.
Alternatively, they are not addressing themselves. Rashi (Shemos 32:4) explains that the word *Yisrael* is not extra because the Eruv Rav are the ones who initiated the egel and because they are outsiders they speak to Bnei Yisrael by calling them *Yisrael*. Why the Torah does not directly inform the readers that the Eruv Rav are behind the egel and the ones saying אֵלֶּה אֱלֹהֶיךָ יִשְׂרָאֵל *These are the Gods, Yisrael*, is unclear.
The Malbim (Shemos 32:1) adds that the word וַיִּקָּהֵל (Shemos 32:1) *and they gathered* implies an emotional reaction and not a well thought-out plan.

on Moshe being an אִישׁ *man*, highlights precisely the point that they do not want a *man* as a middleman.[153] A man, by definition, is mortal. Bnei Yisrael prefer something permanent. If Moshe could disappear, any man could.

Yearning something permanent, as opposed to a mortal man, seems understandable. After all, the plan is for Moshe to descend from Har Sinai with the luchos. The selection of stone tablets may be designed to embody that exact permanence that Bnei Yisrael so deeply desired. Their desire is pure, it is their approach which is not.

Why a Calf?

Once they have begun their search for permanence, perhaps, Bnei Yisrael select a cow because of its symbolism as the source for milk, the source of sustenance. Without their spiritual and political leader, they are in need of an alternative source of sustenance.

That in turn leads to the question of why they select a calf over a cow? Why a calf?

A calf does not serve as an independent source of sustenance, for it still needs support from its mother. A calf captures exactly what Bnei Yisrael are looking for, something that supports and sustains them while simultaneously requiring support and sustenance. The egel impeccably captures the notion of a middleman. The calf serves as the paradigmatic middleman, offering them what they need, a source of sustenance, while itself continuing to rely on Hashem.[154] From their perspective, a calf is the perfect replacement for Moshe.[155]

---

[153] Ohr HaChaim (Shemos 32:1)

[154] According to many, for example the Seforno (Shemos 24:18), the Mishkan, (as well as Kohanim according to the Seforno), are a direct response to the same emotional need for a middleman. According to Rashi (Shemos 31:18) the commandment for the Mishkan (Shemos 25) occurs after the egel (Shemos 32), and therefore is a response to it. It is the solution Bnei Yisrael desperately need. It is a tangible and physical middleman.
Furthermore, the name Mishkan HaEdus (Shemos 38:21) testifies that Hashem forgives Bnei Yisrael for the Chet HaEgel (Rashi Shemos 38:21). Later, the first karban brought in the Mishkan is an egel, as a chatas *sin offering* (Vayikra 9:2), which is for the sin of Chet HaEgel (Targum Yonason 9:2 and Rashi Vayikra 9:2).
By contrast, the Ramban (Introduction to Shemos 25) argues that the Mishkan is not just ideal, but it is the Geula *redemption* which is the zenith of Sefer Shemos.

[155] Alternatively, Bnei Yisrael realize just how fragile they are. When their leader leaves them, they feel lost, like children, missing a parent. They see themselves as calves, not cows;

HASHEM'S RESPONSE

Hashem's initial response is to give up on this nation, not because they are thoroughly wicked, but, rather, because it is easier to start again with Moshe (ibid 32:10). Hashem even labels Bnei Yisrael as עַם קְשֵׁה עֹרֶף הוּא *a stiff-necked nation* (ibid 32:9). Yet, Moshe reminds Hashem that He has committed to working with this nation (ibid 32:13).[156]

This debate between Hashem and Moshe reflects the uncertain status of Bnei Yisrael. True, they fail with the egel, but one must wonder how deeply rooted into Bnei Yisrael's nature this problem is.

Their behavior could be explained by Moshe's departure and their subsequent state of panic. Completely flustered, they mistakenly decide to replace Moshe. Although there is no question that their actions are wrong, their intentions are not. The best proof to that is no one is punished. Alternatively, this sin may be symbolic of a much deeper problem. The fact that they appoint their own middleman is reflective of a severe lack of faith[157] and an inability to rise to the religious standard expected of them.

WHO RECEIVES PUNISHMENT?

The instigators of the egel, Aharon and the bystanders, are not punished, but Hashem does take retribution against those who do not identify with מִי לַיקֹוָק אֵלָי *Who is for Hashem, with me* (ibid 32:26). Why?

Hashem does not punish Bnei Yisrael for sinning in Moshe's absence simply due to the utter confusion and bedlam which permeate completely. Can they really be held accountable under such circumstances? However, when Moshe returns and cries out מִי לַיקֹוָק אֵלָי *Who is for Hashem, with me* (ibid 32:26) thereby offering religious clarity, Hashem is angered by those who still fail to repent. Only a select few, the tribe of Levi, completely identify with Moshe (ibid 32:26). Similarly, only the vast minority, three thousand men, who rebel so

---

immature, young and in need of help.

[156] Because Hashem is not fickle (Rambam Yesodei HaTorah 1:12), He must be testing Moshe to see whether Moshe will communicate thoughts that will placate Him.

[157] Emes L'Yaakov (Shemos 32:1)

vindictively resisting Moshe's pleas are killed (ibid 32:28). Where are the rest? What are the majority of the people thinking? Sadly, they are still confused and spiritually lost.

DRINKING THE EGEL

In addition to breaking the luchos, Moshe subsequently burns and minces the egel before scattering it in water and having Bnei Yisrael drink it. Let us reiterate the previously asked question: why does Moshe do this?

For Bnei Yisrael to have some level of confusion and uncertainty is justifiable. To be slightly unnerved when one fears that Moshe is dead is reasonable. However, to panic, create and then worship avodah zara as a response is not.

The ideological point Moshe makes reflects what physically occurs. By pulverizing the egel into minuscule pieces and having Bnei Yisrael consume it, Moshe is teaching them an important lesson. Having small questions inside is reasonable, allowing them out to create an egel is not. Avodah zara must be destroyed but having tiny pieces inside, symbolizing doubt, is understandable.

THE SOTAH

The Torah presents a detailed description of the laws of a Sotah, a woman who, after being warned by her suspecting husband not to be alone with a particular man, is found secluded with him. Interestingly, the Chet HaEgel narrative contains several surprising parallels to the Torah's account of the Sotah. Let us list the similarities.

1. Both the Sotah and Bnei Yisrael act unfaithfully leading to a situation of deep uncertainty. The Sotah is alone with another man whom her husband has specifically requested that she not be alone with, yet it is unclear whether intimacy took place. Similarly, Bnei Yisrael have clearly erected an egel, but whether or not their motives are malicious remain unclear. In both situations, a clarification is needed.

2. Both Bnei Yisrael and the Sotah drink water with remnants of something destroyed. For the Sotah, it is Hashem's name which is erased, and for Bnei Yisrael, it is the remnants of the egel.

3. Both unfaithful groups are tested. The Sotah is examined by drinking special Sotah-water and Bnei Yisrael are tested via their response to Moshe's statement of מִי לַיקֹוָק אֵלָי *Who is for Hashem, with me* (ibid 32:26). Moreover, the water-drinking in each event is designed to reestablish trust and ultimately a relationship; for the Sotah, with her husband, and for Bnei Yisrael, with Hashem.

4. Hashem acts as the peacemaker between the Sotah and her husband by having His name erased (Bamidbar 5:23-24). Moshe, in his attempt to rescue the relationship between Hashem and Bnei Yisrael, follows in Hashem's ways by requesting that his name be erased as well, אִם תִּשָּׂא חַטָּאתָם וְאִם אַיִן מְחֵנִי נָא מִסִּפְרְךָ *if you forgive their sin (good), but if not, erase me from you book* (Shemos 32:32).

5. Both episodes conclude with the punishment of death for the guilty and total absolution for the innocent.

This fascinating parallel is already alluded to by Chazal (Yoma 44a) regarding Bnei Yisrael's drinking on the minced egel, when they state, וישק את בני ישראל לא נתכוין אלא לבודקן כסוטות *And Bnei Yisrael drank, the goal was nothing but to check them like Sotahs.*[158]

The response to the Chet HaEgel is similar to the response to the Sotah for a simple reason. After that unfaithful act, there is a desperate need to restore trust. Just as the Sotah damages the relationship to the point where an investigation is needed to determine whether moving forward is possible, so too Bnei Yisrael's relationship with Hashem is damaged to the point where He questions whether the relationship with Bnei Yisrael can continue as He says to Moshe, וַאֲכַלֵּם וְאֶעֱשֶׂה אוֹתְךָ לְגוֹי *I will destroy them and make you (Moshe) a great nation* (ibid 32:10).

---

[158] The Sifsay Chochomim (Rashi Bamidbar 32:20 note 30) comments, כי הזונה אחר עכו"ם הוא כאשה המזונה תחת בעלה *because one who is unfaithful after avodah zara is like a woman unfaithful to her husband.* Also, see the Malbim (Shemos 32:20).

OPPOSITE OF THE SOTAH

In addition to the fascinating similarities between our episode and the Sotah, there are several captivating differences as well. Let us list them before attempting to understand the Torah's message.

1. For the Sotah, it is Hashem's name which is erased and consumed. In our episode, it is the egel itself, the idol, that is destroyed, put in water and given to Bnei Yisrael to drink.

2. Hashem serves as the peacemaker in the Sotah's case, allowing His name to be erased in order to reinstate trust between husband and wife. After the Chet HaEgel, it is Moshe, a man, serving as the role of peacemaker.

3. While Hashem's name is actually erased in an attempt to make peace, Moshe's name is not. Moshe does request it from Hashem, מְחֵנִי נָא מִסִּפְרְךָ *erase me from you book* (ibid 32:32), but this request does not come to fruition. Hashem forgives Bnei Yisrael rather than starting anew.

4. The Sotah's unfaithfulness takes place in a private area. By contrast, Bnei Yisrael publicly celebrate their faithlessness with karbanos and partying (Shemos 32:6).

5. The Sotah is specifically warned by her husband not to be secluded with this particular man. Bnei Yisrael are not warned with anything in such a specific fashion.

6. Although both situations have ambiguities, the ambiguities are different. Bnei Yisrael's actions are undoubtedly bad while uncertainty lies in their motivation. The Sotah is the exact opposite, for her actions are uncertain, while her motivation is undoubtedly bad.

7. The Sotah's faithlessness is designed to replace her husband. Just the opposite is true for the egel. It is designed to strengthen their relationship with Hashem, however it is the wrong path to get there. Both fail, but the Sotah fails fully aware of her faithlessness, while Bnei Yisrael fail attempting to be faithful.

8. Unlike the water that the Sotah drinks which is designed to investigate her actions of the past, the water that Bnei Yisrael drink is designed to ensure a better future.

Beyond this list of opposites, the context is radically different. Until this point, Bnei Yisrael were miraculously redeemed from Egypt by Hashem, won a war by having the sea split and then engulf the Egyptian soldiers, received food from the heavens, water from a rock, and were guarded by a magical cloud by day and led by a miraculous fire by night. Nothing like that exists for the Sotah.

This contrast may capture an important difference from the Sotah. Bnei Yisrael are certainly wrong but their intention is unclear. The Sotah's intention is clear, but whether she acted upon it, is not.

The Torah may be illustrating Hashem's unparalleled forgiving nature.[159] In contrast to the Sotah's husband, who might struggle to trust his wife again,[160] Hashem forgives easily. Hashem is pacified (ibid 32:14) and willing to move forward.

THE ROLE OF THE KOHEN

The Kohen assists the Sotah in offering a karban, uncovering her hair,[161] making the necessary oaths, and drinking the Sotah-water (Bamidbar 5). This role of the Kohen, helping the Sotah, may be designed to correct Aharon's mistaken attitude. The character trait of

---

[159] Rabbi Soloveitchik famously compares the plans for building the Mishkan (Shemos 25-27) and designing the clothing of the Kohen Gadol (Shemos 28) to wedding plans. The parable continues with Chet HaEgel representing a bride being unfaithful just before her wedding. In contrast to a standard groom, who presumably would not continue with the marriage, Hashem completely forgives Bnei Yisrael, the Mishkan is built and the Kohen Gadol's clothing are made precisely as originally planned. Not only is there no deviation, the Torah itself continuously stresses that the Mishkan and Kohen's clothing is made exactly כַּאֲשֶׁר צִוָּה יְהֹוָה אֶת־מֹשֶׁה as Hashem commanded Moshe, in accordance with the original plan. Parenthetically, the Beis HaLevi (Parshas Ki Sisa), Rabbi Soloveitchik's great-grandfather and his name sake, draws the opposite conclusion. He argues that Shabbos, which is something central to Torah, is listed after the Mishkan, which is something that offers added kedusha. Yet after the Chet HaEgel, the Torah changes the order. Shabbos is mentioned before the Mishkan. The reason for this, he argues, is that before the sin, building the Mishkan is mentioned first for it captures the natural excitement, yet after the egel, Shabbos comes first because the excitement is diminished and replaced with the responsibility to do necessities.

[160] Even if she is found innocent, the fact that she enters a secluded area with the man her husband warned her not to be alone with undermines any prospect of a complete restoration of trust.

[161] Which, parenthetically, is the source for married women to cover their hair. Whether it is a Mitzvah to cover her hair or an Isur not to, is debated between two opinions found in Rashi (Kesubos 72a, also see Igras Moshe EH 1:57).

flexibility and working with the people is designed for the Kohen to inspire and reinstate trust between man and wife, not facilitate avodah zara. Flexibility is designed to be a virtue in a response to sin, not a facilitator of it.

MORE EGELIM: YERAVAM'S REBELLION

There is another remarkable story which is intertwined with ours as well; that of Yeravam's rebellion and the subsequent schism. Yeravam plans to usurp power from Shlomo. Shlomo responds by sentencing Yeravam to death (Melachim I 11:40). Understandably, Yeravam flees to Mitzrayim and upon Shlomo's death, returns to start a new kingdom in the North and establish a presence in Shachem (ibid 12:25). Fascinatingly, Yeravam's rebellion recalls our episode in several of its vivid details.

1. Most clearly, Yeravam creates gold calves designed for avodah zara (ibid 12:28) as part of a rebellion against the current leadership, unmistakably paralleling our narrative.[162]

2. Yeravam's construction of these calves is motivated by a fear of death. He is concerned that if he allows people to visit Yerushalayim they might be influenced by Rechavam to rejoin the rest of Bnei Yisrael and kill him (ibid 12:27). This too sounds similar to our episode where there is also a great fear of the leader's death.

3. In both situations, the golden calves are constructed to replace something missing, and each time what is missing is a religious in-between designed to serve as a middleman between man and Hashem. In our story, the egel is designed to act as a substitute for

---

[162] Radak (Melachim I 12:28), Ralbag (Melachim I 12:28), Malbim (Melachim I 12:28) Metzudas Dovid (Melachim I 12:28). However, the Abarbanel quoted by the Malbim (Melachim I 12:28) cannot believe that Bnei Yisrael would mistakenly worship an egel again. Instead, he argues, these golden calves symbolize that kingship comes from Yosef's tribes as well as the שור *cow* represents Yosef (Bereshis 49:22 and Devorim 33:17). Furthermore, he adds that there were two egelim representing Menashe and Ephrayim.

Moshe. Similarly, Yeravam constructs two calves designed to replace the Beis HaMikdash (ibid 12:27-28).[163] [164]

4. Yeravam constructs the calves upon returning from Mitzrayim, recalling how Bnei Yisrael also built theirs upon leaving Mitzrayim.

5. Not only does Yeravam worship golden calves and bring extra karbanos, he declares חָג יָרָבְעָם וַיַּעַשׂ *And Yeravam made a Chag (holiday)* (ibid 12:32) using the word חג *holiday* as Aharon has previously at the Chet HaEgel.

6. Yeravam, like Aharon, has a son named Nadav (ibid 15:25).

7. Both narratives tell a story of two leaders not working together. In the first episode, Moshe is on Har Sinai and Aharon leads the people. In the latter case, Yeravam and Rechavam clearly do not work together leading the people to a national schism.

8. Most strikingly, Moshe and Yeravam are each sentenced to death and exiled ultimately to return and lead a group of people into nationhood.

If there is any remaining ambiguity about the association between these accounts, it is surely removed when Yeravam declares, אֱלֹהֶיךָ הִנֵּה יִשְׂרָאֵל אֲשֶׁר הֶעֱלוּךָ מֵאֶרֶץ מִצְרָיִם *These are the Gods, Yisrael, who took you out of Egypt* (Melachim I 12:28) identical to Bnei Yisrael's previous cry, אֵלֶּה אֱלֹהֶיךָ יִשְׂרָאֵל אֲשֶׁר הֶעֱלוּךָ מֵאֶרֶץ מִצְרָיִם *These are the Gods, Yisrael, who took you out of Egypt* (ibid 32:2).

Clearly, the Yeravam narrative is designed to recall the Egel HaZahav episode.

---

[163] Radak (ibid) and Ralbag (ibid). Furthermore, on both occasions the egel is designed to capture the Shechena (Radak ibid). Similar to the Radak, the Ramban (Introduction to Shemos 25) argues Shechena is found in the Aron Kodesh *Ark*. The Seforno (Shemos 30:1) argues that the Shechena is found in many of Kaylim *vessels*, but not the Mizbayach HaZahav *Golden Alter*. The Rambam (Beis HaBechira 6:16) discusses the Shechena in the Beis HaMikdash and Yerushalayim, but not in the context of Kaylim.
For more sources regarding the Shechena, see the Kuzari 4:3, Moreh Nevuchim 1:19 and Ramban (Bereshis 46:1).

[164] The Malbim (Melachim I 12:28) explains that Yeravam does not have the capacity to build a structure as grand as the Beis HaMikdash, and an inferior edifice would not win the people's loyalty. Therefore, he replaces it with two egelim.

THE OPPOSITES BETWEEN THE TWO STORIES

In addition to the remarkable similarities between the two episodes, there are many intentional differences and direct opposites as well. Let us list them before trying to uncover any deeper meaning.

1. Yeravam constructs two golden calves, whereas Bnei Yisrael only fashion one.

2. Although both calves are constructed as part of a coup, one is designed to replace a person, Moshe, the leader serving as the middleman, while the other is intended to replace a building, the Beis HaMikdash.[165]

3. In Sefer Shemos, the rebellion is quashed quickly, whereas Yeravam's rebellion is a division that lasts for generations.

4. In Sefer Shemos, it is the people who push the leader, Aharon, to be involved with constructing the egel, whereas in Sefer Melachim, it is Yeravam, the leader, who pushes the people to worship his golden calves.

5. Bnei Yisrael, in Sefer Shemos, fear losing their leader, Moshe. Just the opposite occurs in Sefer Melachim. Yeravam, the leader, fears losing his nation (Melachim I 12:27).

6. Although Bnei Yisrael incorrectly create the egel, they do so with good intentions. By contrast, Yeravam's intentions are self-serving and greedy.

7. Yeravam encourages the people for his own political purposes, redirecting them to revolt, whereas Aharon, selflessly, tries to divert the people from revolting.

8. Bnei Yisrael construct the egel due to a fear that Moshe, the leader, has already died. By contrast, in Navi, it is the fear that Yeravam, the leader, will die that prompts the construction of the egel.

9. Although both stories have the element of fear of a leader's death, Bnei Yisrael fear Moshe's death, whereas Yeravam, selfishly, fears his own.

---

[165] Although the Radak (Melachim 1 12:32) argues that the karbanos are brought, both in Dan and in Beis El, Rav Yaakov Kamenetsky (Emes L'Yaakov Melachim 1 12:32) argues that they are brought in Beis El only, because it is specifically there, that Yeravam plans to replace the Beis HaMikdash.

10. Although both Aharon and Yeravam have a son named Nadav, their stories are the opposite. Aharon's son does not and cannot continue Aharon's legacy whereas Yeravam's son lives to carry on his father's (Melachim I 15:25-26).

11. In contrast to Bnei Yisrael feeling disconnected to their leader, Moshe, due to his absence, Bnei Yisrael feel disconnected to Yeravam in his presence.

12. Although, as noted, in each story the leader, Moshe and Yeravam, are sentenced to death and exiled. Moshe, however, is exiled from Mitzrayim while Yeravam is exiled to Mitzrayim. Furthermore, Moshe returns to build and strengthen Bnei Yisrael, whereas Yeravam returns to do the exact opposite, divide them.

It is clear that the Navi weaves the Chet HaEgel narrative into Yeravam's rebellion with both parallels and contrasts. Why?

Both stories describe rebellions and both rebellions use an egel to replace a spiritual middleman: Moshe and the Beis HaMikdash. In that sense they are very similar and that explains the similarities.

Yet, in other respects, the stories are diametrically opposed to each other. Whereas Bnei Yisrael incorrectly, but virtuously, look for a middleman, Yeravam fabricates a holiday (ibid 12:33) and employs impostor Kohanim (ibid 12:31). Instead of looking for a way to connect man to Hashem, Yeravam is looking to disconnect them. Instead of leadership designed to bring man close to Hashem, his goal is the opposite, to use religion to service his leadership. The Chet HaEgel story serves as an excellent foil for Yeravam's rebellion. Whereas Bnei Yisrael mistakenly err in using the egel, Yeravam's selfish decision is made with eyes wide open.

APPLYING TEXT TO LIFE: THE HASHKAFIC MESSAGE

The leadership model that Hashem designs, requires balance. On the one hand it synthesizes warmth, love, and flexibility, and on the other, truth and rigidity for the rules. Without proper leadership, values, and morality people will get confused. Moshe and Aharon each excel at their own role and work wonderfully together.

This synthesis represented by Moshe and Aharon, is clearly expressed by Chazal in the Midrash (Shemos Rabbah, Vilna Edition, 5:10), הוי ... משה זה ואמת ... אהרן זה חסד ,נשקו ושלום צדק נפגשו ואמת חסד נפגשו ואמת חסד *Kindness and truth meet, righteous and peace kiss. Kindness is Aharon, and it says… and truth is Moshe … kindness and truth meet.*

Additionally, there is much to learn from Aharon's mistake. There is a time and place for flexibility, and it is definitely not when the threat of idolatry looms. Flexibility should be utilized for granting forgiveness, not condoning sin.

This episode also illustrates what panic can do. Because of their hysteria, Bnei Yisrael make a bad decision. Being unnerved often causes mistaken drastic measures. Important decisions should be made carefully and responsibly.

Lastly, one can learn from Yeravam's mistakes too. Religion should not be changed or desecrated for political purposes. Yeravam takes one of the famous sins and repeats it but in a far worse fashion. Whereas Yeravam uses religion to serve his political agenda, the opposite is correct. One's politics should be designed to facilitate better service of Hashem.

Shaul: The Rise and Fall of the First Jewish King

Shaul's Confusing Religious Nature

The Tanach presents a confusing religious image about the first Jewish king, Shaul HaMelach, *King Shaul.* After being selected by Hashem and informed by Shmuel that he is to be king (Shmuel I 9:15), he immediately unifies Bnei Yisrael to fight and defeat Nachash HaAmoni (ibid 11). This presents Shaul very positively, yet the Navi also records two of Shaul's major sins that relate to and cause his dethroning. First, anxiously, he brings karbanos instead of patiently awaiting Shmuel's arrival (Shmuel I 13). Then, second, he disobeys Shmuel, by not destroying Amalek and worse, lies to shift blame in order to cover up his mistakes (Shmuel I 15).

The tension between these different presentations seems to motivate two diametrically opposite perspectives found in Chazal regarding Shaul. The first school of thought takes a positive perspective on Shaul. The Gemara (Megilla 13b) states, בשכר צניעות שהיה בו בשאול זכה ויצאת ממנו אסתר *as a reward for Shaul's modesty, he merited to have Ester as a descendant.* Shaul is described as modest and appropriately rewarded. The Tosefta (Brachos 4:16), echoing this image and attributing his meriting of kingship to his humility, states אף שאול לא זכה למלכות אלא מפני הענוה *even Shaul merited kingship because of his humility.*

According to Chazal (Brachos 62b) Dovid, himself, sees this quality of humility in Shaul. Shaul attempts to execute Dovid which gives Dovid the right to defend himself, even by killing Shaul. Dovid still chooses to spare Shaul rationalizing, צניעות שהיתה בך *(because of) your modesty.* Here Dovid attests to Shaul's humility, reinforcing the positive image.

Chazal (Yoma 22b) praise Shaul, at the time he ascends to monarchy, by describing his purity as something who לֹא טָעַם טַעַם חֵטְא *never tasted the taste of sin.*[166]

Yet, other statements of Chazal depict a more critical perspective of our inaugural king. One Midrash (Eliyahu Rabbah 29) describes Shaul as גְּסוּת רוּחַ *arrogant,* the exact opposite of the humility described earlier. Another accuses Shaul of מְכַסֶּה פְּשָׁעָיו *(One who) covers up mistakes* (Midrash Tehillim Shachar Tov, Buber Edition 100). This too depicts Shaul negatively; as someone lacking integrity.[167] These two Midrashim portray Shaul far more negatively.

Which is it, good or bad, modest or arrogant? They seem mutually exclusive.

One may simply respond that there is indeed a disagreement regarding Shaul's personality. Different sages approach Shaul differently. However, upon a more in-depth look one may be able to reconcile both opinions and integrate them into a more nuanced perspective of a complicated personality.

THE NAVI'S INTRODUCTION TO SHAUL

The Navi introduces Shaul's narrative peculiarly, focusing on Shaul's father, Kish. It states וַיְהִי אִישׁ מִבִּנְיָמִין וּשְׁמוֹ קִישׁ *And there was a man from Binyamin and his name was Kish* (Shmuel I 9:1-2), as if the upcoming episode is about him.[168] Reinforcing this presentation, the story continues with וְלוֹ הָיָה בֵן וּשְׁמוֹ שָׁאוּל *he had a son named Shaul* (ibid 9:2), unmistakably presenting Kish as the central character and Shaul, peripherally, his son.

---

[166] Another Midrash (Yalkut Shemoni Shmuel II 141) notes that Shaul would kiss great Rabbis when they would teach Torah and still, another (Ester Rabbah, Vilna Edition 6:2) also portraying him positively claims that Shaul's righteousness is implied by the Navi's introduction of him as וּשְׁמוֹ שָׁאוּל *and his name was Shaul* (Shmuel I 9:2).

[167] The Gemara (Yerushalmi Sotah 1:8) critically understands the verse וְאֵין אִישׁ מִבְּנֵי יִשְׂרָאֵל טוֹב מִמֶּנּוּ *And no man in Bnei Yisrael is better than him* (Shmuel 1 2:9) to refer to משכמו ומעלה גבוה *shoulders and up, he is the tallest.* In others words, he excels in height alone.

[168] It is additionally interesting that the Navi lists Kish's ancestry for generations. Although the explanation why is beyond our purview, the observation is noteworthy.

After being introduced to Kish, there is a drastic shift and from this point on the entire story is about Shaul. It covers where he goes, how Shaul searches for his father's lost donkeys and how thoroughly he looks for them (ibid 9:4), his concern that his father may worry about him (ibid 9:5), and how all of this leads to his meeting with Shmuel. The most noticeable description indicating a new focus is the Navi describing, וַתֹּאבַדְנָה הָאֲתֹנוֹת לְקִישׁ אֲבִי שָׁאוּל *And Kish, Shaul's father, lost his donkeys* (ibid 9:3). The frame of reference is completely reversed from Kish to Shaul. What point is the Navi making by beginning the story about Kish and then immediately shifting focus to Shaul? Why would the Navi, during Shaul's introduction, focus so much on Kish?

Are the details recorded about Shaul purely technical, merely providing background information regarding how Shaul arrives at Shmuel's house? If so, there are many extraneous details recorded. However, if the Navi's presentation is designed to introduce us to Shaul, offering important insight into who he is, then we must ask, what insight is it offering?[169]

Daddy's Little Boy

Shaul is extremely attached to his father, and in order to accurately capture their relationship, the Navi adds several details depicting Shaul as "Daddy's Little Boy". Shaul being sent on a mission to retrieve his father's donkeys, his exhaustive search for them, and his concern that his father is worried about him capture precisely that, and therefore serve as the perfect introductory story to Shaul.

By mentioning Kish's concern for Shaul, וְדָאַג לָכֶם לֵאמֹר מָה אֶעֱשֶׂה לִבְנִי *he worries about you saying 'what shall I do about my son'* (Shmuel I 10:2) the Navi reinforces that Shaul is being treated like a young boy by his father. The point is more pronounced because, although we do not know Shaul's exact age, we can be assured that Shaul is a grown man. He must have been for he reigns as king for only two years (Shmuel I 13:1), and while being king, his son, Yonason, is old enough to fight in battle, and even father a son of his own (Dvray HaYamim I 9:40).

---

[169] According to the Malbim (Shmuel I 9:2) the story is designed to illustrate Hashem's hashgacha *providence*. We are going to offer an additional answer.

With this in mind one can suggest why the Navi begins this narrative by focusing on Kish before redirecting its attention to Shaul. Namely, one cannot properly appreciate Shaul without first meeting his father and understanding their relationship.

As a subtle reminder, that Shaul is primarily a son and more, "Daddy's Little Boy", the Navi repeats the phrase בֵּן *son* eight times (ibid 9:1, 1, 1, 1, 1, 2, 2, 3) which subtly underlines who Shaul is; a בֵּן *son*.

SHAUL MEETING SHMUEL

In an effort to find their way back home, Shaul and a Naar, *youth*, accompanying him, decide to seek guidance. Shockingly, neither Shaul or the Naar know any Navi, nor are they even familiar with the concept of one. Neither one knows Shmuel's name nor are they aware of the process of going to a Navi. They mistakenly think that they have to pay him for his prophetic services, as they state וּמַה נָּבִיא לָאִישׁ *and what shall we bring to the man* (Shmuel I 9:7).[170] One would have expected that the future king would not have heard of both the word Navi, and רֹאֶה *seer*, which is their title at the time (ibid 9:9) and the process of meeting one.[171] Instead the Naar describes the Navi's position to Shaul, וְהָאִישׁ נִכְבָּד כֹּל אֲשֶׁר יְדַבֵּר בּוֹא יָבוֹא *And the man is respected, everything he says that will occur, does* (ibid 9:6). Although both Shaul and the Naar have an elementary understanding of Navuah at best, Shaul seems the more uninformed of the two, for it is the Naar who introduces him to this idea.

The Navi, cleverly hints to Shaul's unawareness by employing the language וּמַה נָּבִיא *and what shall we bring* (ibid 9:7) to Shmuel. מַה נביא can also be translated as *what is a Navi*, subtly implying that in

---

[170] Rashi (Shmuel I 9:7) and the Radak (Shmuel I 9:7 and 9:9). Although the text never explicitly states that they are mistaken, presumably they are, for elsewhere there is no expectation to compensate a Navi for his services.
    However, the Malbim (Shmuel I 9:6-7) disagrees arguing that it is common practice to pay Navi'im and this tradition can be traced back to וְלֹא יֵרָאוּ פָנַי רֵיקָם *And you should not see my face (come to Yerushalayim) empty* (Shemos 34:20).

[171] Although the text states that the title "Navi" is not used at this time (Rashi on Shmuel I 9:9), many interpret this to mean that the title "Navi" is not exclusively used, as the term "Roeh" is also in use (Radak on Shmuel I 9:9).

addition to not knowing what a Navi is, they do even realize what they are saying. They do not even know that they do not know.

SHAUL CROWNED KING

In addition to being "Daddy's Little Boy" and presumably to some extent because of it, Shaul is humble and very sheltered. He is from a small tribe (ibid 9:21) and unfamiliar with the aristocracy, including Shmuel (Shmuel I 9:6) who is well-known (ibid 2:26). The Midrash confirms this notion stating, שאול ברח מן השררה והיא רדפה אחריו *Shaul ran from power and (none-the-less) it (the power) chased after him* (Midrash Agada, Buber Edition, Parshas Vayikra 1:1).

When Shaul is publicly introduced to the nation as their new king, shockingly and inappropriately, he is נֶחְבָּא אֶל הַכֵּלִים *hiding among the vessels* (ibid I 10:22) and has to be forcibly pulled out at his own coronation (ibid 10:23). This depicts Shaul as more than humble,[172] or even inexperienced; he is shy, insecure and uncomfortable in front of others in his capacity as a leader.[173] Shaul's modest and unpretentious manner is further manifested when people critique him. Defenselessly, Shaul simply remains quiet, pretending not to notice (Shumel I 10:27). These seem to be the actions of a child more than a visionary, leader or king.

Shaul's response to being crowned king characterizes him this way as well. In stark contrast to someone arrogant who would have jumped at the opportunity to brag about being crowned king, and in contrast to someone confident who might have shared the information respectfully, Shaul withholds it, not even informing his uncle of Shmuel anointing him (ibid 10:16).

Yet the clearest demonstration of Shaul's small self-image is his response to Shmuel when informed that he would be crowned king, הֲלוֹא בֶן יְמִינִי אָנֹכִי מִקַּטַנֵּי שִׁבְטֵי יִשְׂרָאֵל וּמִשְׁפַּחְתִּי הַצְּעִרָה מִכָּל מִשְׁפְּחוֹת שִׁבְטֵי בִנְיָמִן וְלָמָּה דִּבַּרְתָּ אֵלַי כַּדָּבָר הַזֶּה *Am I not from Binyamin, the smallest of tribes, and from an unimportant (young) family among Binyamin. Why*

---

[172] Alshich (Shmuel I 10:22)

[173] Radak (Shmuel I 10:23). The Radak then quotes Chazal who argue that Shaul does not run from power, he is merely uncertain and wants to confirm his legitimacy with the Urim V'Tumim.

did you say this (that I would be crowned king)? (ibid 9:21). Shaul's self-image is self-evident.

SHAUL'S DETHRONING

Both of Shaul's major sins, relate to and cause his dethroning. He mistakenly and impatiently brings the karbanos instead of waiting for Shmuel (Shmuel I 13) and then secondly, he disobeys Shmuel, and lies about it blaming the nation to cover up his mistakes (Shmuel I 15).

Although Shaul knows right from wrong, and is fully aware that he should wait for Shmuel's arrival (ibid 13:11), he nonetheless buckles to the self-imposed pressure created by Shmuel's delay, as alluded to by the Navi וַיָּפֶץ הָעָם מֵעָלָיו *and the nation scattered from him* (ibid 13:8) adjacent to his decision to bring karbanos without waiting for Shmuel (ibid 13:9).[174]

Shaul's second sin of disobeying Shmuel and sparing Amalek's king, Agog, and their animals[175] after being unequivocally warned not to (ibid 15:2-3), further buries his future as a king.

Although Shaul is militarily victorious over Amalek, after the battle he leads the people with an unwanted and undermining mercy on Amalek and their animals, as the Navi states, וַיַּחְמֹל שָׁאוּל וְהָעָם עַל אֲגָג וְעַל מֵיטַב הַצֹּאן וְהַבָּקָר *And Shaul and the nation had mercy on Agog (king of Amalek) and the quality sheep and cattle* (Shmuel I 15:9). Using singular language וַיַּחְמֹל שָׁאוּל *And Shaul had mercy* specifically before וְהָעָם *and the nation* clearly implies Shaul bares personal responsibility for mistakenly affording too much mercy to Amalek.

Shmuel, aware of Shaul's sin, approaches Shaul. However, before Shmuel has the chance to speak, Shaul initiates the conversation with a misleading presentation of his unequivocal success. With his excessive enthusiasm and unprovoked defense of his actions, Shaul greets Shmuel with בָּרוּךְ אַתָּה לַיקֹוָק הֲקֵימֹתִי אֶת דְּבַר יְקֹוָק *Blessed are you Hashem for I have kept the rod of Hashem* (ibid 15:13). Shaul incriminates himself

---

[174] Metzudas Dovid (Shmuel I 13:8)

[175] Interestingly, Rashi (Shmuel I 15:3) explains that the reason that animals are to be killed is because the people have magical abilities to transform into animals.

by appearing to intentionally cover up his disobedience and deny his mistaken actions.[176]

Even after initially being harshly challenged by Shmuel questioning, וּמֶה קוֹל הַצֹּאן הַזֶּה בְּאָזְנָי וְקוֹל הַבָּקָר אֲשֶׁר אָנֹכִי שֹׁמֵעַ *What is this noise of sheep do I hear in my ears and the noise of cows that I hear* (ibid 15:14), Shaul maintains his dishonest position and defends his erroneous actions by repeating, **חָמַל הָעָם** עַל מֵיטַב הַצֹּאן וְהַבָּקָר לְמַעַן זְבֹחַ לַיקֹוָק אֱלֹהֶיךָ *the nation had mercy on the best of the sheep and cows in order to sacrifice to Hashem your God* (ibid 15:15).

Shmuel again expresses disappointment and encourages Shaul to lead the people as opposed to being led by them, אִם קָטֹן אַתָּה בְּעֵינֶיךָ רֹאשׁ שִׁבְטֵי יִשְׂרָאֵל אָתָּה וַיִּמְשָׁחֲךָ יְקֹוָק לְמֶלֶךְ עַל יִשְׂרָאֵל *if you are small in your own eyes, you are still the head of the tribes of Israel and anointed as King of Israel* (ibid 15:17) and continues to reprimands Shaul, וְלָמָּה לֹא שָׁמַעְתָּ בְּקוֹל יְקֹוָק וַתַּעַט אֶל הַשָּׁלָל וַתַּעַשׂ הָרַע בְּעֵינֵי יְקֹוָק *And you did not listen to the voice of Hashem, sparing the spoils and doing what is bad in the eyes of Hashem* (ibid 15:19).

Shaul, again, falsely dismisses the accusation and proceeds to exclusively blame the people, **וַיִּקַּח הָעָם** מֵהַשָּׁלָל צֹאן וּבָקָר רֵאשִׁית הַחֵרֶם לִזְבֹּחַ לַיקֹוָק אֱלֹהֶיךָ בַּגִּלְגָּל *And the nation took from the spoils, the first of the sheep and cattle to sacrifice to Hashem your God in Gilgal* (ibid 15:21).

Ultimately Shaul does utter the word, חָטָאתִי *I sinned* (ibid 24), but whether or not he is sincere remains unclear at best, for he continues with **וְאֶת דְּבָרֶיךָ** כִּי עָבַרְתִּי אֶת פִּי יְקֹוָק *for I violated the word of Hashem and your word*. By adding דְּבָרֶיךָ *your word* and implying that this command came partially from Shmuel, Shaul raises the question of whether he really sees himself as violating Hashem's word or Shmuel is just giving him hard time.

Then Shaul reveals his true colors and further incriminates himself by requesting וְעַתָּה שָׂא נָא אֶת חַטָּאתִי וְשׁוּב עִמִּי וְאֶשְׁתַּחֲוֶה לַיקֹוָק *And now forgive my sin, return with me and I will bow to Hashem* (ibid 15:25). Shaul subsequently offers another insincere apology, חָטָאתִי *I sinned* (ibid 15:30), as seen by an immediate request to be honored publicly עַתָּה **כַּבְּדֵנִי נָא נֶגֶד** זְקְנֵי **עַמִּי וְנֶגֶד יִשְׂרָאֵל** וְשׁוּב עִמִּי וְהִשְׁתַּחֲוֵיתִי לַיקֹוָק אֱלֹהֶיךָ *And now, honor me before the elders of our nation and before Yisrael*

---

[176] Sefer HaIkarim (4:26), Malbim (Shmuel II 12:13)

and return with me and I will bow to Hashem your God (ibid 15:30).[177] Focused only in his reputation, Shaul ignores the severity of his sin and requests of Shmuel כַּבְּדֵנִי *honor me.*[178]

Shaul is solely interested in his public image,[179] even at the cost of properly serving Hashem. Unwilling to admit his mistakes and not wanting to look inadequate, he blames the people,[180] and pays lip service by uttering the word חָטָאתִי *I sinned.* Shaul expresses significantly more concern with returning to the people along with Shmuel than he does with his disobedience.

Arguably, this attitude provides insight as to why Shaul initially has mercy on the Amaleki animals. He would have wanted to use them for a massive celebration, presumably to generate support and create excitement.

Shaul Continues Valuing His Public Image

Focusing on his self-image causes Shaul to make additional bad decisions. Once Dovid starts developing a following and seeing real success, Shaul feels threatened and responds by trying to kill him, knowing full well that Dovid is indeed innocent. Shaul further warns Yonason that Dovid's existence is an existential threat to Yonason's future kingship (Shmuel I 20:31). Shaul sees his primary mission as hanging onto kingship at all costs. Again, Shaul's mistake is overvaluing his reputation.

---

[177] ibid

[178] The Navi further records that וַיַּחֲזֵק בִּכְנַף מְעִילוֹ וַיִּקָּרַע *And he grabbed the corner of his coat and it ripped* (Shmuel I 15:30); however it is unclear if Shaul grabs Shmuel's coat (Radak, Metzudas Dovid and the Alshich all on Shmuel I 15:27), Shmuel grabs Shaul's (Yalkut Shemoni 1:123) or even perhaps, Shmuel rips his own coat (one opinion quoted in the Alshich on Shmuel I 15:27). In response Shmuel remarks קָרַע יְקֹוָק אֶת מַמְלְכוּת יִשְׂרָאֵל מֵעָלֶיךָ הַיּוֹם וּנְתָנָהּ לְרֵעֲךָ הַטּוֹב מִמֶּךָּ *Hashem tore the kingship of Israel from you today and will give it to someone better than you.*

[179] Sefer HaIkarim (4:26)

[180] ibid

The Two Parts of Shaul's Kingship

Shaul's two-year reign contains two separate one-year parts[181] with the Navi clearly marking the midpoint with the verse, בֶּן שָׁנָה שָׁאוּל בְּמָלְכוֹ וּשְׁתֵּי שָׁנִים מָלַךְ עַל יִשְׂרָאֵל *Shaul ruled as king for one year, and for two years he was king of Yisrael* (Shmuel I 13:1). The stories of Shaul's sincerity, humility and success are all during the first year when Shaul's behavior is stellar.[182] The trouble begins in his second, when he struggles and begins worrying about his personal image.

To further contrast Shaul's transformation, the Navi records that during the first year, the רוּחַ אֱלֹהִים עַל שָׁאוּל *sprit of Hashem was on Shaul* (Shmuel I 11:6) and later, during his demise, it departs as the verse unmistakably describes, וְרוּחַ יְקֹנָק סָרָה מֵעִם שָׁאוּל *and the sprit of Hashem left Shaul* (ibid 16:14).

With this perspective in mind, we may resolve our initial contradiction. Understandably, Shaul, before being crowned king, is modest and humble, as the Midrashim that view him positively note. He has incredible potential and is therefore selected as king. However, in the second year, Shaul changes drastically. His insecurities lead to intimidation and he responds poorly. He begins constantly focusing on his reputation and projecting a positive image. Impatiently, he brings karbanos before Shmuel arrives to ensure that the masses take part in the ceremony and then spares the Amaleki king and animals to celebrate his success.

Shaul worries deeply about how Bnei Yisrael see him. Success becomes about him, his own image and not about how the people should follow Hashem. Worrying about and attempting to protect his reputation is precisely what prompts the Midrash to label Shaul as גסות רוח *arrogant* (Eliyahu Rabbah 29) and the Midrash even continues explaining, לפיכך נהרג ונעקרה ממנו מלכות *therefore he was killed and his kingship was uprooted from him* (ibid) underscoring our theory. The

---

[181] Rashi (Shmuel I 13:1), Sedar Olam (Radak on Shmuel I 13:1) Alshich (Shmuel I 13:1). However, according to the Sefer HaIkarim (4:26) the years after Shaul began chasing Dovid, are not counted for Shaul and his rule is significantly longer than two years. The Radak (Shmuel I 13:1) also toys with the possibility that Shaul ruled for three years, one before this point and two after.

[182] Shaul is clean of all sins his first year, (Rashi on Shmuel I 13:1 and 17:38 and the Alshich on Shmuel I 13:1). The Abarbanel (Shmuel 1 9:1) and Malbim (Shmuel 1 9:2) add that Shaul has impeccable middos.

Midrash even continues with its source, 'ויאמר שמואל ומה קול הצאן וגו' ויאמר שאול מעמלקי הביאום *And Shmuel said 'And what is the sound of sheep etc.' and Shaul said 'From Amalek I brought them'* from our narrative further supporting our analysis. This particular Midrash does not deal with why Shaul is chosen as king, it answers why Shaul is dethroned and does so by describing specifically his latter days.

The other critical Midrash (Tehillim Shachar Tov, Buber Edition 100), and one that we have already quoted, echoes Shaul's shortcoming by stating, מכסה פשעיו לא יצליח זה שאול שנאמר ויאמר שמואל (אל שאול) ומה קול הצאן הזה באזני *(One who) covers up mistakes will be unsuccessful' that is Shaul as it says 'And Shmuel said (to Shaul) Is that the sound of sheep that I hear?* Shaul is the paradigm of someone covering up his sins and worrying about his reputation.

Chazal (Megilla 13a-13b) accredit Shaul with both being Ester's ancestor and sparing Agog, which, in turn, spares Haman. The respective associations with Ester and Haman can be traced back to the modesty he displays in the first year and his decision to spare Agog in the second.[183]

Undoubtedly, Shaul has great potential, otherwise Hashem would never have selected him. In addition to having faith in Hashem's decision, we have seen some of Shaul's positive qualities; humility, sincerity and modesty. However, there is a danger associated with too much humility. Inner strength and conviction are critical for leadership. Without enough confidence, one may buckle under pressure resulting in mistakenly worrying too much about what the masses think. When confronted with a difficult political situation, Shaul crumbles under the pressure.

Both of Shaul's sins reflect this shortcoming. Shaul is more concerned about losing crowds and entertaining spectators than waiting for Shmuel to bring karbanos. Additionally, Shaul is more interested in celebrating with Amaleki animals as karbanos than a less celebratory victory with complete obedience to Hashem. In his attempt to gain

---

[183] Perhaps this also accounts for the Tanach's two different presentations of Shaul's death. First the Navi (Shmuel I Perek 31) presents Shaul as taking his own life and then the it (Shmuel II Perek 1) presents Shaul as being killed by an Amaleki boy. Although there are several approaches to resolving this contradiction, one may be based on our thesis. The first presentation takes into account Shaul's image and tells the story the way he would have wanted it told. In order to spare dishonor, Shaul took his own life. In Shmuel II, where Dovid is the focus, the Navi tells the story with historical accuracy.

favor in the people's eyes, with a giant celebration and sacrifices of Amaleki animals, he sacrifices something far more important; religious obedience and commitment to kingly conduct.[184]

SHMUEL'S FEAR

Shmuel knows that anointing Dovid would be seen by Shaul as extremely provocative and that Shmuel would have to fear for his life (Shmuel I 16:2).[185] Moreover, after communicating this fear to Hashem, Hashem does not dismiss this possibility, rather He suggests Shmuel develop a cover story (ibid). The implication of Hashem not protesting or correcting Shmuel, is that Shaul is willing to do anything to save his kingship, even kill Shmuel. Again, in the second year of his reign, Shaul completely loses it.

SHAUL'S NAME

The name שָׁאוּל *Shaul* can be translated as *borrowed*, as if to suggest that his kingship is temporary as Chazal state, וְלָמָה הוּא קוֹרֵא אוֹתוֹ שָׁאוּל שֶׁהָיְתָה הַמַּלְכוּת שְׁאוּלָה בְּיָדוֹ *And why was he called Shaul? Because the kingship was loaned to him* (Bereshis Rabbah 98, Vilna Edition).[186] Shaul is serving as the king, because he has potential to achieve enormous success, but there is a risk involved and therefore does not have a guaranteed long-term kingship. Is it borrowed.

Alternatively, the name שָׁאוּל *Shaul* may come from the word *question*. Perhaps his kingship is under question and its future

---

[184] Commenting on the verse בִּנְיָמִין זְאֵב יִטְרָף *Binyamin, a wolf, he will pray,* the Netziv (Bereshis 49:27) infers that Shaul fights like a wolf, in contrast to Dovid who fights like a lion. Dovid fights utterly fearlessly with an upfront confrontation, the way a lion fights. Shaul, like a wolf, fears shepherds and his rod.

[185] According to the Ralbag (Mishli 21:1) and Malbim (Mishli 21:1) kings have no free choice. The Meshech Chochma (Devorim 17:15) adds once that it has been declared that Shaul will lose his kingship, his free choice is returned and Shmuel's fear is justifiable.

[186] The Abarbanel (Shmuel I 9:1) adds that selecting Shaul as king hints to the fact that kingship is lent to Bnei Yisrael.

undetermined. It can go either way and it depends on how Shaul handles it.[187]

UNCOVERING A PARALLEL FROM SHAUL TO YOSEF

There is a fascinating number of parallels between our narrative and the Yosef one. We are going to list the them as well as the opposites between the stories and see what can be learned. Here are the similarities.

1. Both Yosef and Shaul have uniquely close relationships with their respective fathers with each receiving special care from them. Moreover, that closeness is captured by both stories beginning by describing the respective fathers and quickly transitions to the sons. Yosef's story begins, אֵלֶּה תֹּלְדוֹת יַעֲקֹב יוֹסֵף *These are the generations of Yaakov, Yosef* (Bereshis 37:2); and Shaul's narrative begins with an introduction to his father, Kish, as previously described.

2. Yosef, when separated from his father, encounters a difficult situation which leads to his rise to royalty before ultimately reuniting with his father. Shaul too is separated from his father, also challenged with great difficulties, crowned king, and then also reunited with his father.

3. Yosef and Shaul are each called נער *lad*. Calling Shaul that is particularly pronounced because one would not have thought to address him with a title implying youth when he is an adult.

4. Both Yosef and Shaul have a non-biological father-like figure (Paroh and Shmuel) who unexpectedly brings them to kingship.

5. Yosef is sent on mission by his father to רְאֵה אֶת־שְׁלוֹם אַחֶיךָ וְאֶת־שְׁלוֹם הַצֹּאן *see how your brothers and the sheep are doing* (ibid 37:14). Shaul too, is sent to search for his father's animals.

6. While looking for their father's animals, the central character encounters some peripheral character who redirects him in a life-changing manner. Shaul meets נְעָרוֹת *youthful girls* (Shmuel I 9:11) who direct him to Shmuel, and Yosef meets an אִישׁ *man* who informs

---

[187] There may even be a connection between the two translations of Shaul's name as asking and borrowing both imply a lack of ownership.

him where his brothers are shepherding, which leads to him being sold. Moreover, each interaction leads them to royalty.

7. Yosef and Shaul use strikingly similar phrases while searching. Yosef requests, **הַגִּידָה נָּא לִי אֵיפֹה הֵם רֹעִים** *tell me where they are shepherding* (Bereshis 37:16) and Shaul asks **הַגִּידָה נָּא לִי אֵי זֶה בֵּית הָרֹאֶה** *tell me where is the seer* (Shmuel I 9:18).

8. Yosef keeps a big secret from his family not revealing that he is royalty. Remarkably, Shaul keeps the exact same secret from his family.

9. Yosef wears a special garb which is ultimately ripped symbolizing his demise.[188] This is incredibly similar to Shaul ripping Shmuel's clothing, with precisely the same connotations (Shmuel I 15:30).[189]

This parallel is assumed by the Midrash (Sechel Tov, Buber Edition, Parshas Vayetzei 29:16) which draws upon this connection by stating, מלכות יוסף לשעה ומלכות שאול לשעה *Yosef's kingship was temporary, and Shaul's kingship was temporary*. These are not the only two kings with temporary kingships. The Midrash selects these two examples to bolster our connection. Another midrash (Shachar Tov, Vayetzei 29 and Bereshis Rabbah 70:15) equates Yosef to Shaul by neither bequeathing kingship to their descendants.

The striking parallel between these two narratives is too strong to be seen as coincidental. Why then is the Shaul episode written to recall Yosef's?

THE OPPOSITES BETWEEN SHAUL AND YOSEF

Although there are many similarities between the Yosef and Shaul narrative, the opposites are even more notable. Before offering insight, let us contrast the two stories.

1. Although Yosef and Shaul each lead and build a country, Shaul builds his own country, while Yosef another, Egypt.

2. Yosef travels alone to find his brothers and sheep, while Shaul travels with company, a נער *lad*.

---

[188] After seeing the garb, Yaakov assumes Yosef is dead (Bereshis 37:32-34).

[189] See note 178 for a discussion regarding who ripped what clothing.

3. As a result of meeting the independent party who redirects him, Yosef is further separated from his father, thrown into a pit and ultimately sold to a foreign country. Shaul's meeting with the independent party causes him to quickly return home and reunite with his father.

4. Yosef leaves his father with expectations of being welcomed in by his brothers as family. To his dismay, he is ambushed, thrown into a pit (Bereshis 37:24), excluded from the family dinner (ibid 37:25), and ultimately sold as a slave to a foreign nation (ibid 37:28).[190] The exact opposite happens to Shaul. He meets Shmuel, a complete stranger, expecting to be treated as a stranger and even charged a fee as a formality for his services. Instead of being ambushed and sold, Shaul is welcomed in (Shmuel I 9:23). Instead of being excluded from dinner, Shaul is greeted and invited for dinner (ibid 9:24), and instead of being sold as a slave to another nation, Shaul is promised to become the king of his own nation.

5. Yosef's brothers throw him *down* into a pit in order to prevent his dreams from coming to fruition,[191] fearing that Yosef would ultimately rise to power. Shmuel brings Shaul *up* to his roof (ibid 9:25), the geographical opposite of a pit, and for opposite purposes as well; namely to crown Shaul king and facilitate his rise to power.

6. Yosef ultimately finds what he is looking for, his brothers and the sheep, yet ironically it turns out to be catastrophic for him, for it leads to him being sold. By contrast, Shaul never finds what he is looking for, the donkeys, yet it turns out to be ideal for him, for along with Shmuel communicating that the donkeys are found, he informs Shaul that he will be the future king.

7. Yosef comes from a prestigious family and is sold as a slave. By contrast, Shaul comes from a small and non-prestigious family, yet is elevated to become king.

8. Even though both Yosef and Shaul keep their royalty a secret, Shaul's identity is known by his family, just not his position as king. The exact reverse is true about Yosef. His position is clear, but his identity

---

[190] For the greater significance to this, see Double Take *Moshe and Yosef: A Tale of Two Jewish Princes*

[191] As emphasized by their remark, הִנֵּה בַּעַל הַחֲלֹמוֹת הַלָּזֶה בָּא *behold, the dreamer is coming* (Bereshis 37:19) upon seeing Yosef.

is not, for his brothers know that they are speaking to Egyptian royalty but do not realize that it is Yosef.

9. Although both Yosef and Shaul keep secrets, Yosef thoughtfully keeps his in order to implement his plan,[192] which requires a great amount of confidence and inner strength. Shaul has no plan, and keeps his secret due to his shyness and insecurity.

10. Yosef sees himself as destined for leadership as seen by the content of his dreams. Shaul sees himself entirely different. Coming from the smallest tribe, being "Daddy's Little Boy" and hiding in הַכֵּלִים *the vessels* (ibid 10:22), he demonstrate his self-perception as undeserving of kingship.

Because there are too many comparisons and contrasts to be explained as mere coincidence, we must ask what the point is. Why is Shaul's narrative recorded in a manner that vividly recalls major events in Yosef's life?

On a simple level, the parallels link Shaul and Yosef who both worry exceedingly about their image. Yosef, acting as a נַעַר *youth* (Bereshis 37:2), worries too much about his external beauty, his hair[193] and looks, and Shaul worries about his political image.

Additionally, comparisons are often designed to draw attention to the opposites, and that may be the case here as well. Yosef clearly hits a low before slowly climbing out and rising to power. Yosef is almost killed by his brothers, sold, falsely accused of adultery, sent to jail and is forgotten about there. After hitting the bottom of the pit, both physically and metaphorically, he manages to slowly regain his previous stature. Shaul's life follows the opposite pattern; he climaxes early before falling. Shaul soars for one year, and then fizzles out. By

---

[192] According to the Ramban (Bereshis 42:9), Yosef does all that he does to bring to fruition his dreams of the brothers bowing down to him.

Alternatively, Yosef arranges a situation where his brothers are confronted with the same challenge, forcing them to decide whether to allow their father's favorite son be taken again. Only in the exact same situation can one be assured that sincere Teshuva has been done (Rambam Teshuva 2:1).

A third possibility might be that Yosef, after seeing his brothers arrive in Mitzrayim without Binyamin, assumes that Binyamin is intentionally excluded. Yosef presumes Binyamin, like he himself was, is an outsider and perhaps even in danger from the other brothers. Yosef, fearful and empathetic, concocts a plan to save Binyamin.

[193] Commenting on the term נַעַר *youth* (Bereshis 37:2), Rashi (Bereshis 37:2) says that Yosef would play with his hair to look good. The Seforno (Bereshis 37:2) adds that it is this attitude that causes him to sin by bringing the bad report about his brothers to their father.

contrasting Shaul to Yosef, the Navi highlights Shaul's spiritual path, his quick rise and fall. Whereas Yosef plummets before rising, Shaul rises before plummeting.

Although both Shaul and Yosef worry too much about their image, they do it in opposite ways. Yosef worries about his physical looks whereas, Shaul, his political image.

However, the contrast penetrates significantly deeper. Yosef *begins* worrying about his looks, as a youth. Yet, as the narrative continues, he outgrows that.[194] The exact opposite occurs with Shaul. He begins completely unconcerned with his appearance and political image. He is a simple person as described earlier. However, due to his appointment as king, he develops that insecurity. Whereas Yosef grows out of the fear, Shaul grows into it.

SHAUL AND DOVID

What does Hashem see in Dovid making him fit to be the next king? The Navi hints to the answer when Hashem informs Shmuel that Hashem knows what is in the heart of people,[195] אַל תַּבֵּט אֶל מַרְאֵהוּ וְאֶל גְּבֹהַּ קוֹמָתוֹ כִּי מְאַסְתִּיהוּ כִּי לֹא אֲשֶׁר יִרְאֶה הָאָדָם כִּי הָאָדָם יִרְאֶה לַעֵינַיִם וַיקֹוָק יִרְאֶה לַלֵּבָב *Do not look at his appearance or height as the reason for his (Shaul's) rejection, for Hashem does not see as man sees; because man sees (what is visible) to one's eyes and Hashem sees what is in the heart* (Shmuel I 16:7).

Because the Navi is vague regarding which details Hashem sees inside of Dovid's heart, we should ask what they are, and what it is about Dovid that makes him the ideal replacement for Shaul?

---

[194] Throughout the story, Yosef is extremely well-liked by his superiors including Yaakov, Potifar, the warden in jail, and ultimately Paroh. Yosef's brothers are the only ones jealous of him because of how their father treats him. Yet, his peers are only jealous when he is young. As he grows older, he is equally likable by his superiors, yet no peers express jealousy. Presumably, Yosef outgrows his נַעַר *youth*-like behavior.

[195] This is reiterated when Shlomo inherits Dovid's kingship (Dvray HaYamim I 28:9).

Dovid and Golyas

Dovid's trajectory for kingship really gains traction after his victory over Golyas. The people chant שָׁאוּל בַּאֲלָפָיו וְדָוִד בְּרִבְבֹתָיו *Shaul (beat) thousands and Dovid, tens of thousands* (Shmuel I 18:7). Similarly, after Dovid's victory, Shaul inquires from Avner about his upbringing and background (ibid 17:55-56),[196] implying that, now, he is someone worth keeping an eye on. Furthermore, it is after Dovid's triumph that Yonason develops his affinity for Dovid (ibid 18:1). These details all emphasize how much of a transformative event this is for Dovid.

If beating Golyas propels Dovid towards kingship, then we should ask why. What is so important about this particular victory? How does beating Golyas highlight Dovid as the best replacement for Shaul? A deeper look at their battle should answer this, for it is at this battle that Dovid surpasses Shaul and finds the path towards becoming king.

The Dovid and Golyas narrative begins with detailed descriptions of Golyas' unparalleled power, strength and size (ibid 17:4-7) which sets the tone for his challenge: can anyone defeat him (ibid 17:8-11).[197] When describing Bnei Yisrael hearing, the Navi explicitly states וַיִּשְׁמַע שָׁאוּל וְכָל יִשְׂרָאֵל *And Shaul and all of Yisrael heard* (ibid 17:11). Why does the Navi spell out Shaul's hearing Golyas' challenge independently and separately from the rest of Bnei Yisrael?

---

[196] It is difficult to understand how Shaul is unfamiliar with Dovid until now. Dovid has previously played the harp at Shaul's house and Shaul adores his playing (Shmuel I 16:21). Additionally, Shaul has just given Dovid his armor and sent him to battle against Golyas, seemingly an unforgettable moment. Perhaps Shaul has interacted with, but never paid proper attention Dovid, to the point that he is unfamiliar with his name.
Alternatively, Rashi (Shmuel I 17:55) interprets Shaul's question to be about Dovid's lineage and whether Dovid can take over as king. Either way the point it clear, Dovid is now drawing national attention.

[197] This uncommon form of battle suggests that Bnei Yisrael are not really at war with the Plishitim at this time. Rather this is a contest or compilation which the winner gains great honor. Support can be found by Dovid's reaction to the challenge and to his victory. After victory, Dovid decapitates Golyas, declares how he will throw Golyas' body to the birds and then remarks וְיֵדְעוּ כָּל הָאָרֶץ כִּי יֵשׁ אֱלֹהִים לְיִשְׂרָאֵל *and all of the (people) of the earth will know that there is a God for Yisrael* (ibid 17:46). Then Dovid takes Golyas' detached head to Yerushalayim (ibid 17:54) for all to see. This seems to celebrate national pride more than a military victory.
Alternatively, this style of battle is designed to minimize bloodshed. Instead of many fighting and dying in normative war, this allows for only one man to die.

Continuing, the Navi introduces us to Dovid (ibid 17:12-19) who is small, young and clearly not one of the well-respected brothers in his family.

As Golyas' challenge looms, it becomes clear that Bnei Yisrael are lacking an אִישׁ *man* to represent them and accept the challenge. That fact begs the implicit question; why not? Who should have been that *man*? Who should be the one to stand up to Golyas?

Evidently, Shaul should have been that *man*[198] and the perfect match for Golyas. Beyond being king, and therefore militarily responsible, Shaul is the tallest of Bnei Yisrael (ibid 10:23) and the one most appropriate for the challenge. In fact, Golyas subtly specifically challenges Shaul. He declares, הֲלוֹא אָנֹכִי הַפְּלִשְׁתִּי וְאַתֶּם עֲבָדִים לְשָׁאוּל *Am I not the Pelishti and you are slaves to Shaul?* (ibid 17:8).[199] Golyas does not symmetrically conclude his sentence after *Am I not the Pelishti,* and *Shaul not the Yisraeli.* Instead he replaces it with וְאַתֶּם עֲבָדִים לְשָׁאוּל *you are slaves to Shaul,* subtly implying that Shaul is enslaving Bnei Yisrael by not stepping up and facing Golyas himself. Shaul should be representing Bnei Yisrael, accepting the challenge and he is not. Shaul's cowardly behavior (ibid 17:11) creates a vacuum where there is no *man*? This vacuum leaves space for someone else to step up and lead.

The Navi repeats the word אִישׁ *man* fifteen times (ibid 17:2, 4, 8, 12, 12, 19, 23, 24, 24, 25, 25, 25, 26, 27, 33, and 41) subtly reinforcing that this episode questions who Bnei Yisrael's *man* is. The Plishtim have a *man* and Bnei Yisrael do not.

When Dovid arrives, the Navi repeats the word דבר *speaks* (ibid 23, 23, 23, 27, 28, 28, 29, 30, 30, 31, 31) eleven times. Perhaps the point is that Dovid is ready for action when everyone else is just talking.

Dovid's epic victory enables him to become that *man.* Understandably, this lays the groundwork for his eventual replacing Shaul. In addition to this political gain, the Navi cleverly hints to this replacement with fascinating symbolisms. The visual image of Dovid replacing Shaul occurs when Dovid tries on Shaul's armor to battle Golyas. By wearing Shaul's armor, Dovid is literally filling Shaul's

---

[198] Targum 17:8 and Rashi Shmuel I 17:8

[199] Perhaps Golyas thinks Bnei Yisrael are more likely to accept his challenge if they realize that they have little to lose; either way they are slaves.

shoes and moving into his role as king.²⁰⁰ However, before going out to face Golyas, Dovid removes Shaul's armor (ibid 17:38), indicating something else. More than Dovid replacing Shaul as the *man* Bnei Yisrael so desperately need, Dovid replaces Shaul with his own personal and unique style. Dovid does not need Shaul's armor. He is prepared to fight as himself.

During the conversation that the Navi records between Dovid and Shaul, it becomes apparent that Dovid is the *man* who Shaul fails to be. Dovid is completely confident in Hashem, as he instructs Shaul, עַבְדְּךָ יֵלֵךְ וְנִלְחַם עִם הַפְּלִשְׁתִּי הַזֶּה *your servant will go and we will wage war with this Plishti* (ibid 17:32) while Shaul fearfully responds לֹא תוּכַל לָלֶכֶת אֶל הַפְּלִשְׁתִּי הַזֶּה לְהִלָּחֵם עִמּוֹ כִּי נַעַר אַתָּה וְהוּא אִישׁ מִלְחָמָה מִנְּעֻרָיו *You cannot go to this Plishti to fight, for you are a Naar and he is a warrior (trained) from his (Naar) youth* (ibid 17:33). After Dovid's persistence, Shaul agrees to dispatch Dovid, fully confident that he will lose.²⁰¹

It is at this point where Dovid begins to surpass Shaul. The Navi uses this battle to transition from Shaul's leadership to Dovid's. This story is more than Dovid's first military victory, it foreshadows the change in leadership, highlighting why a change is needed, and why Dovid is selected.

THE DEEPER MEANING

Initially, Dovid is perceived as physically weak, prompting people not to take him seriously at the battlefield: not Golyas, nor his brothers, and not even Shaul (ibid 17:33, 37).²⁰² However, on the inside Dovid is deeply confident and sincere. He has complete faith that he will

---

²⁰⁰ The point is sharpened by Rashi (Shmuel I 17:38) who writes that the armor miraculously shrinks to fit Dovid.

²⁰¹ וַיֵּקִנְק יְהֶיָה עַמָּךְ *And Hashem should be with you* (Shmuel I 17:37) is a prayer or wish (Daas Mikrah Shmuel I 17:37). Alternatively, the Ralbag (Shmuel I 17:37) argues that Shmuel is completely convinced by the story Dovid tells and therefore trusts that Dovid will be victorious. The Abarbanel and Malbim (both on Shmuel I 17:37), too, think Shaul accepts Dovid's argument now because now, Dovid presents his victory as miraculous and not natural.

²⁰² This is seen by how Dovid's brothers speak to him (Shumel I 17:28). At this point, no one, including Shaul, takes him seriously.

succeed.[203] Presumably this is the quality the Navi hints at when it describes Hashem looking into Dovid's heart (ibid 17:16:7).[204]

Shaul appears strong on the outside but is actually weak on the inside which is the opposite of Dovid, who appears weak on the outside, but is actually strong on the inside. Again, the symbolism is incredible. True, Dovid wearing and removing Shaul's armor reflects his replacement of Shaul, and taking it off, reflects doing it in his own way, but it represents much more as well. This event captures the personality difference between the two of them. Shaul values armor, representing the exterior, which is the exact shortcoming he has. He worries about the exterior, symbolizing his reputation and how he is perceived. Dovid, removes that, suggesting that he fights using his inner pureness. He is confident in Hashem and does not have to wear armor to project a serious image.[205]

Until this victory, Dovid is portrayed as a young boy as seen by how his brothers talk down to him criticizing him for coming to watch the battle. It is this victory which grants Dovid remarkable national support, most clearly illustrated by the people's response שָׁאוּל בַּאֲלָפָיו וְדָוִד בְּרִבְבֹתָיו *Shaul (beat) thousands and Dovid, tens of thousands* (Shmuel I 18:7).[206]

THE TOPOGRAPHY

The battle between Golyas and Dovid takes place in a valley directly in between two hills (ibid 17:2). Perhaps that landscape itself encapsulates the significance of the moment. On a simple level, Bnei Yisrael are situated in the valley between two hills. This symbolically represents their political situation, in between two kings, who are likened to mountains.

---

[203] It is Dovid's emotional greatness that leads him to so successfully author Tehillim.

[204] According to the Radak (Shmuel I 16:7), Eliav, Dovid's brother may look appropriate for kingship, however he is not selected כי איננו ישר *because he was not straight*.

[205] Interestingly, both Dovid and Shaul respond to their respective sins with the word חָטָאתִי *I sinned*, but Dovid responds immediately and with profound sincerity (Shmuel II 12:13). Shaul takes his time, making excuses (Malbim Shmuel II 12:13) and trying to defend his image and reputation.

[206] According to the Radak (Shmuel II 17:54) Dovid takes Golyas' head to many other places in addition to Yerushalayim. In doing so, he rallies a lot of national support.

However, there may be another level to unpack. Following the topography, we initially see a hill which is followed by a valley and then another hill. Shaul represents one hill, a physically towering figure who became a valley. Dovid, by contrast, naturally is identified with the valley. It is during this battle that his trajectory of fame and leadership begins, symbolically represented by the second hill, the one on the other side of the valley. Dovid is the valley which grows into the second hill.

MICHAL AND DOVID

Years later, Shaul's daughter, Michal, criticizes Dovid for dancing before the Aron (Shmuel II 6:20). Following in her father's ideological footsteps, Michal disagrees with his behavior worrying about Dovid's public image.[207] By contrast, Dovid dances sincerely before Hashem.

The Navi hints to this difference in perspective twice. Once, by labeling Michal as Michal Bas Shaul (ibid 6:16) hinting at the deep connection between her and Shaul, her father. Additionally, the Navi quotes Dovid describing how he himself dances; לִפְנֵי יְקֹוָק אֲשֶׁר בָּחַר בִּי מֵאָבִיךְ וּמִכָּל בֵּיתוֹ *before Hashem* **who chose me over your father** *and his household* (ibid 6:21). Dovid informs Michal that Hashem does not just select him over Shaul, He selects his approach over Shaul's.[208]

APPLYING TEXT TO LIFE: THE HASHKAFIC MESSAGE

Dovid is chosen to replace Shaul because he excels where Shaul does not. Dovid has deep inner strength. He is selected because וַיִקֹוָק יִרְאֶה לַלֵּבָב *Hashem sees what is in the heart* (Shmuel I 16:7) reflecting his extraordinary character.

---

[207] When describing how Michal looks out the window to watch Dovid, the Navi uses the term נִשְׁקְפָה *let us look* (Shmuel II 6:16); the similarity of this word to *Hashkafa* or ideology connotes she is doing more than innocently observing. She is watching while wearing her ideological glasses. To leave no room for doubt, the Navi records וַתִּבֶז לוֹ בְּלִבָּה *and she loathed him in her heart* (ibid).

[208] As explained by the Malbim (Shmuel II 6:16) למודה בבית אביה שהיה כבודם חשוב בעיניהם מכבוד המקום *she learned this in her father's house, that his honor was more important in their eyes than the honor for Hashem.*

More specifically, Dovid has exceptional faith in Hashem. Fearlessly facing Golyas, he displays his remarkable confidence in Hashem. But more than having conviction, Dovid is open and unabashed about it. He declares גַּם אֶת הָאֲרִי גַּם הַדּוֹב הִכָּה עַבְדֶּךָ וְהָיָה הַפְּלִשְׁתִּי הֶעָרֵל הַזֶּה כְּאַחַד מֵהֶם *I, your servant, also smote the lion and the bear and I can do the same to this Pelishti* (ibid 17:36).[209] Dovid's confidence resonates so clearly, it can inspire others.

There is an additional profound take-home message from the transfer of leadership from Shaul to Dovid. Good leadership is not based on how one appears but who one is. Although Shaul's height enables him to be seen and make a good first impression,[210] that is merely a platform to more easily showcase good leadership. However, more important than that is Dovid's sincerity.

From Shaul's original appointment, one sees how significant potential is; after all, that is why he is selected as king. Yet far more important than having potential is living up to that potential.[211] Dovid achieves actual greatness and does not merely project an image of greatness. It is more important to do right, than celebrate looking right.

Lastly, Shaul should not be seen as profane even at the end of his reign. Dovid deeply respects Shaul and his family and praises him greatly (Shmuel II 1:23). Shaul should be seen as someone who begins as modest and humble with shortcomings who sadly ends up as being described as, גסות רוח היתה בו *arrogant* (Eliyahu Rabbah 29). One should internalize the potential danger that leadership can create, yet steer from it as Dovid does.

---

[209] According to Rashi (Shmuel I 17:26), Dovid realizes then, when he fought the lion and bear, that it was a prelude for his future role in national salvation.

[210] Alshich (Shmuel 1 9:1)

[211] According to the Ramban (Bereshis 22:1), the purpose of all tests that Hashem challenges man with is to allow potential to blossom into actuality.

Political Tension: Mordachi's Critiques

Mordachi's Shocking Unpopularity

After conveying a robust story of how Mordachi heroically facilitates the miraculous Purim salvation, the Megilla concludes with this description of Mordachi: כִּי מָרְדֳּכַי הַיְּהוּדִי מִשְׁנֶה לַמֶּלֶךְ אֲחַשְׁוֵרוֹשׁ וְגָדוֹל לַיְּהוּדִים וְרָצוּי לְרֹב אֶחָיו דֹּרֵשׁ טוֹב לְעַמּוֹ וְדֹבֵר שָׁלוֹם לְכָל־זַרְעוֹ *Because Mordachi, the Jew, was second to the king, great for the Jews, favored by most of his brethren, interested in the well-being of his nation and a spokesman for peace for his people* (Ester 10:3).

At first glance, this verse seems to unreservedly praise Mordachi for his successful efforts. Yet, surprisingly, Chazal (Megilla 16b) interpret this verse differently. וְרָצוּי לְרֹב אֶחָיו *favored **by most** of his brethren*, they argue, implies that there are those, albeit a small number, who do not appreciate Mordachi, as they explain; מלמד שפירשו ממנו מקצת סנהדרין *It teaches that some members of the Sanhedrin separated (from supporting him)*. Rashi (Ester 10:3) adds לפי שנעשה קרוב למלכות והיה בטל מתלמודו *because he (Mordachi) became close with the government and thereby learned less Torah.* Several members of the Sanhedrin, the greatest Rabbinic authoritative body at the time, express great disappointment in Mordachi. They feel that Mordachi should spend more time learning Torah and limit his political involvement.[212]

---

[212] Some do not draw this conclusion, for example, the Rashbam (quoted by the Chachmay Tzarfas Ester 10:3) understands רב *most* to really mean all of his brethren, and the Daas Mikrah Ester (10:3) translates וְרָצוּי לְרֹב אֶחָיו as *favored by many.* Accordingly, there are no critics. Alternatively, others understand that there are critics, but not illustrious members of the Sanhedrin. The Ibn Ezra Nusach Alef (Ester 10:3), for example, notes that it is impossible to win favor in everyone's eyes for there are always those who are jealous. The Rabaynu Yosef (quoted by the Chachmay Tzarfas Ester 10:3) argues that there are people who blame Mordachi for enraging Haman in the first place.

Beyond the incredibly interesting ideological and political debate between that small group within the Sanhedrin and the majority who side with Mordachi, this description is unexpected. One must wonder why the Megilla concludes by raising doubts about Mordachi's character. Why end such a heroic and even glowing narrative of Mordachi with a criticism? Until this point Mordachi is portrayed completely heroically, with nothing but praise. Why end on a downer? Additionally, because Mordachi is the author of Megillas Ester;[213] it is even more strange that he alludes to this critique of himself in such an anticlimactic way.

THE PARALLEL BETWEEN ESTER AND YOSEF

Before directly answering our opening questions, let us take a detour and uncover an interesting character parallel. Both Ester and Mordachi are strikingly similar to Yosef. Many details about each recall and resemble details that describe Yosef in the Torah, hinting that there may be a deeper connection. Let us begin with Ester.

1. Ester and Yosef are both Jewish heroes who save Bnei Yisrael through their political influence on a non-Jewish king.

2. Yosef's mother, Rochel, dies at a young age. Yosef is then separated from his remaining family, ultimately ending up in the palace. Ester too is orphaned and taken from her family, and she too ends up in the palace.

3. Yosef is courted by an aristocrat from the local country in which he finds himself, Ashes Potifar. This is strikingly similar to Ester's selection as Achashvarosh's queen. Ultimately, each marries into the

---

[213] Rashi (Ester 9:20), Ibn Ezra Nusach Alef (introduction to Megillas Ester) and Ra"m Chalev (Ester 9:20).

However, Rashi elsewhere (Baba Basra 15a) contradicts himself, implying that Mordachi did not author Megillas Ester, for Navi'im cannot be written outside of Eretz Yisrael. The Brisker Rav (on the Rambam Megilla 2:9) resolves the contradiction by explaining that Megillas Ester was actually written twice. Megillas Ester was originally written in Persia, then again in Eretz Yisrael, this time with Ruach HaKodesh and to be part of Tanach. This resolution may be hinted to by Rashi (Ester 9:32) himself who reports that Ester requests that the leading Rabbis of the generation accept Megillas Ester as part of Tanach. Here Rashi indicates that the Megilla was written before the Rabbis accepted it into Tanach.

foreign aristocracy; Yosef marries Osnos, Poti Fera's[214] daughter,[215] and Ester marries Achashvarosh.

4. Yosef patiently waits in prison for the king to summon him to his palace. Upon one brief meeting with the king, his life is metamorphized, as he transforms from a powerless peasant to an incredibly influential and dominant force in the government,[216] which facilitates his ability to save Bnei Yisrael. Ester too, waits for the king to summon her. Her life too, is transformed based on that brief meeting, and she too, rises to power, enabling her to help save Bnei Yisrael.

5. Both Ester and Yosef initially withhold their true identity from family, Yosef from his brothers and Ester from, her husband, Achashvarosh. More astonishing is that after initially hiding who they really are, they each ultimately reveal their true identities in an incredibly dramatic manner; one that serves as the central turning point in each story. In essence, each one reveals themselves by saying "Surprise! I'm Jewish" and from thereon out salvation is just a matter of time.

6. Yosef brilliantly crafts a clever plan, falsely accusing his brothers of espionage, capturing Shimon and ultimately isolating Binyamin. Ester, in an equally ingenious fashion, invites Achashvarosh to a party, leading to another party and ultimately accusing the unsuspecting Haman of mass genocide.[217]

7. Each story includes a major accusation leading to the story's crescendo. Ester accuses Haman of genocide and Yosef accuses Binyamin of stealing his goblet.

8. Both stories end similarly, albeit sadly. After saving Bnei Yisrael, each hero remains behind as the only Jew in the foreign and secular palace. Yosef stays with Paroh and Ester stays with Achashvarosh.

Chazal (Sifri Bamidbar, Parshas Naso 41, Sifri Zuta 6) bolster this parallel thematically and linguistically by comparing Ester to

---

[214] Potifar

[215] Bereshis Rabbah, Vilna Edition 85:2

[216] Here is where Ester begins to amass power. For more on Ester's accumulation of power, see the chapter entitled *The Transformation from a Quiet Jewish Girl into a Heroine.*

[217] For greater detail on Haman and Achashvarosh's relationship, see the chapter entitled, *Achashvarosh's Important Religious Role in the Megilla.*

Yosef, noting that they are both attractive youth described as נַעַר *youth* (Bereshis 37:2 and Ester 2:2, 4) who find חֵן *favor* in the eyes of others; Yosef in the eyes of the warden (Bereshis 39:21) and Ester in the eyes of all who see her (Ester 2:15).

THE PARALLEL BETWEEN MORDACHI AND YOSEF

There are a number of similarities between Mordachi and Yosef as well, reinforcing the connection between these two characters. Chazal in a Midrash (Bereshis Rabbah, Vilna Edition 87:6) designed to illustrate this parallel list several comparisons.

Both Yosef and Mordachi are challenged daily by an aristocratic character in their respective stories; Yosef by Ashes Potifar, desiring an intimate relationship (Bereshis 39:10), and Mordachi by Haman demanding he bow down to him (Ester 3:4). The Megilla even uses the exact same language יוֹם וָיוֹם *daily*, quoting the Torah into order to emphasize this parallel.

In both episodes, the respective kings empower both Yosef and Mordachi with important decision-making responsibilities by resigning their ring to these two trusted individuals (Bereshis 41:42 and Ester 8:2).

Additionally, they are both dressed up and then paraded around the city's capital as declaration of their elevated status (Bereshis 41:42-43 and Ester 6:11).

In another Midrash, Chazal (Midrash Lekach Tov, Vayeshev 40 and Rabaynu Bachaya on Bereshis 40:2) compare both stories as in each the king becomes angry with two of his assistants for bringing him bad food. Achashvarosh gets upset with Bigson and Seresh and Paroh with Sar HaMashkim and Sar HaOfim. In both narratives, Yosef and Mordachi find themselves right in the middle.

In addition to what Chazal list, there are numerous other parallels between Mordachi and Yosef.

1. Megillas Ester's introduction to Mordachi (Ester 2:6) focuses on his exile from Israel by mentioning it four times.[218] Yosef too is exiled and sold as a slave into a foreign land by his brothers. Yet, despite

---

[218] Rashi (Ester 2:5) claims that Mordachi is introduced as a Yehudi (Ester 2:5) precisely because he is exiled with Yehuda.

being exiled from the land of Israel and finding themselves in foreign lands, both Mordachi and Yosef quickly rise to political power.

2. They each become advisors to the king and ultimately second only to the king himself (Bereshis 41:44 and Ester 10:3). To illustrate this, Mordachi is labeled as מִשְׁנֶה לַמֶּלֶךְ *Second to the King*.

3. Each rises to power primarily based on a single act of helping the king by providing him with important information; for Mordachi it is notifying him of a planned assassination and for Yosef it is interpreting his dreams.

4. The Megilla's language of וַיַּפְקֵד הַמֶּלֶךְ פְּקִידִים *And the king appointed* parallels the Torah's, יַעֲשֶׂה פַרְעֹה וְיַפְקֵד פְּקִדִים *And Paroh appointed officials*.[219] Similarly, וַיִּקְרָא לְפָנָיו *and he called before him* in Megillas Ester (6:11) is nearly identical to וַיִּקְרְאוּ לְפָנָיו *and they called before him* (Bereshis 41:43). The Navi also says וַיַּרְכִּיבֵהוּ *and they rode him* (Ester 6:11) mimicking וַיַּרְכֵּב *And he rode him* (Bereshis 41:43).[220]

Not only are there many similarities, but the fact that both heroes mentioned in Megillas Ester, Mordachi and Ester, are both compared to Yosef makes it far less likely to be coincidental.

THE DIFFERENCES BETWEEN THE MEGILLA AND YOSEF

Although the question begs to be asked as to why the Megilla would present both main characters in parallel to Yosef, it is worthwhile to first note the contrasts between Ester, Mordachi and the entire Megillas Ester narrative on the one hand, and Yosef on the other, before offering a theory.

1. In contrast to how Yosef is exiled, as an individual apart from his family, Mordachi is exiled as part of a nation (Ester 2:6). Moreover, Yosef is exiled by his brothers where Mordachi, by contrast, is exiled by a stranger, a foreign king (ibid 2:6).

2. Although both kings ask for advice, they do so in different manners. Achashvarosh asks his most-trusted assistant, Haman for advice.

---

[219] Baal HaTurim Bereshis 41:34

[220] The Rashbam (Bereshis 43:14) adds that וַאֲנִי כַּאֲשֶׁר שָׁכֹלְתִּי שָׁכָלְתִּי *And as for me as I am bereaved, I am bereaved* (Bereshis 43:14) is echoed by וְכַאֲשֶׁר אָבַדְתִּי אָבָדְתִּי *and if I am lost, then I am lost* (Ester 4:16).

Paroh does the exact opposite, consulting with a complete stranger, an imprisoned Hebrew slave. However, the contrast is even more profound because Haman is the first individual Achashvarosh asks while Yosef is asked last, summoned only when all other options are exhausted.[221]

3. Although each king listens to both Yosef's and Haman's advice, their intentions as well as subsequent results are opposite. Yosef has a selfless agenda, and is elevated to become second to the king. Haman, by contrast, attempts to selfishly become second to the king, does not succeed. Instead he is hanged.

4. Although both Yosef and Mordachi are both given special clothing, Yosef receives his as a permanent gift from his father, while Mordachi's is temporary and from the king. Moreover, and more importantly, Yosef receives special clothing which directly leads to his misfortune. By contrast, Mordachi's success directly leads to him receiving special clothing (ibid 8:15).

5. Ester is taken as a wife by the one courting her, Achashvarosh,[222] which makes her queen. Ashes Potifar is unsuccessful at courting Yosef, and subsequently he is incarcerated. Whereas Ester rises to the top of society, Yosef tumbles to the bottom.

6. Although ultimately both Ester and Yosef reveal their true identities, Ester communicates that Achashvarosh does not know her upbringing and past, while Yosef says the exact opposite; he tells his brothers that

---

[221] One may even suggest that Paroh unsuccessfully questioning his assistants is actually part of the dream itself. At the end of Paroh's first dream, the Torah clearly indicates the conclusion of the dream with וָאִיקָץ *and I awoke* (Bereshis 41:21). Yet in Paroh's second dream, there is no clear phrase indicating that Paroh wakes up and וָאֹמַר אֶל הַחַרְטֻמִּים וְאֵין מַגִּיד לִי *and I said to the Chartumim and no one could tell (explain it) to me* (Bereshis 41:24) may be part of Paroh's dream. Paroh may trust Yosef's interpretation, and not the Chartumim's because in the dream their interpretations are rejected.

[222] How this is Halachikally permissible is subject to dispute. There are two in independent problems that have to be addressed. Ester is married to Mordachi, and beyond that, the sin committed is done publicly. Either of these sins should have prevented her from being intimate with Achashvarosh, even at the cost of her life. The Gemara (Sanhedrin 74) addresses the second problem offering two resolutions. According to Abaya, Ester acts like קרקע עולם *merely land,* meaning passive (Rashi Sanhedrin 74b), while Rava says הנאת עצמו שאני *his own pleasure is different.* Achashvarosh's intention for self-pleasure, as opposed to making a theological point, allows for her to do this.
Regarding the first question, Ester being married, Tosfos (Sanhedrin 74b and Kesuvos 3b) offers two answers. According to the Rivam, the previous answers of Abaya and Rava solve this problem as well whereas the Rabaynu Tam disagrees arguing that intimacy with a non-Jew does not carry with it the obligation to surrender one's life.

they do know his history and past. When revealing her identity, Ester further tells her husband, "You think we are family, but, in truth, you do not know me" while Yosef conversely reveals to his brothers: "You think that you do not know me – surprise – we are family."

7. Yosef waits in jail until he is summoned into Paroh's palace (ibid 41:14). The opposite happens to Achashvarosh twice. First Haman enters his house uninvited at night (Ester 5:4). Later, Ester bursts into the inner chamber of the king uninvited, breaking the law and endangering her own life.

8. Yosef's primary intention is to assist Paroh and save the Egyptian kingdom while Mordachi's primary mission is to save Bnei Yisrael. Transforming the city into וְהָעִיר שׁוּשָׁן צָהֲלָה וְשָׂמֵחָה *The city of Shushan was cheerful and happy* (Ester 8:15) is a byproduct that happens only peripherally.[223]

9. In one story the king takes a wife from the primary character, and in the other the king gives a wife to the primary character. Achashvarosh takes his wife Ester from Mordachi. Paroh, instead of taking a wife, gives one to Yosef (Bereshis 41:45).[224]

10. Yosef is alone in Egypt without support or communication with his family. Ester, by contrast, is in constant communication with Mordachi and has his full support as well.

11. Although both kings have two assistants who bring bad food, Achashvarosh's, Bigson and Seresh, maliciously attempt to poison him, while Paroh's act carelessly in their service of him.

12. Although both stories conclude with an accusation, Yosef falsely accuses Binyamin while Ester accurately accuses Haman. Moreover, after the accusation, Haman is hanged whereas Binyamin is freed.

13. Perhaps the most astute contrast is that in Yosef's story, redemption begins at night with Paroh's dreams as he sleeps. The dreams prompt him to look for advice and ultimately enable him to find Yosef to interpret them. By contrast, it is Achashvarosh's insomnia, his

---

[223] The Brisker Rav (on Kesuvim 198) asks why the Megilla includes taxes that Achashvarosh imposes on his people (Ester 10:1). He answers that it reflects Achashvarosh's kingdom being even stronger than before. Part of the miracle is that after the small battle, Achashvarosh grows in power and control. The Megilla includes this detail to illustrate Persia's political improvement.

[224] The contrast is even stronger because Mordachi is married to Ester (Megilla 13a).

inability to sleep at night, that causes to him to look for advice which ultimately leads to Mordachi and Ester's salvation.

UNDERSTANDING THE PARALLEL

Returning to why the Megilla concludes with a hinted criticism of Mordachi, we can suggest that it is Mordachi, just like Yosef, who facilitates salvation from the foreign government.[225] The Megilla stresses Mordachi's political success echoing Yosef's. But the reason for the parallel may be stronger, for in neither episode is an overt miracle performed, yet each instance of redemption clearly displays Hashem working behind the scenes. The numerous unlikely coincidences that occur, one after another, can only be traced back to Him. Yosef faithfully trusts Hashem that his being sold, falsely accused of adultery, imprisoned and then ultimately crowned as the second to the king are all parts of Hashem's larger plan. Mordachi, equally devoted, expresses his faith when he requests Ester's help. He confidently communicates to Ester that we cannot know Hashem's larger plan, אַל תְּדַמִּי בְנַפְשֵׁךְ לְהִמָּלֵט בֵּית הַמֶּלֶךְ מִכָּל הַיְּהוּדִים כִּי אִם הַחֲרֵשׁ תַּחֲרִישִׁי בָּעֵת הַזֹּאת רֶוַח וְהַצָּלָה יַעֲמוֹד לַיְּהוּדִים מִמָּקוֹם אַחֵר וְאַתְּ וּבֵית אָבִיךְ תֹּאבֵדוּ וּמִי יוֹדֵעַ אִם לְעֵת כָּזֹאת הִגַּעַתְּ לַמַּלְכוּת *Do not be silent with your soul escaping from all the Jews, for if you are silent now, salvation will come to the Jews from another place and you and your father's house will be lost. And who knows if for this moment you became queen* (Ester 4:14).

However, although it is speculative, perhaps we can further hypothesize why the Megilla is written in the shadow of the Yosef narrative. Perhaps Mordachi, as the author, is subtly defending himself against the critics. By the Megilla paralleling Mordachi to Yosef, it is subtly addressing the critique that the small group of members of the Sanhedrin have. Yosef is a religious paradigm and an excellent precedent for significant government involvement, proving his approach is at least a legitimate one. Yosef too, lives among a foreign nation, assisting and abetting a foreign government. Yosef too is second to the king and perhaps also sacrificed some of his time – that could have been devoted to Talmud Torah – instead involved in Egyptian political

---

[225] Midrash Lekach Tov, Lech Lecha 12

affairs. Perhaps including the parallels between the stories subtly hints to a defense of both Mordachi and Ester, who are criticized for their heavy involvement in the Persian government.

In addition to the numerous similarities listed above, we listed many opposites as well. By contrasting these stories, Mordachi, the author, may be further explaining and justifying his intimate involvement in the Persian government. Because, unlike Yosef, whose intentions are to save himself and yet are completely legitimate, Mordachi and Ester are tasked with the salvation of the Jewish people, a significantly more altruistic ambition. Moreover, Yosef has a happier ending. He reunites with his family, while Ester, by contrast, remains a wife to Achashvarosh, a significantly bigger sacrifice. If Yosef is justified in his conduct, as Mordachi's critics would presumably concede, then Mordachi and Ester's government interaction should be justified as well.

However, there may be an additional defense for Mordachi's character. Even if one disagrees with Mordachi's ideological position with regards to involvement in government rejecting the comparison to Yosef, Mordachi can still claim that he is well-intentioned. In other words, even if he acts incorrectly, which the author, Mordachi, does not accept, he certainly does not act selfishly. This may be precisely the conclusion of the Megilla. Immediately after communicating that Mordachi is וְרָצוּי לְרֹב אֶחָיו *favored by most of his brethren* the Megilla adds that he is דֹּרֵשׁ טוֹב לְעַמּוֹ *interested in the well-being of his nation* and דֹּבֵר שָׁלוֹם לְכָל־זַרְעוֹ *spokesman for peace for his people,* unequivocally stating Mordachi's motivations are pure.

The phrase וְרָצוּי לְרֹב אֶחָיו *favored by most of his brethren* hints to the comparison with Yosef. Yosef too is not appreciated by his peers. Yosef too is not liked by all, including those who benefit from his efforts. Moreover, the Megilla may be using the term הַיְּהוּדִי *the Jew* and וְגָדוֹל לַיְּהוּדִים *great for the Jews,* as a subtle hint to Yehuda, who is most responsible for Yosef's sale.[226] Lastly, calling וְדֹבֵר שָׁלוֹם *spokesman for peace* may allude to וְלֹא יָכְלוּ דַּבְּרוֹ לְשָׁלֹם *They could not speak peacefully with him* (Bereshis 37:4), referring to Yosef's brothers.

---

[226] For a greater look at Yehuda's role in Mechiras Yosef *sale of Yosef,* see the chapter *Yosef and Yehuda: The Impact of Mechiras Yosef*

APPLYING TEXT TO LIFE: THE HASHKAFIC MESSAGE

Beyond Mordachi's unwavering dedication to his people, and exceptional efforts to save them, he has extraordinary humility. It would have been far too easy to undermine his critics by outwardly attacking them as ungrateful and unappreciative. Instead, Mordachi maintains his composure while responding. Instead of dismissing or insulting them, Mordachi presents their opinion, then defends himself and his own opinion.

Humility is always a virtue, but even more impressive after being criticized and especially after succeeding so greatly. Perhaps this is what prompts the Midrash (Ester Rabbah, Vilna Edition 6:2) to compare his humility with Moshe's, איש יהודי היה בשושן הבירה איש מלמד שהיה מרדכי שקול בדורו כמשה בדורו דכתיב ביה והאיש משה ענו מאד 'A *Jewish man (Ish) from the capital Shushan'. 'Ish' teaches us that Mordachi in his generation was just like Moshe in his generation, and it is written 'And the man Moshe was most humble of all'.*

Mordachi further demonstrates how one should disagree; respectfully. He presents a convincing argument, his success, his precedence and lastly, his motivation, without maliciously undermining others. Mordachi shows us how to convincingly and respectfully defend oneself.

Lastly, the previous two aforementioned points may be connected. It is Mordachi's humility that enables him to disagree with the Sanhedrin members so respectfully. Anger emanates from entitlement, which is clearly linked to arrogance,[227] which causes disrespect. It follows that the opposite is true as well: humility enables respect.

---

[227] Igeres HaRamban

Yehoshua's First Battle

A Peculiar Battle Plan

The first military conflict Bnei Yisrael enter upon leaving Mitzrayim is against Amalek (Shemos 17:8-13). Numerous questions must be asked, for the battle is strange on several levels, most overtly is Bnei Yisrael's peculiar military strategy. Surprisingly, it is Yehoshua, not Moshe,[228] who leads Bnei Yisrael into this first battle as a nation (ibid 17:9). Even more perplexing is the excuse Moshe offers as to why he cannot lead them to fight: מָחָר אָנֹכִי נִצָּב עַל רֹאשׁ הַגִּבְעָה וּמַטֵּה הָאֱלֹהִים בְּיָדִי *for tomorrow I will stand on a hilltop with the staff of Hashem with me* (ibid 17:9). Is sitting on a mountaintop with a staff a sufficiently important prior engagement to miss leading his people into battle?

Additionally, Moshe's activities during the battle itself are bizarre. He ascends a mountain and raises his hands. When his hands are up, Bnei Yisrael win, and when they are not, they lose. The seemingly arbitrary positioning of Moshe's hands determines the fate of the battle. Why? What do these hand movements mean?

Then, when Moshe's hands become heavy after raising them for an extended time, Aharon and Chor bring him a rock to sit on and even help him raise him hands. Is that not cheating? His hands just have to be in the air, even without him raising them? Additionally, what significance is there in Aharon and Chor assisting Moshe by providing him a rock to rest upon and hold up his hands?

---

[228] Typically, Moshe leads the people into battle (Rashi on Bamidbar 27:17) as seen with Sichon and Og.

Seemingly this is an important aspect of the story, as the Torah focuses its attention on Moshe's hands far more than the actual battle itself.

OTHER ODDITIES IN THE WAR WITH AMALEK

Beyond the peculiarities in military strategy, there are several other details in the story which also seem strange. Firstly, the episode abruptly begins with the phrase וַיָּבֹא עֲמָלֵק *and Amalek came* (Shemos 17:8). וַיָּבֹא *and he came* is usually a response to a previous event, not an introduction to a story.[229] Then, the Torah adds the location of the battle, רְפִידִם *Rifidim* (ibid 17:8). This information appears to be irrelevant and unnecessary. Why include it?

Moreover, upon a careful reading of the text, there is confusion as to who actually wins this war. It is clear that Yehoshua weakens Amalek, as the Torah states, וַיַּחֲלֹשׁ יְהוֹשֻׁעַ אֶת עֲמָלֵק וְאֶת עַמּוֹ לְפִי חָרֶב *And Yehoshua weakened Amalek and his nation via the sword* (Shemos 17:13). However, it seems like Bnei Yisrael are weakened as well, for who else would עַמּוֹ *his nation* (ibid 17:13) be?

Lastly, when Moshe ascends to the mountaintop, why does he take the Matteh *staff*? What purpose does it serve?[230]

THE FIRST POST-EXODUS BATTLE

This conflict's status as Bnei Yisrael's first military encounter since leaving Mitzrayim gives it special significance. The Torah reports that Yehoshua gathers soldiers together to form an army (Shemos 17:9), which highlights just how new war is for them, as well as how different this battle is from the Exodus from Egypt, their first victory over an enemy nation.

In truth, there are several elements about the way they wage war here which stand diametrically opposed to the way they left Mitzrayim.

---

[229] Classically, stories begin with וַיְהִי *and it was* or וַיֹּאמֶר *and he said.*

[230] Presumably carrying it only makes his hands heavier and tougher to keep raised.

1. The war with Mitzrayim is long and drawn-out, both in how long it takes and how much coverage the Torah allocates to the story, spanning a dozen perekim (Shemos 3-15). The Amalek story is significantly shorter; totaling just six verses (Shemos 17:8-13).

2. The Exodus story is introduced with a detailed historical background dating back to Yosef and his brothers. The battle with Amalek begins abruptly. No real history is previously mentioned regarding Amalek. The Torah begins the narrative with וַיָּבֹא עֲמָלֵק *and Amalek came.*

3. While combatting Amalek, Bnei Yisrael seem relaxed. There is no panic or hysteria like there is at the Yam Suf. The attitude Bnei Yisrael have when fighting Amalek is presented completely differently.

4. The battle against Amalek is fought without miracles, and in a mundane manner. The war against Mitzrayim, by contrast, is fought by Hashem in a completely miraculous fashion.[231]

5. Bnei Yisrael fight for themselves against Amalek, in contrast to the war with Mitzrayim where Hashem fights for them, as the Torah records, יְקֹוָק יִלָּחֵם לָכֶם וְאַתֶּם תַּחֲרִשׁוּן *Hashem will fight for you and you should remain silent* (ibid 14:14).

6. Instead of Moshe being in command, it is his assistant, Yehoshua, who takes the lead.

The Previous Episode: Maaseh U'Mirevah

As we noted, the phrase וַיָּבֹא *and he came* (ibid 17:8), in reference to Amalek coming, implies that we are in the middle of a story and not beginning a new one. Accordingly, we can infer that the battle against Amalek is somehow connected to the previous episode where Bnei Yisrael have no water and complain so bitterly and forcefully to Moshe that he actually fears for his life (ibid 4). Hashem commands Moshe to hit the rock with his staff (ibid 5). When Moshe does, water flows from the rock, enabling the people and animals to drink (ibid 6).

There are many similarities between the two stories, reinforcing the connection. Both episodes occur in רְפִידִם *Rifidim* (ibid 17:1 and

---

According to the Ramban (Shemos 13:16), the Exodus is unmistakably designed to break nature so that parents could use this story to convey belief in Hashem to their children for generations.

8), and the Torah makes note of it. In each account, Bnei Yisrael are involved with conflict; in Maaseh U'Mirevah with Moshe and in our episode, with Amalek. Additionally, similar language is used as well: for example הִנְנִי עֹמֵד לְפָנֶיךָ שָּׁם עַל הַצּוּר בְּחֹרֵב *I stand here before you on a rock in* **Chorev** and וַיַּחֲלֹשׁ יְהוֹשֻׁעַ אֶת עֲמָלֵק וְאֶת עַמּוֹ לְפִי חָרֶב *And Yehoshua weakened Amalek and his nation via the sword* **(Chorev)**(ibid 17:6 and 13). The Torah stresses Moshe's location, the word *Chorev,* and other specific information otherwise unnecessary, to support the linkage between the two.

Both stories have the same characters doing similar things. Each time Moshe leaves the nation with a smaller selective group. Additionally, and far more unmistakably, both stories contain the exact same props. In each episode Moshe uses a rock and a staff. And in each circumstance, it is the staff in Moshe's hand which facilitates a miracle that ultimately saves them.

What is the significance of that connection? How does the previous account of Maaseh U'Mirevah connect to the Amalek episode?

MAASEH U'MIREVAH

Any attempt to understand the linkage between the two episodes necessitates a deeper look at the Maaseh U'Mirevah narrative.

During this episode Bnei Yisrael quickly become exceedingly negative. They first bicker with Moshe about the lack of water (ibid 17:2). This reflects particularly negatively on them because they complain even before they get thirsty (ibid 17:3).[232] Worse than that is how quickly they jump to their despondent conclusion לָמָּה זֶּה הֶעֱלִיתָנוּ מִמִּצְרַיִם לְהָמִית אֹתִי וְאֶת בָּנַי וְאֶת מִקְנַי בַּצָּמָא *Why did you take us from Egypt to kill me and my son, my flock with thirst?* (ibid 17:3). And beyond the verbal attack, the Torah highlights their underlying selfish concerns by quoting them with a singular language, לְהָמִית אֹתִי וְאֶת בָּנַי וְאֶת מִקְנַי *to kill me and my son, my flock.*

Astonishingly, it gets so bad that Moshe sincerely fears that Bnei Yisrael will stone him, as he communicates to Hashem, מָה אֶעֱשֶׂה לָעָם הַזֶּה עוֹד מְעַט וּסְקָלֻנִי *What should I do with this nation, in a little bit they will stone me* (ibid 17:4). Although the Torah is unclear whether they are really going to kill him[233] Moshe's fear alone speaks volumes.

This colossal failure on Bnei Yisrael's part comes directly on the heels of the *mann* story where they fail as well, distrusting and disobeying Hashem.[234]

UNCOVERING THE STRUCTURE OF MAASEH U'MIREVAH

Interestingly, the Torah crafts this story with a chiastic structure. Here is the episode's layout.

1. Initially, Bnei Yisrael begin traveling עַל פִּי יְקֹוָק *according to the word of Hashem* (ibid 17:1) and they conclude by questioning, הֲיֵשׁ יְקֹוָק בְּקִרְבֵּנוּ אִם אָיִן *Is Hashem in our midst or not?* (ibid 17:7). Both phrases underscore the significance of Hashem's presence being felt when they travel, albeit one time they completely feel it, and the other, they completely do not.

2. Moshe challenges Bnei Yisrael by asking them, מַה תְּרִיבוּן עִמָּדִי מַה תְּנַסּוּן אֶת יְקֹוָק *Why do you (Riv) fight with me and why do you (Tinasoon) test Hashem* (ibid 17:2). The Torah repeats the same two words of *Riv* and *Nasosum* as it offers the reason for naming the place מַסָּה וּמְרִיבָה *Maaseh U'Mirevah* (ibid 17:7); מַסָּה וּמְרִיבָה עַל רִיב בְּנֵי יִשְׂרָאֵל וְעַל נַסֹּתָם אֶת יְקֹוָק *Maaseh U'Mirevah because of the (Riv) fight of Bnei Yisrael and the (Nasosum) testing of Hashem* (ibid 17:7).

3. Bnei Yisrael demand water, תְּנוּ לָנוּ מַיִם וְנִשְׁתֶּה *Give us water and we will drink* (ibid 17:2) and, subsequently, Hashem delivers, וְיָצְאוּ מִמֶּנּוּ מַיִם וְשָׁתָה *and water came out and they drank* (ibid 17:6).

4. The phrase וַיִּצְמָא שָׁם הָעָם לַמַּיִם *the nation was thirsty for water* (ibid 17:3) clearly correlates with וְשָׁתָה הָעָם *and the nation drank* (ibid 17:6).

What is showcased in the center of the chiasm are the two worst elements. Bnei Yisrael whine, לָמָּה זֶּה הֶעֱלִיתָנוּ מִמִּצְרַיִם לְהָמִית אֹתִי וְאֶת בָּנַי וְאֶת מִקְנַי בַּצָּמָא *Why did you take us from Egypt to kill me and my son,*

---

[233] Perhaps because they themselves did not know.

[234] Hashem has given them *mann* as a result of their complaining (Shemos 16:12). Additionally, Moshe instructs Bnei Yisrael not to take more than they need (ibid 16:19), yet they disobey him collecting extra (ibid 16:20). Again, Moshe instructs them (ibid 16:26) not to collect *mann* on Shabbos (ibid 16:25-26) and again they disobey (ibid 16:27).

my flock with thirst? (ibid 17:3) revealing a deep distrust in Hashem. Moreover, Moshe responds מָה אֶעֱשֶׂה לָעָם הַזֶּה עוֹד מְעַט וּסְקָלֻנִי *What should I do with this nation, in a little bit they will stone me* (ibid 17:4).

The chiasm demonstrates that Bnei Yisrael act selfishly and lose faith. They should not question Hashem's presence (ibid 17:7); after all, they are traveling intimately with Him (ibid 17:1). The episode begins with Bnei Yisrael initially traveling עַל פִּי יְקֹוָק *according to the word of Hashem* (ibid 17:1) and concludes with their challenge, הֲיֵשׁ יְקֹוָק בְּקִרְבֵּנוּ אִם אָיִן *Is Hashem in our midst or not?* (ibid 17:7). This short segment illustrates that Bnei Yisrael are losing faith.

In order to illustrate the power of Bnei Yisrael's temerity and how their spiritual state deteriorates, the Torah uses a chiastic structure, for it emphasizes what is at its center.

THE BIG QUESTION

Based on this, there is sufficient reason to question Bnei Yisrael's religious mindset. Their complaining and challenging Hashem casts serious doubt on their readiness to enter Eretz Yisrael, for success requires both selflessness and faith.

The major question that needs to be asked now is whether Bnei Yisrael are ready for Har Sinai,[235] Kabbalas HaTorah and entering Eretz Yisrael. After displaying such a deep lack of faith, further investigation has to be conducted to determine whether they are indeed ready to receive the Torah and continue on into Eretz Yisrael. Are they ready to face and bring about their destiny?

MOCK-ERETZ YISRAEL BATTLE

Because there are now deep concerns regarding whether Bnei Yisrael are ready to enter Eretz Yisrael, a test case is orchestrated. The battle with Amalek is an experiment conducted to determine whether they are ready for Eretz Yisrael because it is a mock-Eretz Yisrael

---

[235] Perhaps using the specific word חורב *Chorev* (Shemos 17:6), another name for Har Sinai, while describing their doubts hints to their not being ready to receive the Torah at חורב *Chorev.*

situation which is created.[236] How would Bnei Yisrael fare against an Eretz Yisrael enemy, Amalek,[237] and fighting in an Eretz Yisrael style war; that is, natural and non-miraculous?[238]

Because Moshe will have died when Bnei Yisrael enter Eretz Yisrael, he does not lead them into this battle.[239] Instead Yehoshua does, for he is destined to lead Bnei Yisrael into Eretz Yisrael.[240] He is, therefore, the perfect choice to lead them in the mock-Eretz Yisrael battle. And what better place for Moshe than on top of a mountain, representative of him passing on and ascending up into the heavens? Aharon and Chor also join Moshe on the mountain, for they too will have passed on. Bnei Yisrael could look to him for religious inspiration, which is exactly what Moshe's hands represent in the mock-Eretz Yisrael situation.

WHO WON THE WAR

Who won this war? At the end of this incident, the Torah comments וַיַּחֲלֹשׁ יְהוֹשֻׁעַ אֶת עֲמָלֵק **וְאֶת עַמּוֹ** לְפִי חָרֶב *And Yehoshua weakened Amalek and his nation via the sword* (ibid 17:13). Clearly Yehoshua comes out on top. It is equally clear that Amalek is weakened and not defeated. However, the biggest surprise is that עַמּוֹ *his nation*, Bnei Yisrael, seem

---

[236] Alternatively, Amalek comes as a punishment for their lack of faith (Chazal quoted by Malbim Shemos 17:8).

[237] Destroying Amalek is only an obligation once Bnei Yisrael have entered Eretz Yisrael and have established a king (Sanhedrin 20b and Rambam Melachim 1:1).

[238] Malbim (Shemos 17:13). The wars fought in Eretz Yisrael in Sefer Yehoshua are almost exclusively fought naturally. In fact, the Netziv (Introduction to Bamidbar) posits that Sefer Bamidbar transitions to a more mundane existence, specifically through the medium of war.
The Tzror Hamaor (Shemos 13:27) adds that if Bnei Yisrael could only weaken Amalek and not completely beat them, they have no chance of defeating the thirty one nations living in Eretz Yisrael.

[239] Netziv (Bamidbar 13:2). Even at this point, the plan is for Yehoshua, not Moshe, to lead Bnei Yisrael into Eretz Yisrael (Midrash Tanchuma Parshas Beshalach 28, Bava Basra 119b, Rashi Shemos 15:17, 17:14 and Bamidbar 11:28, Chizkuni Shemos 23:20, Rabaynu Bachaya Bamidbar 11:28, Meshech Chochma Bamidbar 13:30 and 16:12).

[240] Alternatively, because Yosef's decedents are destined to fight and beat Amalek (Bava Basra 123b).

to be weakened along with Amalek.[241] They survive, but by the skin of their teeth.[242]

If this physical war corresponds with their spiritual level, then they are above average, but barely. That is exactly what is reflected by Moshe's hands. He is, or more specifically his hands are, a barometer of Bnei Yisrael's religious status which is exactly what the Mishneh (Rosh Hashana 29a) conveys.[243]

'And it was that Moshe's hand were raised, Yisrael won.' Did Moshe's hand determine victory or defeat? Rather (it is recorded) to teach you that all the time the Bnei Yisrael were looking to the heavens and dedicating their hearts to their father in heaven, they were victorious, and if not, they would fall.	והיה כאשר ירים משה ידו וגבר ישראל וגומר וכי ידיו של משה עושות מלחמה או שוברות מלחמה אלא לומר לך כל זמן שהיו ישראל מסתכלים כלפי מעלה ומשעבדין את לבם לאביהם שבשמים היו מתגברים ואם לאו היו נופלין

Moshe's hands do not directly cause victory. Rather, they symbolize Bnei Yisrael's level of faith. The Torah focuses predominately on Moshe's hands because they tell the story that the Torah wants told. They symbolize Bnei Yisrael's religious status.

This may be captured singularly by the Torah's declaration וַיְהִי יָדָיו אֱמוּנָה *Moshe's hand were Emunah* (Shemos 17:12). His hands are indicative of how much trust[244] Bnei Yisrael have. That is precisely why they reflect Bnei Yisrael's success or lack thereof in war.

Moshe informs Yehoshua that he is going up מָחָר *tomorrow* (ibid 17:9). Perhaps מָחָר *tomorrow* hints to the future. Moshe communicates to Yehoshua that in the future, meaning in Eretz Yisrael, he will no longer be around, and he instructs Yehoshua to lead the people without him.

---

[241] However, the Seforno (Shemos 17:13) disagrees, arguing that עַמּוֹ *his nation* refers to mercenaries that Amalek recruited.

[242] Meshech Chochma (Bamidbar 13:30)

[243] Tanchuma Parshas Beshalach 27. The Mishneh (Rosh Hashana 29a) and Midrash (ibid) extend this phenomenon to the Nachash HaNechoseh *Copper Snake* (Bamidbar 21) and the Midrash (ibid) even extends it to placing blood on the doorposts (Shemos 12). These miracles only work when Bnei Yisrael direct their attention to Hashem.

[244] Rav Shimshon Rafeal Hirsch translates Emunah as trust, not faith (Bereshis 15:6).

Bnei Yisrael do succeed, but barely. After some time, Moshe's hands become tired, and he requires assistance from Aharon and Chor. This reflects Bnei Yisrael's struggle sustaining proper faith. Due to their failings, Moshe needs help. Aharon and Chor provide the assistance.

Using Aharon and Chor and resting on the rock is not cheating because Bnei Yisrael are not competing against anyone. Instead, their help being necessary further attests to Bnei Yisrael's lukewarm religious condition.

WHY AMALEK?

On a simple level, Bnei Yisrael fight with Amalek because Amalek attack them. Yet because Amalek is a nation from Eretz Yisrael, it is a perfect opportunity to determine whether Bnei Yisrael are ready to fight and conquer Eretz Yisrael. However, symbolically, there may be more to this. Amalek represents doubt.[245] When Bnei Yisrael fight Amalek, the war exists on two levels; physically, against the nation Amalek as well as symbolically, against doubt, which is exactly what Bnei Yisrael are currently struggling with. This is captured with their final question, הֲיֵשׁ יְקֹוָק בְּקִרְבֵּנוּ אִם אָיִן *Is Hashem in our midst or not?* (ibid 17:7).[246] This episode is designed to determine whether Bnei Yisrael have enough trust in Hashem to progress onward.

MOSHE TAKING WATER FROM A ROCK

If the Maaseh U'Mirevah episode captures Bnei Yisrael's lack of trust in Hashem and raises the question of whether they are ready to

---

[245] Shem M'Shmuel (Vayikra), Mishneh Sachir (Moadim, Megillas Ester). Rashi (Devorim 25:18) interprets the word קָרְךָ *happened* from אֲשֶׁר קָרְךָ בַּדֶּרֶךְ *that he happened on the way* (Devorim 25:18) describing Amalek's attack as לשון מקרה *a language of happen (by chance)* reinforcing Amalek's ideology. Chazal compare Amalek attacking Bnei Yisrael to a man jumping into a hot bath to remove the sting (Tanchuma, Parshas Ki Tetzei, Rashi Devorim 25:18). Amalek are willing to get burned in order to minimize Bnei Yisrael's ability to remove doubt by teaching the world about Hashem. Many reinforce this theory using the gematria of the word Amalek, which is 240, the same as the word ספק *doubt.*

[246] As the Netziv (Shemos 17:7) summarizes ובשביל חסרון אמונה זו בא מלחמת עמלק *And because of this lack of faith, there is a war with Amalek.* The Meor V'Shemesh (Parshas Beshalach) adds that religious doubt always precedes Amalek's attack.

enter Eretz Yisrael, it may also be used as a foil for the next time Moshe is to miraculously take water from a rock (Bamidbar 20:7-13).

Later in Sefer Bamidbar, Bnei Yisrael again drink water supernaturally taken from a rock; however, there is one significant difference. In Bamidbar, when Moshe is supposed to take water from the rock, he sins. That Moshe sins is unmistakable, as the verse records, לֹא הֶאֱמַנְתֶּם בִּי לְהַקְדִּישֵׁנִי לְעֵינֵי בְּנֵי יִשְׂרָאֵל *(he) did not have faith to sanctify Hashem before the eyes of Bnei Yisrael* (ibid 20:12), but the exact nature of the sin is unclear.[247]

Famously, Chazal (Midrash Agada and quoted by Rashi Bamidbar 20:12) attribute Moshe's mistake to hitting the rock when he is supposed to speak to it.

If the goal really is sanctifying Hashem's name, what is the difference between hitting the rock as opposed to speaking to it? Either way, taking water from a rock should be impressive enough of a miracle to sanctify Hashem's name. Yet apparently hitting it does not suffice. Why not?

Furthermore, Hashem Himself instructs Moshe to take the staff, קַח אֶת הַמַּטֶּה *take the staff* (Bamidbar 20:8), fully aware that on the previous occasion Moshe has been commanded to hit the rock (Shemos 17:6). It is certainly reasonable for Moshe to assume that hitting the rock is expected of him.[248] One could have chalked this up to a simple oversight or misunderstanding on behalf of Moshe. Why is Moshe not allowed to enter Eretz Yisrael for this seemingly minor infraction?

---

[247] Ohr HaChaim lists ten different opinions as to what Moshe does wrong. 1. Moshe hits the rock as opposed to speaking to it (Rashi). 2. Moshe fights with Bnei Yisrael, loses focus and has to hit the rock a second time before the water comes out (Ibn Ezra). 3. Moshe hits the rock a second time. 4. Moshe does not sing when he brings out water from the rock. 5. Moshe speaks too harshly to Bnei Yisrael, saying שִׁמְעוּ נָא הַמֹּרִים *listen now rebellious ones.* 6. Moshe gets angry at Bnei Yisrael (Rambam). 7. Moshe does not give credit to Hashem for taking out the water (Rabaynu Chananel and Ramban). 8. Moshe mistakenly says הֲמִן הַסֶּלַע הַזֶּה *from this rock* implying that Hashem cannot take the water out of the rock (R"m HaKohen). 9. Moshe and Aharon lack faith by not realizing that they can take the water out from the rock themselves (Sefer HaIkarim). 10. Initially, Moshe and Bnei Yisrael could not agree on the location of the rock from which to draw water. Moshe ultimately gets so frustrated, he throws his staff out of anger. Luckily it hits a rock and the water subsequently emerged. (Baal Maaseh Hashem).

[248] Especially because, initially, the water come out in drops (Tanchuma Parshas Chukas 9, and Rashi Bamidbar 20:11).

Lastly, Hashem's reaction is complicated. Because of Moshe's mistake, he is not allowed to enter Eretz Yisrael, yet Hashem does not express anger as He does elsewhere.

THE ROLE OF THE STAFF

Perhaps the detail with which to begin in order to decipher this disarray is why Hashem instructs Moshe to take his staff when he is not supposed to use it. What is the role of the staff supposed to be?

Until this point, the staff has been an instrument of wondrous miracles: it turned into a snake before Moshe's eyes (Shemos 4:2), swallowed the staffs of the Egyptians (ibid 7:12), served as an instrument to bring the Makkos against Mitzrayim (ibid 8:12), split the sea (ibid 14:16), and was used for taking water from the rock the first time (ibid 17:6). All of these miracles frame Moshe's staff as representing the supernatural manner in which Bnei Yisrael leave Mitzrayim. The Torah unequivocally identifies the staff's role the first time Moshe is commanded to take it, וְאֶת הַמַּטֶּה הַזֶּה תִּקַּח בְּיָדֶךָ אֲשֶׁר תַּעֲשֶׂה בּוֹ אֶת הָאֹתֹת *And take the staff in your hand for you will perform miracles with it* (ibid 4:17). It is designed to perform miracles.

Throughout Sefer Bamidbar[249] and even into Sefer Yehoshua, Bnei Yisrael transform from a nation operating on a metaphysical and supernatural level, fighting wars miraculously and eating mann, into a physical and natural one, fighting wars in a mundane fashion and eating regular food (Yehoshua 5:12). This metamorphosis is the prerequisite for entering Eretz Yisrael.

Moshe's sin may be misunderstanding that the staff is now outdated.[250] Although the people need water and Hashem decides to miraculously give them water from a rock,[251] He does not want

---

[249] The Netziv (Introduction to Bamidbar) elaborates that the theme of Sefer Bamidbar is this transformation from the supernatural existence they live upon leaving Mitzrayim to the normal one preparing for Eretz Yisrael. The initial wars after the Exodus are fought miraculously whereas the later ones, naturally. Even the title Sefer HaPikudim, *Book of Numbers*, refers to the two times Bnei Yisrael are counted, capturing these two distinct stages of Bnei Yisrael's development; Post-Mitzrayim and Pre-Eretz Yisrael.

[250] The Netziv (Bamidbar 20:5, 8, 10, and 12) similarly argues that praying for water is a hallmark of Eretz Yisrael. Moshe and Aharon's sin was hitting the rock, not praying.

[251] In fact, according to the Rambam (Yesodei HaTorah 8:1), miracles are prompted by

the water to come out via striking of the rock with a staff. On the contrary, He wants Moshe to hold the staff and take water from the rock specifically without hitting it, specifically without using the staff.[252] Although it necessary to do something miraculous, Hashem at least wants to illustrate that the staff is not being used.

It is not a sin that prevents Moshe from entering Eretz Yisrael as much as it is reflective of Moshe's inability to לְהַקְדִּישֵׁנִי *sanctify me* (Bamidbar 20:12). Moshe is an unparalleled leader and ideal for the previous generation. This new generation, the younger generation, will greatly benefit from a different leader, one who is himself a contemporary.[253] By using the staff and hitting the rock with it, Moshe reveals that he belongs to the previous generation, the one that left Mitzrayim. Yehoshua, by contrast, never uses a staff. Yehoshua fights wars naturally and performs significantly fewer miracles.[254] [255] This is

---

a technical need. The Ramban (Shemos 13:16) disagrees, arguing that miracles are designed to inspire Bnei Yisrael to believe in Hashem and pass that faith forward to future generations.

[252] There are those who previously thought that Moshe could only perform miracles with the staff (Rabaynu Bachaya Shemos 14:16).

[253] Rav Soloveitchik

[254] Still, Bnei Yisrael defeat Yericho miraculously, eat *mann* until they enter into Eretz Yisrael (Yehoshua 5:12) and benefit from the sun seemingly remaining in sky in the battle against Givone (Yehoshua 10:13).
Regarding the sun remaining in the sky in Givone, the Ralbag (Yehoshua 10:12) limits the extent of this miracle by arguing that Hashem does not deviate from the laws of nature; rather Hashem assists Bnei Yisrael in defeating the Givonim quickly, achieving the same effect as if the sun had remained longer in the sky. By contrast, the Maharal (second introduction to Gevuros Hashem) argues that Hashem breaks the laws of nature by having the sun set for the Givonim, and simultaneously, not set for Bnei Yisrael.
It should be noted that many (Rambam Moreh Nevuchim 1:75, 3:15 and Rav Saadah Gaon Emunah V'Daos 2:13) believe Hashem is limited by the laws of logic, math and science. The inability to do the impossible does not limit Hashem for He can do whatever can be done. Logic does not rule Hashem, because it reflects truth, or Hashem Himself, as the Rambam notes, Hashem and His knowledge are one (Yesodei HaTorah 2:10 and Teshuva 5:5). The Maharal (Derech Chaim 5:6) argues that Hashem is above logic. Thinking logically is something He does, not who He is. He created logic but is not limited to it. Accordingly, the Rambam (Avos 5:6) struggles with miracles which break the laws of nature. In order to solve that problem, he broadens the definition of nature, arguing that Hashem inserted many of the things that seem to break the laws of nature into nature itself. These things are created specially during creation on the sixth day (Avos 6:5). Not surprisingly, the Maharal (Derech Chaim 5:6) rejects this position of the Rambam.

[255] This may explain why, according to Rashi (Devorim 3:23), Moshe thinks he has a better chance of entering Eretz Yisrael after beating Sichon and Og (See the Netziv's introduction to Sefer Bamidbar). Since he wins the battle in a natural manner, he reasons that he might be able to take Bnei Yisrael into Eretz Yisrael in a natural fashion.

precisely why Hashem does not get angry at Moshe for sinning. Moshe is not punished; rather, it is time for Yehoshua to lead.

On both occasions Moshe hits the rock to take out water for Bnei Yisrael to drink, and in each case a test is being conducted to determine whether the tested party (first Bnei Yisrael and later Moshe) is in a position to go into Eretz Yisrael. Moreover, both times a party comes up short because that party is not ready to enter in Eretz Yisrael. In Shemos, Bnei Yisrael are not ready to progress forward, whereas Moshe is, and in Bamidbar, it is Moshe not ready, whereas Bnei Yisrael are.

Trust in Hashem is a criterion for Bnei Yisrael to enter Eretz Yisrael. In Sefer Shemos Bnei Yisrael are not ready for that challenge. In Sefer Bamidbar, Yehoshua is needed to accomplish that.

HAR SINAI

There are numerous hints to a connection between the Amalek episode and Kabbalas HaTorah on Har Sinai. The Har Sinai episode is introduced with וַיִּסְעוּ מֵרְפִידִים וַיָּבֹאוּ מִדְבַּר סִינַי *And they traveled from Rifidim and they came to the Sinai desert* (ibid 19:2), clearly linking the two events. However, there are several other similarities.

1. Both events, Matan Torah, *the giving of the Torah*, and the war with Amalek occur on mountains.

2. Both times Moshe leaves the nation below as he ascends a mountain.

3. Chor only appears twice in the Torah, our narrative and Har Sinai (Shemos 17:10 and 24:14).[256] Moreover, both times he partners with Aharon.

4. Bnei Yisrael fear death each time (ibid 17:3 and ibid 20:16).

5. Each story involves a test. The Maaseh U'Mirevah episode is where Bnei Yisrael clearly test Hashem, מַסָּה וּמְרִיבָה עַל רִיב בְּנֵי יִשְׂרָאֵל וְעַל נַסֹּתָם אֶת יְקֹוָק *Maaseh U'Mirevah because of the Riv fight Bnei Yisrael and the (Nasosum) testing of Hashem* (ibid 17:7). At Har Sinai, Moshe explains that the purpose is כִּי לְבַעֲבוּר נַסּוֹת אֶתְכֶם *in order to test you* (ibid 20:17).

---

256 Chor's lineage is mentioned later (Shemos 38:22).

6. The Maaseh U'Mirevah episode occurs in two places, Rifidim (ibid 17:1) and Chorev (ibid 17:6). Har Sinai occurs in the exact same locations, as Bnei Yisrael travel from Rifidim (ibid 19:2) to Midbar Sinai, which is Chorev (ibid 33:6).

In addition to these parallels, it pays to contrast the episodes as well, for there is much to uncover.

7. Although, each story involves tests, in Maaseh U'Mirevah Bnei Yisrael clearly test Hashem (ibid 17:7), and at Har Sinai, the opposite occurs as Hashem tests Bnei Yisrael (ibid 20:17).

8. At Maaseh U'Mirevah, Bnei Yisrael selfishly act in a disunited manner, each person worrying for themselves as seen most clearly from their complaint, לָמָּה זֶּה הֶעֱלִיתָנוּ מִמִּצְרַיִם לְהָמִית אֹתִי וְאֶת בָּנַי וְאֶת מִקְנַי בַּצָּמָא *Why did you take us from Egypt to kill me and my son, my flock with thirst?* (ibid 17:3). At Har Sinai they united כאיש אחד בלב אחד *like one person with one heart* Rashi 19:2) as the verse hints וַיִּחַן שָׁם יִשְׂרָאֵל נֶגֶד הָהָר *And they, Yisrael, camped across from the mountain* (Shemos 19:2).

9. At Maaseh U'Mirevah, Bnei Yisrael lack faith in Hashem, whereas at Har Sinai, in reciting נַעֲשֶׂה וְנִשְׁמָע *we will do and we will listen* (ibid 24:7), Bnei Yisrael display an unparalleled deep trust in Hashem.

10. Although Chor appears on both occasions, accompanied by Aharon, in our episode they assist Moshe. At Har Sinai, they remain separate.

11. At Maaseh U'Mirevah, Bnei Yisrael question whether Hashem is among them. Bnei Yisrael doubt Hashem and at Har Sinai, all doubt is removed as Hashem displays revelation in an incomparable manner.[257]

12. At Maaseh U'Mirevah, Bnei Yisrael challenge Hashem, asking why He has taken them from Mitzrayim; Har Sinai is the answer.

The point may be that at Maaseh U'Mirevah, Bnei Yisrael act selfishly and are unable to muster up enough faith in Hashem. The question is whether Bnei Yisrael have the faith needed to succeed in Eretz Yisrael. Har Sinai is the answer. Yes. At Har Sinai Bnei Yisrael have what they lack at Maaseh U'Mirevah.[258]

---

[257] Rambam Yesodei HaTorah 8:1, Sefer HaIkurim 4:18

[258] According to the Gr"a (Mishlei 22:19), the reason for giving the Torah is to facilitate

This theory is already found in Chazal (Mechelta D'Rebbe Shimon Ben Yochi 19) when they state,

And what does it mean when it says, "And they traveled from Rifidim and came to Midbar Sinai? Just like traveling from Rifidim, they were testing and fighting with Hashem, saying, "Is Hashem in our midst or not?" so too when they camped at Midbar Sinai, they were testing and fighting saying "Is Hashem in our midst or not?" It comes to show you how great the power of repentance is. Once Bnei Yisrael repent, it is immediately accepted.	ומה ת"ל ויסעו מרפידים ויבאו מדבר סיני אלא מקיש נסיעתן מרפידים לחנייתן במדבר סיני מה נסיעתן מרפידים בני מסה ובני מריבה היש ה' בקרבנו אם אין (שמ' יז ז) אף חנייתן במדבר סיני בני מסה ובני מריבה היש ה' בקרבנו אם אין. להודיעך כמה הוא כוחה שלתשובה שבשעה קלה שעשו ישראל תשובה מיד נתקבלו

In truth, this may even be hinted to in the verses. When the Torah records וַיִּסְעוּ מֵרְפִידִים וַיָּבֹאוּ מִדְבַּר סִינַי *And they traveled from Rifidim and they came to the Sinai desert* (ibid 19:2), it may refer to more than a geographical relocation. Traveling to Har Sinai captures their spiritual journey from doubt to faith.

APPLYING TEXT TO LIFE: THE HASHKAFIC MESSAGE

Bnei Yisrael's selfishness and pessimism lead to their attack on Moshe and criticism of Hashem. Coupled with their bad attitude is their lack of faith in Hashem. Bnei Yisrael struggle fighting with and challenging Hashem. Selfishness leads to a distrust in others, for the more one worries exclusively about oneself, the more difficult it is to trust others. Bnei Yisrael's selfishness leads to a distrust in Hashem.

This lack of faith in Hashem is particularly troubling as Bnei Yisrael anticipate entering Eretz Yisrael for entering Eretz Yisrael is designed to be done naturally. Instead of seeing Hashem in an overt fashion as they did as they left Mitzrayim and in the desert, Bnei Yisrael are now supposed to become a normal nation which fights natural battles, eats normal food and lives a common life, while simultaneously recognizing that Hashem is the one assisting them in a concealed

profound faith in Hashem.

fashion. That is the greater religious level, when awareness of Hashem exists without Him having to constantly prove Himself.[259]

An additional and more nuanced conclusion to draw is that sometimes it is better to appoint a leader like Yehoshua[260] who can properly lead and inspire the next generation, even over Moshe, a leader who reaches the highest heights man can reach. Moshe reaches the spiritual and intellectual zenith.[261] He is both the greatest prophet ever to live (Devorim 34:10) and is the most humble man to ever live (Bamidbar 12:3). He singlehandedly delivers the Torah from Hashem to man.[262] However, leadership is about finding the right match for each generation, and Yehoshua is the right match, able to connect with the nation and understand their mindset.[263]

---

[259] Ramban (Shemos 13:16) echoes this explaining ומן הנסים הגדולים המפורסמים אדם מודה בנסים הנסתרים שהם יסוד התורה כלה *from the great public miracles, man recognizes the hidden miracles which are the foundation of Torah.*

[260] After Moshe dies, the nation struggles to view Yehoshua with the admiration they held for Moshe. For a greater discussion, see Double Take, the chapter *Yehoshua and The Challenges of Following in Moshe's Footsteps.*

[261] Rambam (Yesodei HaTorah 1:10)

[262] Avos (1:1)

[263] Based upon this idea, the Netziv (Devorim 17:14) explains that the Mitzvah of appointing a king is one form of government among many. It is impossible to create only one model due to the differences in different cultures and societies.

THE TRANSFORMATION
FROM A QUIET JEWISH GIRL INTO A HEROINE

ESTER IN THE EYES OF CHAZAL

Ester is understandably remembered as one of the heroes of Jewish history. She bravely risks her life for the sake of the Jewish people's survival. Yet while Chazal make numerous comments expanding on this, many seem cryptic not revealing much about her at all.

One example is how Chazal in a Midrash (Yalkut Shemoni on Tehillim 22) draw a parallel between Ester and the morning. The Midrash extends the metaphor by likening fading stars at daybreak to the declining fortunes of Haman and his sons.

Why was Ester compared to the morning? To tell you that just like the morning rises and the stars diminish, so too was Ester in Achashvarosh's house. She shone, while Haman and his sons diminished.

למה נמשלה אסתר לשחר לומר לך מה השחר עולה והכוכבים שוקעים אף אסתר בבית אחשורוש היא היתה מאירה והמן ובניו שוקעין

What profound insight does this comparison offer?

In an equally enigmatic fashion, another Midrash (Midrash Tehillim Shachar Tov 22) draws upon similar imagery in stating that והיה אור ישראל זו אסתר שהאירה את ישראל כאור שחר *And it was the light of Yisrael, this is Ester, for she shined light upon Yisrael like the light of the morning.* Here too, we must ask what there is to glean from this comparison.[264]

Chazal (Shemos Rabbah, Vilna Edition 15:6) extend the comparison between Ester and the moon with the use of another parable:

Ester is compared to the moon: just like the new moon appears after thirty days, so too Ester said, 'And I was not called to the king for thirty days'	שנדמית אסתר ללבנה כשם שהלבנה נולדה לשלשים יום כך אסתר אמרה ואני לא נקראתי לבא אל המלך זה שלשים יום

While it is true that Ester has not been called for thirty days, a period equal to the duration of the moon's orbit, it is not immediately obvious what Chazal intend to convey with this specific comparison.[265]

In order to decode Chazal's descriptions of Ester, it pays to develop a better understanding of who Ester is. With that newfound perspective, we can revisit these statements and develop an understanding of what lies behind Chazal's perception of Ester.

ESTER: QUIET AND PASSIVE

Throughout the first three chapters of the Megilla, Ester is portrayed primarily as beautiful,[266] quiet, passive and obedient. This is certainly expressed in the Megilla's introduction to her, וַיְהִי אֹמֵן אֶת הֲדַסָּה הִיא אֶסְתֵּר בַּת דֹּדוֹ כִּי אֵין לָהּ אָב וָאֵם וְהַנַּעֲרָה יְפַת תֹּאַר וְטוֹבַת מַרְאֶה וּבְמוֹת אָבִיהָ וְאִמָּהּ לְקָחָהּ מָרְדֳּכַי לוֹ לְבַת *And he had brought up Hadasah, that is Ester, his cousin, for she had no father or mother, and the girl was beautiful and pleasant to look at and when her father and mother died, Mordachi took her in as a daughter* (Ester 2:7).

---

[264] Chazal elsewhere (Yoma 29a) repeat this, comparing Ester to the morning, למה נמשלה אסתר לשחר לומר לך מה שחר סוף כל הלילה אף אסתר סוף כל הנסים *Why is Ester compared to the morning? To tell you, just like the morning is the end of night, so too Ester is the end of all miracles.*

[265] The Shut Beis Yitzhak Tzalos Habayis (YD Drush 4) suggests that it is through the merit of Kiddush HaChodesh *sanctifying the moon* that Bnei Yisrael are saved. Still, the Midrash implies that Ester, herself, is like the moon, a comparison that requires explanation.

[266] One opinion in the Gemara (Megillah 16a) lists Ester as one of the four most beautiful women. Interestingly, another claims that ירקרוקת היתה she was *green* (Megillah 13a) yet selected because וחוט של חסד משוך עליה *there was a string of mercy upon her.*

Although beautiful, Ester's initial circumstances evoke compassion from the reader. Both of her parents have died[267] and, seemingly, she is unprepared to live independently.

The Megilla reinforces this image by noting that Ester obeys Mordachi's command to remain utterly silent[268] [269] and specifically to not inform anyone of her religion or nationality (Ester 2:10-11).[270]

Ester is then taken into the palace for a special party (ibid 2:18). There, the people are deeply impressed with her beauty (ibid 2:16). The Megilla then reiterates how she remained docile, not revealing her nationality, as Mordachi has instructed her (ibid 2:20).[271] These descriptions reinforce our image of Ester as beautiful, quiet and obedient.

In fact, Ester only speaks once in the opening three chapters, when she informs Achashvarosh of Bigson and Seresh's plans to assassinate him (ibid 2:21-23). Furthermore, even in this one instance when she

---

[267] To further illustrate the point, the Torah Temimah (Ester 2:19) quotes the Rambam (Daos 6:10) who describes how difficult and tragic it is to be an orphan.

[268] The Gemara (Megilla 13b) notes that because of the unique level of modesty Rochel has, she is rewarded with Shaul as a descendent and that Shaul HaMelech is rewarded with Ester as a descendent for his having that same quality. Furthermore, the Midrash (Bereshis Rabbah, Vilna Edition 71:5) traces this virtue to both Rochel and Binyamin, Ester's ancestors.
In truth, roots of the battle between Ester and Haman can be traced back to Shaul, Ester's ancestor, and Agag, Haman's. Interestingly, it is Rochel's descendants who fight Amalek: Yehoshua from Shevet Ephrayim (Bamidbar 13:8) fights in Sefer Shemos (17:8-16), Shaul (Shmuel 1 15:2-9) from Shevet Binyamin, Mordachi from Shevet Binyamin (Ester 2:5) and Ester. Presumably, the Midrash (Otzer Midrashim, Yaakov Avinu and Pisikta Rabasi (Ish Shalom) Pisikta 13 Mani Efraim) draws on this when it states, אין זרעו של עמלק נופל אלא ביד בנה של רחל the descendants of Amalek will be wiped out by Rochel's son.

[269] The Gemara (Megilla 13a) even suggests that the meaning of Ester's name, hidden, is based on her hiding her nationality. Presumably if her name captures that quality, it is a central one.

[270] The Ibn Ezra Nusach Alef (2:10) offers three reasons why Ester keeps her religion and nationality a secret. First, Mordachi, mistakenly, is fearful that the king would not take her if he knows that she is an outsider. Secondly, he has Navuah that via Ester, Bnei Yisrael would be saved. Thirdly, he wants to make it easier for her to keep Mitzvos in the palace. Rashi (Ester 2:10), however, disagrees, explaining that because she is a descendant of Shaul, keeping her nationality a secret decreases the likelihood of the palace detaining her. Additionally, the R"I Nachmiash (Ester 2:8) suggests that in order to keep her nationality a secret, before being taken by the king, she moved from Mordachi's house to a neighbor's.

[271] Although Rashi (Ester 2:18 and 5:8) argues that Achashvarosh is very interested in her nationality and religion. In fact, Rashi continues, when Ester tells Achashvarosh, at the second party, that she will answer his request (Ester 5:8) it refers to his request to know her nationality. However, many (Ibn Ezra Nusach Alef, Ralbag, Ri"d and Chachmay Tzarfas all on 5:8) disagree assuming that Ester is referring to the reason why she arranged the first party.

does speak, she does not convey her own words or thoughts; rather, she simply relays Mordachi's discovery and does so because of his command (ibid 2:22).[272] This sole communication is the exception which proves the rule.

Ester is not just quiet and passive; she seems to be controlled by others, specifically men. She almost blindly obeys Mordachi to keep her nationality secretive (ibid 2:10, 20). Additionally, she is taken forcefully to the palace (ibid 2:8)[273] first as a prospect to marry the king and ultimately, as a wife to the king (ibid 2:17).[274] None of these actions taken appear to be of her own volition. The verse stating וַתִּלָּקַח אֶסְתֵּר And Ester was taken (ibid 2:16) is more than a mere description of her movements; it captures who she is.

Ester is an innocent girl taken for the king because of her beauty. She is in over her head, and completely unprepared for the situation in which she finds herself.

ESTER AS A HEROINE: POWERFUL AND AUTHORITATIVE

There is a stark contrast between Ester in the first (chapters 1-3) and second parts (chapters 4-10) of the Megilla. In the second segment, she is exceedingly active. Ester initiates and organizes three days to fast and mourn (ibid 4:15-16). She enters Achashvarosh's inner courtyard unannounced (ibid 5:1-2) putting her life in peril (ibid 4:11).[275] On top of that, she throws two parties for Achashvarosh and Haman, and at the second one, she accuses Haman of plotting mass extermination.

Ester's transformation entails a stark role reversal. In her newly active role, she exerts dominance over men, and specifically the same

---

[272] It is from here that Rebbi Eliezar, quoting Rebbi Chanania, concludes that כל האומר דבר בשם אומרו מביא גאולה לעולם *All who say something in the name of the original author bring redemption to the world* (Megilla 15a).

[273] Ibn Ezra Nusach Beis (2:8 and 16)

[274] Although Ester's age is not mentioned explicitly in the Megilla, some assume that she is significantly older than one might have otherwise expected. The Midrash (Bereshis Rabbah, Vilna Edition 39:13) offers three opinions: forty, eighty and seventy-five (seventy-five is also found in the Targum Ester 2:7). Accordingly, it is surprising that Mordachi still cares for Ester as an orphan. Perhaps this supports our theory that Ester is not completely independent.

[275] The Ralbag (Ester 5:3, 6) adds that Achashvarosh must have realized that Ester has a serious and important request if she is willing to risk her life to ask.

men who had previously controlled her. The Megilla unmistakably presents her as having the upper hand over Mordachi, Achashvarosh, and Haman.

Instead of indiscriminately following Mordachi, she now directs him. She commands him to gather the Jews to fast (ibid 4:16) and he complies, as the Megilla relays, וַיַּעַשׂ **כְּכֹל אֲשֶׁר צִוְּתָה עָלָיו אֶסְתֵּר** *And he (Mordachi) did **everything that Ester had commanded*** (ibid 4:17). By stressing כְּכֹל אֲשֶׁר צִוְּתָה *everything that Ester had commanded* the Megilla communicating more than the Mordachi listens to Ester, but rather that she is in command.

Instead of Achashvarosh throwing a party for Ester, she now throws two parties for him.[276] Rather than being the subject of the party, she is the hostess. Ester also dictates the terms of her relationship with Achashvarosh. On four separate occasions, Achashvarosh asks what he can do to fulfill her will (ibid 5:3, 5:6, 7:2, and 9:12). The magnitude of this transformation can only be properly appreciated when one recalls the typical woman's role in ancient Persia, and more specifically under Achashvarosh's rule. In order to discourage women from controlling marital relationships, Achashvarosh had killed Vashti.

She further demonstrates her influence over Achashvarosh by convincing him to issue an additional royal decree allowing the Jews to defend themselves (Ester 8:3-6). Ester's accumulation of power is unmistakably reinforced when Haman, pleading for his life, turns to Ester, rather than Achashvarosh (ibid 7:7). Even Haman realizes that Ester is now the one calling the shots. Haman begs Ester for his life because, clearly, she has the power. This visual illustration further reinforces Ester's commanding role.

Additionally, Ester's advice is accepted because Ester has replaced Haman as Achashvarosh's trusted advisor.[277] At the end of the story, Ester no longer listens to others. Instead others listen to her.

---

[276] According to the Ibn Ezra (Nusach Alef 5:8), Ester waits to reveal her identity until the second party because she wants to first see Hashem send some type of sign. When Mordachi gains political power, she knows it is time.

[277] This is part of a larger theme of the Megilla וְנַהֲפוֹךְ הוּא *And it was switched around* (Ester 9:1).

ZERESH IN THE MEGILLA

Zeresh, Haman's wife, plays a relatively insignificant role in the Megilla. She appears only twice, on each occasion offering Haman advice (Ester 5:14 and 6:13). Her negligible role raises the question of why she is even included in the narrative.

One possibility is that, at least in part, Zeresh appears in the Megilla to serve as a foil for Ester. Contrasting Ester to Zeresh further highlights the transformation that Ester undergoes.

Their commonalities only accentuate their fundamental dissimilarities. Both Ester and Zeresh are wives of the two central characters[278] who each guide their husbands' actions from behind the scenes. Zeresh influences Haman's plan to hang Mordachi on a tree (Ester 5:14), while Ester encourages Achashvarosh to protect Mordachi and the Jewish people. However, as previously mentioned, the contrasts between the characters is far more striking.

1. There is very little recorded about Zeresh in the Megilla because she is a peripheral character. By contrast, Ester is the central character, after whom the book is named.

2. Ester emerges as victorious via her husband, whereas Zeresh loses via hers.

3. Zeresh tries to have the Jewish people exterminated and fails. Ester sets out to save the Jewish people and succeeds in that endeavor.

---

[278] Ester is at least Achashvarosh's wife. Whether Ester is married to Mordachi as well is subject to debate. The Gemara (Megilla 13a) quoting Rabbi Meir assumes that she is, based upon the verse לקחה מרדכי לו לבת *Mordachi took her as a daughter* which is interpreted as אל תקרי לבת אלא לבית *Do not read it as 'Daughter' but 'house' (wife)* (See Tosfos Sanhedrin 74b, Kesubos 3a for a discussion as to why Ester does not violate Arayos *illicit relations,* which carry a Halacha of יהרוג ואל יעבור *(Better to) be killed and not violate (the Isur))*. Others disagree. The Midrash (Shachar Tov on Tehillim 22) writes that Mordachi's wife nursed Ester. Presumably, Ester is taken into their house as an orphan, and not as Mordachi's wife. Interestingly, the Meiri (Kesuvos 51b) writes that according to the Drash, Ester is married to Mordachi. This implies that according to the Pshat, she is not. Additionally, the Chachmay Tzarfas (Ester 2:7) compare Mordachi taking in Ester לְקָחָהּ מָרְדֳּכַי לוֹ לְבַת *He took her as a daughter to him* to Bas Paroh taking in Moshe וַיְהִי לָהּ לְבֵן *And he was a son to her,* implying that the relationship is not of man and wife. However, the R"I Nachmiash is clearest in stating לא אשתו *not as a wife.* He then continues comparing Mordachi taking in Ester to Bas Paroh taking in Moshe. His proof is that Achashvarosh gathers all the besulos *virgins* (Ester 2:2-3) when looking for a wife, and since Ester is chosen, it is unlikely that she is married to Mordachi if she is a Besulah *virgin.*

4. Those who identify with Ester, her family and nation, are initially threatened but ultimately saved. By contrast, Zeresh's husband, Haman, originally feels safe, yet in actuality, it is he and his sons who are hanged.[279] This contrast penetrates deeper, for both women are also the only exceptions to the rule. Ester's family is initially threatened whereas she is not, and Zeresh's family is ultimately hanged, while she is not.

5. Zeresh aggressively instigates and encourages Haman's evil attempt at mass extermination. By contrast, Ester is passive. She only enters the political realm when she is absolutely forced to do so.

6. Ester remains faithful to Mordachi throughout the entire story. Her commitment to Mordachi and her people never wavers even when it would have been much easier to abandon them. Zeresh does just the opposite. She abandons Haman at a time of need as she remarks, אִם מִזֶּרַע הַיְּהוּדִים מָרְדֳּכַי אֲשֶׁר הַחִלּוֹתָ לִנְפֹּל לְפָנָיו לֹא תוּכַל לוֹ כִּי נָפוֹל תִּפּוֹל לְפָנָיו *if Mordachi, of whom you have started to fall (before), is of Jewish seed, you will not succeed, rather you will fall before him* (Ester 6:13).[280] In contrast to Zeresh who discards her husband, Ester remains loyal and devoted.

This contrast between Ester and Zeresh may be more clearly captured by a simple statement of Chazal (Yerushalmi quoted by Tosfos Megilla 7b): ארורה זרש ברוכה אסתר *Zeresh is cursed while Ester is blessed.* Looking at the larger context – ארור המן ברוך מרדכי זרש ברוכה אסתר ארורים כל הרשעים ברוכים כל ישראל *Haman is cursed while Mordachi is Blessed, Zeresh is cursed while Ester is blessed, Wicked people are cursed while Jews are Blessed,*[281] – further illustrates that Ester and Zeresh are opposites.

The myriad of distinctions draw our attention to these two characters in order to give prominence to the contrast between them. Ester is humble, faithful and non-demanding, while Zeresh is entitled, selfish and greedy. Beyond showcasing Ester's tremendous character, the

---

[279] Although we do not know of other sons from Megillas Ester itself, according to the Gemara (Megilla 15b) Haman has thirty sons, and according to the Targum Yonason (Ester 9:14) Zeresh flees with seventy other sons that Haman has.

[280] The word נפילה *fall* is repeated several times (Ester 6:13), highlighting how quickly she turns on Haman.

[281] Others have a slightly different text, ארורים כל הרשעים ברוכים כל הצדיקים *Wicked people are cursed while righteous people are blessed.*

contrast highlights Ester's transformation. As the aggressive Zeresh loses control, the unassuming Ester gains control. Zeresh starts out powerful and plummets whereas Ester begins helpless but grows stronger. This too buttresses our theory that Ester's role in the beginning of the Megilla is vastly different from that at the end.

VASHTI IN THE MEGILLA

Vashti, like Zeresh, may also be featured as a foil for Ester. There are numerous noticeable similarities between Ester and Vashti which, like Zeresh, highlight the difference. The most prominent one is that they are the two Persian queens married to Achashvarosh. Moreover, both women are beautiful. Both are designed to be the center of a royal party.[282] The parallel continues when each queen breaks protocol by not listening to Achashvarosh; Vashti disobeys by not heeding his request to appear at the party and Ester does so by entering his chamber uninvited. The Megilla highlights the connection between the two, by stating וַיַּמְלִיכֶהָ תַּחַת וַשְׁתִּי *And he appointed her queen in place of Vashti* (Ester 2:17);[283] Ester is not just the new queen; she is the successor and substitution for Vashti.

Ester supplanting Vashti as queen is precisely what prompts Chazal to state that כל אותן השנים משעה שנהרגה ושתי עד שנכנסה אסתר לא שככה חמתו של אחשורוש *all the years from the time he (Achashvarosh) killed Vashti until Ester entered (in place of her) Achashvarosh's anger was not soothed* (Ester Rabbah, Vilna Edition 3:14).

In addition to the similarities between Ester and Vashti, there are a number of important contrasts.

1. Ester is Jewish while Vashti is not.

---

[282] (Ester 2:18). According to the Ibn Ezra Nusach Alef (Ester 1:3), the original party that lasts one hundred eighty days is to celebrate Achashvarosh's marriage to Vashti. This greatly strengthens the parallel, for Achashvarosh throws a party when marrying Ester as well. The Ibn Ezra Nusach Alef (ibid) also quotes two other reasons why Achashvarosh throws this party; either because the time for the Galus has ended and Bnei Yisrael have not yet been redeemed or because the wars have ended and they are entering a time of peace.

[283] Ester is a descendant of Shaul, while Vashti's ancestor is Nevuchadnetzer (Megilla 10b). Moreover, Vashti too is an orphan (Ester Rabbah 3:5).

2. Vashti is the queen in the beginning of the Megilla, whereas Ester is queen at the end.

3. Vashti declines the king's invitation to his party, while Ester extends an invitation to the king and in further contrast, her invitation is accepted.

4. Achashvarosh intends to show off Vashti's beauty to his guests, inappropriately sharing his wife with the other men at the party. Later, Ester invites Haman with Achashvarosh to a party, subtly insinuating that she might be inappropriately shared with Haman.[284]

5. Achashvarosh kills Vashti because she refuses to attend the party where he plans on sharing her with foreign men. Later, he kills Haman because he is paranoid that his wife is unfaithful (Ester 7:8), or in other words, being shared with a foreign man.

6. Whereas Vashti is stubborn, insisting on what *she* wants, Ester is extremely flexible, consistently obeying and following others reflecting her humble nature.[285] Ester listens to others, particularly Achashvarosh. Vashti, by contrast, stubbornly disobeys him.

7. Arguably the most pronounced contrast is that Vashti does not heed Achashvarosh's summons, and is surprised[286] with a death sentence.[287]

---

[284] For more on Achashvarosh fearing that Ester may be shared with Haman, see the chapter entitled *Achashvarosh's Important Religious Role in the Megilla.*

[285] Even when Ester requests an exclusive party for her, Haman and Achashvarosh, she asks humbly, אִם עַל הַמֶּלֶךְ טוֹב יָבוֹא הַמֶּלֶךְ וְהָמָן הַיּוֹם אֶל הַמִּשְׁתֶּה אֲשֶׁר עָשִׂיתִי לוֹ *If it pleases the king, will the king and Haman come to a party that I made for him* (Ester 5:4) and again אִם מָצָאתִי חֵן בְּעֵינֵי הַמֶּלֶךְ וְאִם עַל הַמֶּלֶךְ טוֹב לָתֵת אֶת שְׁאֵלָתִי וְלַעֲשׂוֹת אֶת בַּקָּשָׁתִי יָבוֹא הַמֶּלֶךְ וְהָמָן אֶל הַמִּשְׁתֶּה אֲשֶׁר אֶעֱשֶׂה לָהֶם *if I have found favor in the eyes of the king and if it pleases the king to grant my wish and answer my request, will the king and Haman come to a party that I made for them (ibid 5:8).*

[286] There is no indication that Vashti would have been aware of this punishment. The reason for Vashti's refusal to listen to Achashvarosh is unclear from Megillas Ester itself; however, several theories have been suggested. One opinion (Megilla 12b, Rashi Ester 1:12) is that she is plagued with Tzaraas *leprosy* and embarrassed to be seen publicly. Another, she is arrogant and insulted that she is only summoned by the king's men and not Achashvarosh himself (Ralbag Ester 1:12) to which Achashvarosh's drunken state only exacerbates the issue (Ra"m Chalev Ester 1:12). Alternatively, she does not want to leave the party she is hosting for the women (Ra"m Chalev Ester 1:12).

[287] Although the Megilla is not explicit about Achashvarosh killing Vashti, the Midrash (Vayikra Rabbah, Margolis 11:1) unequivocally states ביקש להכניסה ערומה ולא קיבלה עליה לפיכך קצף עליה והרגה *He requested that she come naked and she refused, so he became mad and killed her.* Most Midrashim (Ester Rabbah, Vilna Edition 5:2, Psichta D'Ester Rabbah, Vilna Edition 9, Shachar Tov 22:26) as well as other commentaries (Rashi Ester 1:19, R"A Kohen Tzedek Ester 1:10) concur. The Ralbag (Ester 1:19) agrees that Achashvarosh kills Vashti, but not as a punishment; rather because of a legal technicality in that he is unable

Instead of being summoned, Ester enters the king's court without an invitation expecting a death sentence, yet is surprised by the king's unanticipatedly warm reception.

8. Achashvarosh initially kills his wife, Vashti, because of his advisors,[288] yet later he kills his central advisor, Haman, because of his wife, Ester. As Chazal (Psichta D'Ester Rabbah, Vilna Edition 9) put it שהרג את אשתו מפני אוהבו ופעם אחרת הרג את אוהבו מפני אשתו *he killed his wife because of his loved ones and on another occasion killed his loved one because of his wife.*

Chazal (quoted by Rashi Ester 1:12) reinforce this contrast by recounting Vashti's oppressive treatment of the Jews on Shabbos. Although Ester does not have to, she saves Bnei Yisrael. Vashti, by contrast, persecutes them.

This contrast draws further attention to both Vashti's stubborn personality and her loss of power. Ester, by contrast, is flexible, submissive and passive. And as with Zeresh, the contrast with Vashti accentuates Ester's evolution over the course of the Megilla.

The two other female characters in the Megilla, Zeresh and Vashti, both begin in positions of power and that power is taken from them. Including them and their stories highlights Ester's transformation in the opposite direction.

Ester's Transformation, Reflective of Bnei Yisrael's

As we have seen, Ester undergoes a metamorphosis, transforming into a strong and outspoken leader. This dynamic shift carries significance on two levels. On a personal level, she grows into a heroine. However there is a more significant impact. Her transformation sparks a national renaissance captured by the defining phrase in the Megilla וְנַהֲפוֹךְ הוּא *And it was switched around* (Ester 9:1). Bnei Yisrael begin

---

to marry a different queen.

Others (Rav Saadah Gaon Ester 1:19, Ibn Ezra Ester Nusach Beis 1:21, Chachmay Tzarfas Ester 1:19, Ra"m Chalev 1:21, Ri"d Ester 1:19) argue that Achashvarosh does not kill her. He merely divorces or dethrones Vashti.

Interestingly the R"I Nachmiash in different comments (Ester 1:19 and 2:1) implies different things.

[288] The contrast is strengthened because Mimuchan is Haman (Megilla 12b).

powerless but grow in strength, taking inspiration from Ester's example to defend themselves (ibid 9:15-16).

THE POINT OF TRANSFORMATION

Uncovering the stark transformation Ester undergoes in the Megilla raises the important question of what precipitates this change? What motivates Ester to behave so differently?

The turning point in Ester's behavior occurs immediately after a powerful conversation with Mordachi. At the climax in the narrative, Mordachi powerfully exclaims, אַל תְּדַמִּי בְנַפְשֵׁךְ לְהִמָּלֵט בֵּית הַמֶּלֶךְ מִכָּל הַיְּהוּדִים כִּי אִם הַחֲרֵשׁ תַּחֲרִישִׁי בָּעֵת הַזֹּאת רֶוַח וְהַצָּלָה יַעֲמוֹד לַיְּהוּדִים מִמָּקוֹם אַחֵר וְאַתְּ וּבֵית אָבִיךְ תֹּאבֵדוּ וּמִי יוֹדֵעַ אִם לְעֵת כָּזֹאת הִגַּעַתְּ לַמַּלְכוּת *Do not be silent with your soul escaping from all the Jews, for if you are silent now, salvation will come to the Jews from another place and you and your father's house will be lost. And who knows if for this moment you became queen* (Ester 4:14).

Upon hearing this challenge, Ester is deeply inspired and risks everything, including her life, to save her nation. Without hesitation, Ester responds, לֵךְ כְּנוֹס אֶת כָּל הַיְּהוּדִים *Go and gather all of the Jews* (ibid 4:16) instructing them וְצוּמוּ עָלַי וְאַל תֹּאכְלוּ וְאַל תִּשְׁתּוּ שְׁלֹשֶׁת יָמִים *Fast and do not eat or drink for three days* (ibid).

RETURNING TO UNDERSTANDING CHAZAL

Perhaps this perspective on Ester can help us better understand some of Chazal's puzzling comments.

By comparing Ester to the morning in a general sense, Chazal profoundly allude to the subtle initial transition from night to morning. At first, one can see the sky becoming progressively lighter, yet day still dawns with a certain suddenness. This timeline models Ester's evolution. In the first part of the Megilla, Ester is like darkness. She passively refrains from all activity. Then, as morning slowly approaches, she begins implementing her plan and the fruits of her efforts slowly become visible. She takes small steps – inspiring the masses to fast, arranging two parties – before her involvement grows dramatically. She shares her troubles with Achashvarosh and accuses Haman of planning mass murder against her people. By the time Haman is sentenced to death, there is a sense of surprise at the speed with which events have overtaken the narrative.

The Midrash's description of the morning sun outshining the stars captures the way in which Ester eclipses Haman and his sons as the principal influence on both Achashvarosh and the broader course of events. This shift, symbolized by the fading of the stars, comes at Haman's expense, as Ester, represented by the sun, outshines him and his sons. Ester, like the morning, develops slowly, gains power and almost in a moment, like night transforms into day, becomes a heroine.

This theory may also elucidate Chazal's comparison of Ester to the moon. The moon renews itself after thirty days. Although it is the same moon as before, it appears anew. By likening Ester's thirty days of not being called into the king's inner chamber to the moon's thirty days of renewal, the Midrash emphasizes how Ester's claim of וַאֲנִי לֹא נִקְרֵאתִי לָבוֹא אֶל הַמֶּלֶךְ זֶה שְׁלוֹשִׁים יוֹם *And I have not been called to go before the king for thirty days* (Ester 4:11) occurs immediately before her transformation and the Megilla's turning point. Just like the moon, Ester renews herself. It is the same woman but with a new mission: saving Bnei Yisrael.

Textual support may come from the juxtaposition between וַאֲנִי לֹא נִקְרֵאתִי לָבוֹא אֶל הַמֶּלֶךְ זֶה שְׁלוֹשִׁים יוֹם *And I have not been called to go before the king for thirty days* (Ester 4:11), and her proactive response, לֵךְ כְּנוֹס אֶת כָּל הַיְּהוּדִים *Go assemble all the Jews* (ibid 4:15). Immediately after Ester communicates that she has not been called for thirty days, two things happen. First Mordachi shares his inspiring words with Ester, and then she responds by commanding him to gather the Jews. Ester's transformation comes right after the verse that Chazal cite when comparing her to the moon. This reinforces our theory that comparing Ester to the moon is designed to communicate to the reader Ester's extraordinary transformation.

APPLYING TEXT TO LIFE: THE HASHKAFIC MESSAGE

Ester's transformation is truly remarkable. Her personal evolution can be explained in one of two ways. Either Ester always has the charisma and leadership to orchestrate the plan she executes and just originally opts not to display those qualities because there is no need to do so. Ester's unique leadership, fused with the lack of need to deploy it, and outstanding self-control, serves as a spectacular combination. The alternative, an equally remarkable one, would be her ability to adapt and quickly grow into the heroine needed to save Bnei Yisrael. Both of these two understandings of Ester's shift in behavior offer an important lesson in leadership. Ester, like the moon, is the same person, but with an entirely new dimension; heroism, leadership and a hunger to assist Bnei Yisrael.

Perhaps as impressive as Ester's transition, is what motivates it. For she is profoundly impacted by Mordachi's powerful message. Ester is inspired by a message of faith. She displays great trust that Hashem will not abandon His nation and will continue to protect and care for His people. Yet more impressive is her desire to take advantage of the opportunity and contribute. Ester is willing to risk it all to help save what she believes in, Am Yisrael. Ester's sacrifice to help Bnei Yisrael is what enters her into a category of her own. She is a true heroine.

THE GANGSTER AND THE GODFATHER

WHY DOES ESUV NOT FOLLOW YAAKOV TO LAVAN'S HOUSE?

In order to receive the blessing that Yaakov is entitled to from his father Yitzhak, he has to disguise himself as Esuv and evoke deception while Esuv is out hunting. When Esuv returns, he discovers that Yaakov has received the blessing. Raging with anger, Esuv vows to kill his brother Yaakov, once Yitzhak dies (Bereshis 27:41).[289] Upon discovering Esuv's intentions,[290] Rivka sends Yaakov to her brother Lavan's house for protection.[291]

---

[289] From the verses, it is unclear why Esuv decides to wait for Yitzhak's death rather than act immediately. Several answers are offered. The Ramban (Bereshis 27:41) has two; either Esuv does not want to pain his father, or he fears being cursed by him. Along the lines of the first explanation, the Daas Zekenim M'Baalay HaTosfos (Bereshis 27:41) adds that Esuv fears this might hasten his father's death.
Yonason Ben Uzial (Bereshis 27:41) understands Esuv's motives differently. Esuv sees that after Cain killed Hevel, Adam had another son, Shes, with whom Cain had to share his inheritance. Esuv fears the same could happen, therefore he plans to wait until Yitzhak dies and fathering another child is impossible. In a similar vein, the Chizkuni (Bereshis 27:41) argues that Esuv fears Yitzhak would have another son who might one day kill Esuv. According to the Kli Yakar (Bereshis 27:41), Esuv plans to wait for Yitzhak's death, and as Yaakov mourns, and learning Torah becomes forbidden (Shulchan Aruch YD 384:1), he will no longer have the Divine protection, making him more easily susceptible to being hurt or killed.
Alternatively, the Bechor Shor (Bereshis 27:41), and Malbim (Bereshis 27:41) understand that Esuv intends to kill Yaakov immediately and cause his father to be an אבל *mourner*. With this approach, one can easily explain that Rivka sends Yaakov out immediately. This saves him from an imminent threat.
Although beyond our purview, the previously mentioned explanations all have different vantage points regarding Esuv's identity, agenda and relationship with his father.

[290] There is a variety of explanations how Rivka discovers this information. According to Rashi (Bereshis 27:42), Hashem informs Rivka either with Ruach HaKodesh, *a Divine revelation*, or prophecy (Bereshis Rabbah, Vilna Edition 67:9). By contrast, the Ibn Ezra (Bereshis 27:41) argues that Rivka is informed naturally. Esuv reveals his plans to a friend or family member and presumably word travels to Rivka.

[291] According to Chazal, Yaakov spends years learning at Beis Aver before arriving at Lavan's

Two questions emerge from this account. Firstly, why Lavan? Is there no more secretive location than a family member's house? Secondly, and more strangely, why does Esuv not barge into Lavan's house to kill Yaakov? The Torah spells out that Esuv is fully aware that Yitzhak has sent Yaakov to Paden Aram to find a wife (ibid 28:5-6). Esuv knows where Yaakov is. Additionally, Esuv knows exactly when Yaakov leaves Lavan's house, for when Yaakov does eventually leave, Esuv has already assembled four hundred men to approach Yaakov (ibid 32:7).[292] Esuv is clearly keeping a close watch on Yaakov. Seemingly Esuv could have killed Yaakov whenever he pleases. Therefore we must ask, would killing Yaakov in Lavan's house not fit Esuv's plans?[293] [294]

Perhaps after a closer look at Lavan, we will better understand why Rivka specifically choose his residence as a place for Yaakov to hide and why Esuv, though enraged with a desire for revenge, does not enter Lavan's home. Instead Esuv, in an uncharacteristically patient fashion, waits for twenty years until Yaakov leaves.

Let us take a closer look at how the Torah presents Lavan.

(Bereshis Rabbah, Vilna Edition 68:11 and quoted by Rashi Bereshis 28:11). Rav Yaakov Kamenetsky (Emes L'Yaakov Bereshis 28:11) explains that this is in order to prepare for the Lot's house, for preparing for the outside world is Yeshivas Shem V'Aver's specialty. Otherwise, he adds, Yaakov would remain with Yitzhak and learn Torah there.

Parenthetically, Rav Yaakov Kamenetsky (Ibid) assume that Yeshivas Shem V'Aver is one place and not two separate places, Beis Midrasho Shel Shem and Beis Aver, like the simple reading of Rashi (Bereshis 25:22 and 28:11) suggests.

[292] Although the Torah never informs us of Esuv's intention, many assume (Bereshis Rabbah, Vilna Edition 75:7 and Rashi Bereshis 32:7-8, 33:4), that Esuv is now attempting to carry out his original plan against Yaakov.

However, surprisingly, the Rashbam (Bereshis 32:7) disagrees, arguing that Esuv brought four hundred men to greet Yaakov after being away for so long. Also, see the Rashbam (Bereshis 25:34).

[293] According to Rashi (Bereshis 29:11), Esuv does send his son, Elifaz, on a mission to locate and eliminate Yaakov. It is curious that Esuv does not pursue after Yaakov himself. When Elifaz returns, Esuv disappointed and angrily confiscates all of Yaakov's possessions that Elifaz is given (Sefer HaYashar Parshas Toldos). Once Esuv knows that Elifaz has left Yaakov alive, the question resurfaces. Why does Esuv not pursuit Yaakov at Lavan's?

The same question can be asked assuming Yaakov goes to Beis Aver (Bereshis Rabbah, Vilna Edition 68:11), why does Esuv not and kill him there?

[294] Although Esuv initially wants to wait until Yitzhak dies, he does gather four hundred men (ibid 32:7) to attack Yaakov (Rashi Bereshis 32:7) while Yitzhak is alive, for Yitzhak only dies later (Bereshis 35:28).

WHY DOES LAVAN SWITCH WIVES?

Before analyzing Lavan's character, let us ask one more central question. Why does he switch wives on Yaakov? It comes as no surprise that Lavan is unethical and dishonest, but that does not explain his motives for tricking Yaakov into marrying both Rochel and Leah. What does Lavan gain by tricking Yaakov into marrying Leah?

It is difficult to imagine that he acts as a loving father, interested in protecting and caring for his daughter, Leah. He certainly does not think that this secret is a long-term solution for Leah, for it is bound to be discovered quickly. And the consequences for Leah are disastrous. She becomes שְׂנוּאָה *hated* (ibid 29:30). Moreover, Lavan completely ignores Rochel's interests and almost ruins her life. Where is his sensitivity for Rochel? Whose best interests are in Lavan's mind?[295]

With these questions in mind, let us look at the narrative where the Torah portrays Lavan, Yaakov's arrival and subsequent time at Lavan's.

UPON YAAKOV'S ARRIVAL IN CHARAN

Even before Yaakov's arrival at Lavan's house in Charan, the Torah documents a seemingly uneventful interaction that Yaakov has

---

[295] One might suggest that Lavan only cares about Leah and not Rochel and therefore arranges for her to marry Yaakov even though it ruins Rochel's life. Support can even be found from the fact that only Rochel is recorded as shepherding the sheep (Bereshis 29:6), an inferior job not typically given to woman. The Chizkuni (Bereshis 29:18), in fact, accepts this approach and adds that Lavan favors Leah because she is older (Chizkuni on Bereshis 29:9).

However, according to most commentaries, this theory seems to be incorrect as Lavan treats Rochel well. Upon marriage, Lavan gives Rochel a Shifcha *maid-servant* (ibid 29:30), as a gift, just as he had given one to Leah (ibid 29:24). Additionally, just before Yaakov leaves Lavan's house to return home, and he communicates that their father sees them as outsiders (ibid 31:14-15), Rochel is in as much disbelief as Leah. From her perspective, her father loves and cares for her. Maybe one can claim that Rochel is even more surprised based upon the Torah's language וַתַּעַן רָחֵל וְלֵאָה וַתֹּאמַרְנָה לוֹ הַעוֹד לָנוּ חֵלֶק וְנַחֲלָה בְּבֵית אָבִינוּ *And (she) Rochel and Leah responded and they said 'Do we have no longer an inheritance in our father's home'.* Using the singular language וַתַּעַן *And (she) respond, "she",* when describing both Rochel and Leah, yet placing Rochel first, may indicate that Rochel is even more surprised (for precedence, see Rashi Bereshis 9:23). If Rochel is indeed treated poorly, it would be difficult to understand why she is more surprised.

Regarding why Rochel is the only shepherd, perhaps it is because Leah's eyes are weak and too much sun may be damaging (Ramban Bereshis 29:9) or because she is still young and in less need of protection from unwanted gentleman callers (Ramban ibid).

with several shepherds at a well. There the shepherds make small talk answering Yaakov's basic questions about Lavan by informing Yaakov that they, in fact, do know Lavan and that he is doing well (ibid 29:4-6). This seemingly insignificant conversation is exactly the type of information we would expect the Torah to omit. Is it important for the readers to be informed that the strangers at the well are from Charan, that they know Lavan and communicate to Yaakov that he is fine? What does the Torah accomplish with this episode?[296]

LAVAN'S COMPLEX NATURE

Lavan's character is very confusing. He welcomes Yaakov warmly, with a hug and kiss commenting (ibid 29:13) אַךְ עַצְמִי וּבְשָׂרִי אָתָּה *You are my flesh and blood* (ibid 29:14). Additionally, he initially insists on paying Yaakov a salary (ibid 29:15), both seemingly positive and welcoming actions. Yet, later, Lavan dishonestly changes Yaakov's salary tens of times (ibid 29:41, 31:7), and he tricks Yaakov into marrying Leah. For someone who mistreats Yaakov so greatly, why does Lavan welcome Yaakov so warmly?

Lavan's response to hearing Yaakov's desire to marry Rochel is strange and impolite. Lavan remarks, טוֹב תִּתִּי אֹתָהּ לָךְ מִתִּתִּי אֹתָהּ לְאִישׁ אַחֵר *Better to give her to you than someone else* (ibid 29:19), implying that Yaakov is the best option in a bad situation. It seems as if Lavan prefers for his daughter not to get married at all, but if she has to, then choosing Yaakov is the least bad option. Does he not want Rochel to get married? Does he not worry about her happiness? Then, strangely, Lavan adds שְׁבָה עִמָּדִי *stay with me*. How is that relevant?

Lavan's behavior further confuses us, for he gives each of his daughters a Shifcha, *maid-servant,* a generous wedding gift, again seemingly displaying deep care and concern for his daughters.

---

[296] Interestingly, this conversation is bookended with identical language, presumably highlighting its importance. Before this passage, the Torah notes וְנֶאֶסְפוּ שָׁמָּה כָל הָעֲדָרִים וְגָלְלוּ אֶת הָאֶבֶן מֵעַל פִּי הַבְּאֵר וְהִשְׁקוּ אֶת הַצֹּאן וְהֵשִׁיבוּ אֶת הָאֶבֶן עַל פִּי *And the shepherds would gather there and roll the rock off of the opening of the well and give the sheep (water) to drink and the return the rock to the opening* (ibid 29:3) and afterwards, the shepherds, themselves express that no water can be drawn until later, וְנֶאֶסְפוּ כָל הָעֲדָרִים וְגָלְלוּ אֶת הָאֶבֶן מֵעַל פִּי הַבְּאֵר וְהִשְׁקִינוּ הַצֹּאן *And the shepherds gather there and roll the rock off of the opening of the well and give the sheep (water) to drink* (ibid 29:8).

In order to develop answers to these questions, it pays to first continue asking several questions from the events that occur at Lavan's house and later with Yaakov's departure from it. We will use these questions and other clues we can gather to develop a comprehensive theory and return to address these questions.

PLANNING TO LEAVE LAVAN'S HOUSE

After Yaakov's wealth increases (Bereshis 30), Lavan's perspective towards Yaakov changes in an irreversible way (ibid 31:2). Why is it that Yaakov's financial success reshapes their relationship? Is Lavan jealous? Is he not extremely wealthy himself?

Later, when Yaakov plans on leaving Lavan's house with his wives and sons to return home, he informs his wives, Rochel and Leah, of several things. He communicates his intentions to leave Lavan's house as well as two other things: their father's manipulations (Bereshis 31:6-9) and that they are no longer welcome in Lavan's home (ibid 31:5). Rochel and Leah have both anticipated the duplicity but are nevertheless shocked that their father no longer welcomes their family, as they remark together, הֲלוֹא נָכְרִיּוֹת נֶחְשַׁבְנוּ לוֹ *Are we considered strangers* (ibid 31:15). Rochel and Leah assume Lavan is a caring father with his house always open to them. Again, we must ask, how do they see Lavan and what does it say about him?

YAAKOV'S DEPARTURE

When Lavan is away tending his flock, Yaakov secretly gathers together his family and escapes. The Torah records that this departure is heartbreaking for Lavan (Bereshis 31:20), again insinuating that Lavan sincerely cares.[297] Yet, Lavan, upon returning home and realizing Yaakov has left, crafts a plan to kill Yaakov. Only because Hashem intervenes and warns Lavan not to touch Yaakov does he refrain from doing so.[298]

---

[297] Targum Onkelus. However, others (Targum Yonason Ben Uziel, Ibn Ezra on Bereshis 31:20 and Radak on Bereshis 31:20) interpret this to mean that Yaakov simply misleads Lavan, and the Torah reveals nothing about how it impacts Lavan.

[298] Rav Yosef Dov HaLevi Soloveitchik (Festival of Freedom 126-127). This certainly explains

²⁹⁹ How can someone who cares so deeply for Yaakov be willing to hurt him so severely?

Eventually, Lavan catches up with Yaakov and accuses him of stealing his Terafim.³⁰⁰ Yaakov responds to Lavan by challenging him to search through his belongings for the lost Terafim, and by adding a condition that if anyone is found to be the thief, that person should be punished with death.³⁰¹ Only after Lavan does not discover them does Yaakov react strongly (ibid 31:36), verbally attacking Lavan and releasing built up complaints of decades of deceit. For years Yaakov has restrained himself, why does Yaakov only respond so harshly when Lavan cannot find his Terafim (ibid 31:36-42)?

Lavan communicates honestly to Yaakov that he was devastated upon discovering that Yaakov snuck away when Lavan was not home.

how Chazal (Hagadah and Rashi Devorim 26:5) understand אֲרַמִּי אֹבֵד אָבִי *An Aramite attempted to destroy my father* to be referring to Lot's attempt to obliterate Yaakov. However, it should be noted that the Rashbam (Devorim 26:5) understands אֲרַמִּי אֹבֵד אָבִי *My father was a wandering Aramite*, to be referring to Avraham's wandering.

²⁹⁹ Interestingly the Tzrur HaMaor (Bereshis 31:20) adds that Yaakov leaving without informing Lavan reflects a lack of faith in Hashem.

³⁰⁰ Rashi (Bereshis 31:19) states that Terafim are Avodah Zara *idols* and Rochel steals them to prevent her father from worshiping them. This may even be implied from the verse's extra phrase, וַתִּגְנֹב רָחֵל אֶת הַתְּרָפִים אֲשֶׁר לְאָבִיהָ *And Rochel stole the Terafim that were her father's.* אֲשֶׁר לְאָבִיהָ *that were her father's* is not superfluous if the Torah is teaching Rochel's religious motivation (Sifsey Chochomim Bereshis 31:19).
The Rashbam (Bereshis 31:19), Malbim (Bereshis 31:19) and Netziv (Bereshis 31:19) agree that the Terafim are Avodah Zara, but disagree as to why Rochel takes them. They argue that the Terafim have some magical tracking power and Rochel steals them to prevent Lavan from using them to find them. (For a discussion regarding whether or not powers such as these actually exist see the Rambam (Hilchos Avodah Zara 11:13, 16), who thinks they do not, and the Ramban (Devorim 18:9,13 and Mitzvah Asay L'Daas HaRamban 8) who thinks they do, but are nonetheless forbidden).
The Ramban (Bereshis 31:19) understands that Rashi distinguishes between different types of Terafim, for not all are designed to be worshiped. After all, Dovid and Michal have Terafim and they are not used for Avodah Zara. The Meshech Chochmah (Bereshis 31:19) also agrees that Terafim refer to Avodah Zara, but argues that her taking them facilitates Hashem appearing to Lavan to warn Lavan not to harm Yaakov.
The Ramban (Bereshis 31:19) understands Terafim to be a vessel that can answer questions about the future.
For other options regarding what Terafim are, see the Ibn Ezra (Bereshis 31:19).

³⁰¹ As the Meshech Chochma (Bereshis 31:32) notes, death is the punishment for theft for Bnei Noach (Rambam Melachim 9:9).
This is why Rochel dies early according to Rashi (Bereshis 31:32). Alternatively, the Ramban (Bereshis 26:5) who limits the Avos' observance of Mitzvos to Eretz Yisrael argues Yaakov could marry two sister outside of Eretz Yisrael, but upon return to Eretz Yisrael, Rochel dies. Lastly, the Midrash (Bereshis Rabbah, Vilna Edition 74:4) blames Rochel for speaking before (cutting off) her sister וַתַּעַן רָחֵל וְלֵאָה וַתֹּאמַרְנָה *And Rochel and Leah answered* (Bereshis 31:14).

Then he adds that he would have thrown Yaakov a grand and musical going-away-party (ibid 31:27). It is difficult to imagine that Lavan would have even been willing to let them go, as Yaakov himself attests (ibid 31:31), but it is almost impossible to believe that Lavan would have thrown a party. Again, what picture does the Torah paint of Lavan?

Lastly, Yaakov shares with Lavan why he left by informing him, כִּי יָרֵאתִי כִּי אָמַרְתִּי פֶּן תִּגְזֹל אֶת בְּנוֹתֶיךָ מֵעִמִּי *Because I feared, and said 'lest he take my daughters from me'* (ibid 31:31).[302] Again, what does this say about Lavan and how Yaakov sees him?

ANSWERING THE CENTRAL QUESTION: WHO IS LAVAN?

Lavan is a selfish, egocentric, and self-absorbed man.[303] The entire world is owed to him and he owes nothing back. Lavan manipulates whoever he needs to, because the ends justify the means, and the ends are often seen though his own selfish and warped perspective.

Furthermore, Lavan lies, but never in a manner in which he can be caught. Everything is defendable and he has an answer for everything. Lavan is no amateur; he is a professional criminal.

Lavan truly cares for his family, but for completely selfish reasons. He views them as an extension of himself and he undoubtedly cares for himself. Additionally, Lavan wants to keep them close by. He gives them gifts ensuring that they remain close and from his position, it is moving money from one pocket to the other. He gives his daughters Shifachos, *maid-servants*, as wedding gifts and offers Yaakov a salary. Both of these acts reflect his desire to care for his family members as well his obsession with controlling them and keeping them near to him. Furthermore, offering Yaakov a job creates a financial dependence and ensures that Yaakov remains in his possession. Continuously changing the price is rationalized because the entire salary he offered was never intended to go to Yaakov as a separate entity anyway.

---

[302] The Tzrur HaMaor (Bereshis 31:27) proves from the word וָאֲשַׁלֵּחֲךָ *and I will send you* which is written singularly, that Lavan had planned on withholding everyone besides Yaakov.

[303] Rashi (Bereshis 24:50) comments that Lavan even as a young boy interrupts his father. Lavan has always been self-absorbed.

Lavan[304] sees growth in the number of sheep as a symbol of his own success even though such a view is unfounded in reality. And it is only when Yaakov achieves his own financial success that Lavan can no longer view Yaakov the same way. Until now, Lavan saw Yaakov as part of his own possessions. Once Yaakov develops some financial independence, Lavan, threatened and unnerved, can no longer look at Yaakov the same way.

Based upon this hypothesis, we can further explain why Leah and Rochel are shocked to be seen as outsiders. Knowing their father well, they expect his skullduggery, but expelling his own family members is completely uncharacteristic and unexpected. Lavan is not a good man, but he is a family man.

Yaakov thought that Lavan's missing Terafim claim was a cheap excuse for Lavan to follow them. Only when nothing is found, does Yaakov explode, because then it becomes clear to him that he is correct and thinks that this is just another one of Lavan's crafty tricks. This pushes Yaakov too far, at which point he gets angry and lets Lavan know it (ibid 31:36).

Beyond manipulating and controlling his family and household, Lavan appears powerful in Charan. He is able to both arrange a wedding where the entire city attends,[305] yet simultaneously, ensure that no one reveal to Yaakov that he is due to marry the wrong girl.[306] The townsmen keep it a secret for they both deeply respect and fear Lavan.[307]

---

[304] and his sons (Bereshis 31:1)

[305] Lavan arranges a party to help hide his deception and cover himself from embarrassment if Yaakov discovers the truth. By arranging the event in a public place, it is more likely for Yaakov to go along with the wedding plans or keep quiet rather than publicly embarrassing Leah. The point is especially poignant assuming wedding parties are uncommon at the times of Tanach; there are no others recorded wedding reception parties. However, the Radak (Bereshis 29:22) argues that wedding reception parties were common at the time.

[306] Presumably the townsmen are aware of Lavan's trick, for it is otherwise almost unimaginable that no one would have revealed the secret to Yaakov at the wedding. And, even if the townspeople are unaware, that too speaks to Lavan's ability to manipulate the entire village, an equally considerable feat. Either way Lavan is clearly a powerful individual.
Interestingly, according to the Malbim (Bereshis 29:22), Lavan assembles the townsmen in order to institute the custom of not having a younger daughter marry before an older one. Incidentally, this explains how Yaakov works in Charan for seven years completely oblivious to the village's practice. How does he not notice this or hear of it from someone who knows that he is working for Rochel? The answer is that the practice does not previously exist. This too reinforces Lavan's great influence and power.

[307] One may argue that deception is a quality that the entire town possesses. Support may be found from the fact that the shepherds keep a big rock on the well, presumably fearing

This also answers why the Torah makes a point to include Yaakov's meeting the local shepherds. The point is to communicate Lavan's power and prestige by reporting that everyone in Charan knows Lavan. That short dialogue depicts Lavan as a well-known and important man in Charan.[308] People in Charan all know Lavan.

In truth, it should not come as such a surprise that Lavan runs the city of Charan; it was probably in their family's control for generations. After all, the Midrash (Yalkut Shemoni 190, Parshas Chaya Sarah) records that his father, Bisuel, was the king, and moreover, was entitled to jus primae noctis. Indeed, the city was referred to as Ir Nachor (ibid 24:10), the city of Lavan's grandfather.[309]

Although Lavan undoubtedly acts deceitfully, he never lies in an indefensible manner. There is nothing that he says that can be proven untrue and he can always cover his tracks. Eventually, he does give Rochel to Yaakov, it is just after seven more years of work.[310] Additionally, it cannot be disproven that Lavan had no intention of throwing Yaakov a musical going-away party (ibid 31:27).[311] This all fits Lavan's persona as a disingenuous charlatan.

Lavan is a white-collar criminal, a skilled and polished maneuverer, a powerful and manipulative individual who cares for no one besides himself and those directly around him, who he can include as extensions of himself.

---

that others would steal from them.

[308] Alternatively, the Torah records this in order to teach the proper way to come as a guest, learning a little about the host in advance (Seforno Bereshis 29:6).

[309] Although the Torah addresses Lavan as Nachor's son (Bereshis 29:5), biologically Nachor is in fact his grandfather. Because Lavan identified with his ancestor who ran the city, he is associated with Nachor, and called Nachor's son (Ramban on Bereshis 29:5).

[310] Radak (Bereshis 31:26). Moreover, the Malbim (Bereshis 29:26) adds, השיב לו, לא תחשוב שעשיתי זאת מפני שאני רוצה לשנות לתת לך את רחל, או שאני רוצה להכריח אותך תשתא את לאה שלא כרצונך, שבהפך, שעשיתי זאת למען אוכל למלא את אשר הבטחתי לך לתת לך את רחל, ומנהג המקום מעכב He responded, 'Do not think that I did this because I do not want to give you Rochel, or I want to force you into marrying Leah against your will, for the exact opposite is true. I did this in order to fulfill my promise that I would give you Rochel; the community's customs were otherwise preventing me.'

[311] After all, Lavan protested last time Yaakov tried to leave (Bereshis 30:25-27).

Lavan in the Eyes of Chazal

Chazal provide support for this image. On the one hand, they explain that when Lavan welcomes Yaakov, he searches Yaakov's pockets and mouth for hidden jewels (Bereshis Rabbah 70:13), clearly attesting to his subtly deceptive character. However, they also recognize that Lavan will not utter an outright lie. He is far too skillful for that. By agreeing to work for Lavan before marrying Rochel,[312] Yaakov assumes Lavan will abide by what he pledges (Rashi Bereshis 29:18). This illustrates that Yaakov believes Lavan has some level of credibility. Twist or manipulate his words, Lavan might do, but overtly break them, he would not.

Why Lavan Does Not Hurt Yaakov

When Lavan does catch up to Yaakov, he suppresses his anger and does not hurt Yaakov because Hashem warns him not to. Unsurprisingly, Lavan displays compete self-control.[313] This also supports our theory. Lavan is not inexperienced and does not act impulsively based upon emotion. He is a well thought out mastermind, completely in control of his actions.

The Final Confrontation

After Lavan fails to produce the stolen Terafim, Yaakov believes he has confirmation that Lavan's entire claim was fabricated and he unleashes twenty years of stored-up complaints.[314] After patiently

---

[312] Yaakov asks for רָחֵל בִּתְּךָ הַקְּטַנָּה *Rochel, your youngest daughter.* By mentioning three descriptions, Yaakov repeats the details, trying to pre-empt any possible lie that Lavan might concoct (Rashi Bereshis 29:18). Yaakov is not afraid that Lavan will deny the agreement. He is afraid that Lavan will manipulate it.

[313] Even when Lavan's heart is broken by Yaakov leaving without informing Lavan (Bereshis 31:20), Lavan completely maintains his composure.

[314] Interestingly, Yaakov omits Lavan switching brides at the wedding. At first glance this should be shocking for it is Lavan's greatest trick of all. Rav Shalom Schvadron, the Maggid of Yerushalayim, suggests that Leah is unaware of Yaakov plans to marry her sister, Rochel, and not her. No one had ever informed Leah otherwise and she therefore assumes, consistent with the local custom, that she, as the oldest daughter, is Yaakov's intended wife. For more

listening to Yaakov's complaint, Lavan reveals his true colors by replying הַבָּנוֹת בְּנֹתַי וְהַבָּנִים בָּנַי וְהַצֹּאן צֹאנִי וְכֹל אֲשֶׁר אַתָּה רֹאֶה לִי הוּא *The daughters are my daughters, and the sons are my sons, the sheep are my sheep and all that you see is mine* (ibid 31:43). Nowhere more than here are we exposed to Lavan's outrageous sense of entitlement. He sees everything as his own. Lavan, with his warped perspective, sees himself as entitled and, moreover, the victim.[315]

In fact, this is exactly the concern that Yaakov has feared, כִּי יָרֵאתִי כִּי אָמַרְתִּי פֶּן תִּגְזֹל אֶת בְּנוֹתֶיךָ מֵעִמִּי *I was afraid because I thought that you would steal your daughters from me* (ibid 31:31).

LAVAN'S GREATEST TRICK

We had questioned why Lavan arranges for both of his daughters, Leah and Rochel, to marry Yaakov. Whose best interest is he looking out for? Lavan is not looking out for Leah's welfare, nor Rochel's. He is looking out for his own welfare. Lavan, in a selfish attempt to tie down Yaakov, orchestrates a plan tricking Yaakov into marrying both sisters. Selfishly, Lavan wants Yaakov to become part of his family which he sees as his possessions.[316] This is exactly why after telling Yaakov he is the best of all options for Rochel, טוֹב תִּתִּי אֹתָהּ לָךְ מִתִּתִּי אֹתָהּ לְאִישׁ אַחֵר *Better to give her to you than someone else* (ibid 29:19), he states שְׁבָה עִמָּדִי *stay with me* (ibid 29:19). שְׁבָה עִמָּדִי *stay with me* is Lavan slightly revealing his cards.

In fact, שְׁבָה עִמָּדִי *stay with me* has two elements to it. On a simple level, Lavan invites Yaakov to remain with him as a guest, but on a deeper level, the Torah is hinting to Lavan's entitlement. Lavan wants Yaakov to join his family and become his property.

---

on this theory, see *Double Take* footnote 353.

[315] This is the perspective of Lavan's sons as well (Bereshis 31:1); presumably one that they heard from him.

[316] The Netziv (Bereshis 29:14) understands this to be the reason why Lavan welcomes Yaakov in and treats him like family, in contrast to Esuv, whom Lavan agrees to protect Yaakov from. It is clearly not Yaakov's status as a biological nephew alone that gains him favor, for Esuv would have gained the same favor. Rather Yaakov is a pawn for Lavan to use and therefore Lavan welcomes him in, looking to keep him there.

Lavan's agenda is simply to enlarge his family and attain greater wealth and possessions.[317]

THE THREE STORIES TOLD OF LAVAN

In total the Torah communicates three episodes regarding Lavan. Firstly, how Lavan welcomes Yaakov to Charan (Perek 29); secondly, how he struggles with Yaakov's accumulation of wealth and sheep (Perek 30); and thirdly, how poorly he responds when Yaakov sneaks out at night (Perek 31).

All three stories capture Lavan's greed, his unceasing sense of entitlement and his willingness to lie and cheat in pursuit of power and wealth.

LAVAN AND SHAUL

In the episode of Shaul chasing Dovid and searching for him at Michal's house, the Navi (Shmuel I Perek 19) subtly inserts numerous similarities to our story, insinuating that there may be a deeper connection.

1. The episode in Navi tells of Dovid, an innocent shepherd, running from his self-absorbed and power-hungry father-in-law, Shaul.[318] Yaakov, too, runs from his self-absorbed and power-hungry father-in-law, Lavan.

2. In each story, the innocent sons-in-law, Dovid and Yaakov, are originally employed by their unappreciative fathers-in-law and each is forced to separate.

3. A central element in the Navi is when Michal lies and hides something from her father in an attempt to save Dovid's life. Rochel,

---

[317] Lavan may have been motivated by Rivka's decision to leave as a young girl, marry Yitzhak, and never return. Lavan now insist on having Yaakov remain at his house.

[318] For more about Shaul's hunger for power, see the chapter entitled *Shaul: The Rise and Fall of the First Jewish King.*

too, lies and hides something from her father to save someone's life, her own.[319]

4. Both Lavan and Shaul, who are interested in harming Dovid and Yaakov respectively, are instructed not to. Lavan is commanded by Hashem whereas Shaul is told by, his son, Yonason.

5. Lavan switches his daughters, causing Yaakov to marry Leah when Yaakov actually works for Rochel. In a stirringly similarity, Shaul replaces Merav with Michal when Dovid works for Merav (Shmuel I 18:17 and 19).[320] More than just switching wives for the story's hero, an extremely uncommon phenomenon in Tanach, each father-in-law has a selfish ulterior motive for doing so.

6. Besides the narrative similarities, the account involving Dovid and Shaul uses language that is reminiscent of Yaakov and Lavan's story. Both episodes use the phrase כִּתְמוֹל שִׁלְשׁוֹם *like earlier days* (Bereshis 31:2 and Shmuel I 19:7), but more importantly, and most prominently, Michal hides Dovid by placing תְּרָפִים *Terafim* in the bed. Not only is the word Terafim a very uncommon word for Tanach, but both tricks include hiding something, and they both involve Terafim. In Lavan's case, the Terafim are hidden from the persecutor, and for Shaul they are used to hide Dovid.

Perhaps the reason that the Navi weaves details from our story into the Shaul, Dovid and Michal narrative, is to portray just how insane Shaul has become. Lavan is the paradigm of a self-absorbed and greedy patriarch. Shaul, following his path, has developed the same warped perspective. Entitled to everything, he chases an innocent man, his son-in-law, to satisfy his selfish desires.

Beyond the remarkable connection between Shaul and Lavan, Shaul's fears seem to be identical to Lavan's, particularly stemming from the concern that his daughters might leave him. This association may very well be what inspires the Midrash (Shemos Rabbah 1:33)[321] to articulate Shaul's fear, having his daughters taken from him, like Lavan,

---

[319] Bereshis 31:32

[320] However, there are some (Sanhedrin 19b, Tosefta Sotah 11:9) who say that Dovid marries both, first Merav and then, after her death, Michal.

[321] Another Midrash (Tanchuma Shemos 12) makes a similar comparison.

I (Shaul) know that Yaakov, your father,   יודע אני שיעקב אביכם כשנתן
when Lavan gave him his daughters as   לו לבן בנותיו נטלן והלך לו
wives, he (Yaakov) took them and left   חוץ מדעתו שמא אם אתן לך
without his (Lavan's) knowledge. Maybe   את בתי אתה עושה לי כך
if I give you my daughter, you will do the
same to me.

Undoubtedly, the Midrash interprets Shaul's fear based on our aforementioned parallel.

LOT AND LAVAN

In addition to the list of similarities to the Dovid and Shaul episode, there is another parallel to be uncovered. Lavan can be compared to another character as well, Lot. There are numerous similarities between the two as well.

1. Both Lot and Lavan are biologically related[322] as well as through marriage[323] to the right family, that of the Avos, but remain peripheral characters in Sefer Bereshis.

2. Lavan and Lot each fight about sheep with one of the Avos immediately before separating from that Av. Lot's shepherds fight with Avraham's (ibid 13:7) and Lavan fights directly with Yaakov (ibid 30).[324]

3. Lot and Lavan each have an unnamed wife who is peripheral to the story, highlighting the identity of the central characters: each father and his two daughters.

4. Both narratives tell of two sisters, each part of a deception that leads to a night of relations with an unsuspecting family member. Lot's daughters are intimate with Lot, and Leah, with Yaakov, her cousin.

---

[322] Additionally, Lot is a biological nephew of Avraham and Lavan is a great great nephew of Avraham.

[323] Avraham marries Sarah, Lot's sister (according to Rashi Bereshis 11:29 because Sarah is Iskah) and Yitzhak marries Rivka, Lavan's sister.

[324] Reinforcing the parallel, the Midrash Tanchuma (Parshas Vayetzei 10) adds that when Avraham and Yaakov separate from Lot and Lavan, they receive prophecy that they could not have otherwise received while still around Lot and Lavan.

Lot is unaware of his relations with his daughters, and Yaakov, misled, thinks that he is with Rochel, when in fact he is with Leah.

5. Both Lot and Lavan offer their daughters away in a terribly unethical manner. Lot offers his daughters to a lust-hungry mob while Lavan switches his daughters, offering Leah as the bride instead of Rochel.

6. In each of the stories, the two sisters display remarkable teamwork[325] enabling the deception to occur. Lot's daughters also work together in intoxicating and being intimate with their father.

7. After each story, the sisters each have sons who ultimately build great nations. Rochel and Leah build Klal Yisrael while Lot's daughters build Amon and Moav.

8. In both stories the older sister enters the relationship before the younger one. Lot's older daughter has relations with Lot first, before his younger daughter. Similarly, Leah, the older sister, marries Yaakov before Rochel.

In addition to the thematic elements of the stories that parallel to each other, there are linguistic one as well. Both stories use the language of בְּכִירָה *first born* (Bereshis 19:31,34) and צְעִירָה *younger one* (ibid 29:26) in describing the sisters. This linguistic parallel is more pronounced when taking into account that the Torah usually calls Lavan's daughters הַגְּדֹלָה *big one* and הַקְּטַנָּה *small one* (ibid 29:16). Arguably, the intention is to add to the list of similarities.

In each story, there is an announcement regarding the intimacy that occurs, stating that it is not ideal. Lot's daughters declare, וְאִישׁ אֵין בָּאָרֶץ *And there is no man in the land* (Bereshis 19:31) explaining why they must revert to intimacy with their father. Lavan too remarks, טוֹב תִּתִּי אֹתָהּ לָךְ מִתִּתִּי אֹתָהּ לְאִישׁ אַחֵר שְׁבָה עִמָּדִי *Better to give her to you than someone else, stay with me* (ibid 29:19) implying that Rochel marrying Yaakov is not ideal.

---

[325] Perhaps no where is their teamwork more apparent than when Rochel gives Leah Yaakov's signs to avoid embarrassment (Rashi on Bereshis 29:25).

THE DIFFERENCE BETWEEN THE LOT AND LAVAN NARRATIVES

In addition to the comparisons between these stories, there are fascinating contrasts as well. Before offering any explanation as to why the contrast exists, it pays to list them first.

1. Lavan has ruled a city that is controlled by his family for generations.[326] Just the opposite is true of Lot. He is a newcomer to a city that does not fully accept him.[327]

2. Although both attempt to offer their daughters in an unethical manner, Lavan successfully does so whereas Lot does not.

3. The Torah omits the names of Lot's daughters, presenting them as peripheral characters, while Lavan's daughters are not just named – they are two of the most central figures in Tanach.

4. Lot's daughters are proactive in developing and instituting their plan. Lavan's daughters, by contrast, are totally passive, following their father's instruction.

5. Although both stories tell of someone unaware of who he has intercourse with, Lavan, in a masterful but deceptive fashion uses his daughters as he orchestrates trickery. Lot does not trick others; he is tricked by his daughters.

6. Lot's daughters selflessly and sensitivity intoxicate Lot attempting to minimize his awareness. Lavan, selfishly, takes no such steps to minimize the pain his plan will inflict on Yaakov and his daughters.

7. Although both Lot and Lavan separate themselves from one of the Avos (Avraham and Yaakov respectively), Lot leaves Avraham, as opposed to Lavan, who is left by Yaakov. However, the contrast is really deeper, because Lot, searching for his freedom and independence, desperately wants to leave Avraham, whereas Lavan desires the dependency of others.

---

[326] The city was even called Ir Nachor (Bereshis 24:10), after his grandfather.

[327] The city-dwellers of Sdom challenge him by saying הָאֶחָד בָּא לָגוּר וַיִּשְׁפֹּט שָׁפוֹט *And one comes to live among us and he judges us* (Bereshis 19:9). For more insight on Lot's outsider status, see *Double Take*, the chapter entitled *Noach, Yonah, Lot and Avraham* — "*What it Takes to Start up a Nation.*"

8. Lot is deceived in a cave, an extremely private place. By contrast, the Lavan story takes place in a public arena, a wedding celebration in front of the whole community.

9. Both sets of daughters find themselves fleeing for their lives, but Lot's daughters flee with him from Sdom (Bereshis 19:14-16), while Lavan's flee from him (ibid 31:21).

10. Although both of Lot's daughters as well as Rochel and Leah give their children names revolving around the event, they do so very differently. Lot's daughters crassly name their children about the past, and how they were intimate with their father, מוֹאָב *from (my) father* and בֶּן עַמִּי *son of my nation* (Bereshis 19:37-38) while Leah and Rochel name their children to reflect their future dreams and desires.

What is the point of the Torah doing this? Why craft the Lavan story in a fashion that recalls the Lot episode yet in other respects uses it as a foil? Perhaps comparing them draws our attention to the difference. Contrasting Lavan to Lot highlights who Lavan really is.

While Lot is a uniquely selfless man, Lavan is exceptionally selfish. Unlike Lot, who sincerely cares for guests, and shows no concern for his daughters, as seen by his decision to offer them to a lustful mob, Lavan does the exact opposite. He cares for his family and nobody else.

Lot sees his family as an extension of himself to the point where he can justify acting selflessly on their behalf, Lavan is the opposite. He sees his family as an extension of himself to the point where he can justify acting selfishly on their behalf.[328]

LAVAN AND ESUV

Having developed a hypothesis and applied it to answer many of our questions, we can now attempt to explain why Esuv does not attack Yaakov at Lavan's home. Esuv though infuriated and committed to killing Yaakov is deeply afraid to intrude into Lavan's house. Esuv is

---

[328] For a better perspective on Lot, see the previous *Lot and the Karban Pesach* chapter and *Double Take*, the chapter entitled *Noach, Yonah, Lot and Avraham* — *"What it Takes to Start up a Nation."*

scared to take something that Lavan sees as his own. Taking something from Lavan is tantamount to filling out one's own death certificate.[329]

With this we can add insight as to why the Torah does not just record the first half of Yaakov's conversation with the shepherds at the well where they all know Lavan. It is important to know that Lavan's daughter, Rochel, shepherds her flock freely, fearless of anyone stealing from her.[330] People know very well not to take anything from Lavan.

Esuv is a hoodlum, a gangster, where as Lavan is the Godfather.[331] This gangster knows very well not to enter the Godfather's turf and take something that belongs to him. No one appreciates this better than Rivka. Fully aware of her brother's personality, she sends Yaakov to Lavan.[332] Lavan's house is selected, by Rivka, as protection for Yaakov, not a secret place to hide.[333]

WHITE AND RED

However, this aforementioned theory about Lavan and Esuv may penetrate deeper and offer greater insight. Lavan's name may capture his attitude for it means *white*. After all, Lavan is a professional criminal wearing the mask of innocence, represented by the color white. Lavan is a white collared criminal and the master of "white lies". Chazal[334] capture this point by stating הידעתם את לבן בן נחור הידעתם את מי שהוא עתיד ללבן עונותיהם כשלג *'Do you know Lavan the son of Nachor' the one who will whiten his sins like snow.* This perspective connects Lavan to

---

[329] This is precisely why Yaakov fears leaving Lavan's house and has to sneak out when Lavan is gone.

[330] Malbim (Bereshis 29:5-6)

[331] Malbim (Bereshis 28:5)

[332] Malbim (Bereshis 27:43-44)

[333] According to the Netziv (Bereshis 29:14), Lavan communicates this to Yaakov. Furthermore the Malbim (ibid 29:14) adds that Lavan favors Yaakov over Esuv simply because Rivka does.
Based on this one might be able to understand an otherwise difficult Midrash (Midrash Agada, Buber, Parshas Vayetzei 29:12) which claims that the first thing Yaakov communicates to Lavan is what occurs with Elifaz. Perhaps Yaakov is ensuring Lavan's protection.
By contrast, the Chizkuni (Bereshis 29:18) notes that Yaakov fears marrying Leah because Esuv might come attack him at Lavan's house for taking Esuv's planned wife. Accordingly, Yaakov does not feel safe at Lavan's house. Presumably, Yaakov fears are unjustified for even after marrying Leah, Esuv does not dare enter Lavan's house.

[334] Yalkut Shemoni, Parshas Vayetzei

the color white and reaffirms our theory that עתיד ללבן עונותיהם כשלג *whiten his sins like snow.*

Not only is Lavan associated with the color white, but Esuv is associated with a color too, red. Esuv is Edom, *red* while Lavan is *white*. Esuv is raw, and he acts impulsively, completely based upon emotion. He does not intelligently weigh all the options and decide rationally. Esuv's attitude is best captured by the color red.

However, there is a difference between Esuv's association with red and Lavan's association with white. The name *Lavan* actually means white, while Esuv's name does not mean red. It actually means *complete* or *done* because that is how he is born, hairy (Bereshis 25:25), grown up and complete. Although there is an allusion to Esuv's redness, וַיֵּצֵא הָרִאשׁוֹן אַדְמוֹנִי כֻּלּוֹ כְּאַדֶּרֶת שֵׂעָר *And the first one came out reddish, like a hairy mantle,* Esuv really only acquires the association with red when he trades the birth-right. The Torah records וַיֹּאמֶר עֵשָׂו אֶל יַעֲקֹב הַלְעִיטֵנִי נָא מִן הָאָדֹם הָאָדֹם הַזֶּה כִּי עָיֵף אָנֹכִי עַל כֵּן קָרָא שְׁמוֹ אֱדוֹם *And Esuv said to Yaakov 'Give me from the red red (food) for I am tired' therefore call his name Edom red.*

Esuv's association with red is a turning point in life, for it is when he trades his birth-right. Until that point he is similar to Yaakov (Bereshis Rabbah, Vilna Edition, 63:10) and could have continued on the proper path. Esuv's spiritual deterioration[335] begins with that trade and continues with the acquisition of a new identity, one identified with red, anger.[336]

---

[335] For a greater look at Esuv's religious potential, see *Double Take*, the chapter entitled *Yaakov's Two Hats*

[336] What fuels Esuv's fire of anger is the cognitive dissonance that exists within him. Ideologically he understands what Hashem values, for he is raised in Yitzhak's house with Yitzhak's values, yet he chooses short term enjoyment and can not live up to his own religious standards.

Along these lines, Esuv cries uncontrollably when Yitzhak realizes the significance of Yaakov taking the Bracha (Bereshis 27:34). Why? Intellectually, Esuv knows right from wrong but can not live up to his value system. Esuv is disappointed with what he sees in the mirror and weeps bitterly (Lubavitcher Rebbe).

Moreover, Chazal (Sotah 13a) say Esuv dies by decapitation and his head is buried in Ma'aras HaMachpaleh. Chazal symbolically emphasize the divide between Esuv's ideology and actions. His head, representing his ideals, belongs in Ma'aras HaMachpaleh, but his body, representing his actions, do not.

WHY EACH LAVAN AND ESUV DO NOT ATTACK YAAKOV

Neither Lavan nor Esuv attacks Yaakov but for different reasons. Lavan does not attack Yaakov because Hashem intervenes warning him not to. Esuv also has an opportunity to attack Yaakov after he leaves Lavan's house. Esuv's anger may have just been soothed. After time, gifts and Yaakov's proper handling of the situation calms Esuv down.[337] Esuv reacts impulsively, gets angry quickly, and even maintains the anger for a while, but can be calmed down.[338] By contrast, Lavan's decision are not affected by anger because he acts based on intellect, not emotion. He would hold the grudge forever and that is precisely why Hashem has to intervene.

LAVAN'S AND ESUV'S GREETING

The contrast between Chazal's understanding of how Esuv and Lavan each greet Yaakov is very telling. Both Esuv and Lavan approach Yaakov with unfriendly motives. Esuv embraces Yaakov with the intention of biting Yaakov's neck but it miraculously turns into

---

[337] Yaakov prepared to meet Esuv with prayer, gifts, and a readiness to fight. (Koheles Rabbah 9:1).
Moreover, according to one opinion in Rashi (Bereshis 32:5), Yaakov tells Esuv אינך כדאי לשנוא אותי על ברכות אביך שברכני הוה גביר לאחיך, שהרי לא נתקיימה בי *You have no reason to hate me, for your father's bracha 'Rule over your brother' was not fulfilled in me which may be what Esuv wanted to hear, more than what Yaakov wanted to say* (For more about this see the chapter in *Double Take* entitled *Yaakov's Two Hats*).

[338] According to the Rashbam (Bereshis 25:34), Esuv is young and immature when he foolishly exchanged his birth right and he later he came to regret his decision.
By contrast, Rashi (Bereshis 25:34) argues that Esuv trades away the birthright because he dislikes anything associated with Torah. Perhaps these two interpretations revolve around Esuv's religious character. According to Rashi, Esuv is absolutely wicked, while according to the Rashbam, Esuv is immature and foolish (See Rashi and Rashbam on Bereshis 32:7 for a further picture of how each viewed Esuv).
Lastly, the Ibn Ezra (Bereshis 25:34) offers a third explanation. Esuv scorns the firstborn rights because it has little financial value, as Yitzhak had lost the family fortune. The Ibn Ezra continues by proving that Yitzhak, in fact, has lost the family fortune. Yitzhak loves Esuv because he brought food for the family, something they so desperately need. Additionally, Esuv trades his firstborn rights for food. Presumably there is no other food in the pantry, otherwise he could have eaten that instead. Furthermore, Yitzhak sends Esuv hunting for food before blessing him, again, because he is hungry. Lastly, Yaakov comes to Lavan empty-handed, with no clothing or food, because their family has none to send him with. The Ramban (Bereshis 25:34) strongly disagrees, arguing Yitzhak does not lose the family fortune.

marble and Esuv cries of pain (Bereshis Rabbah, Vilna Edition 78:9).[339] Lavan discreetly checks his pockets while hugging Yaakov and after finding nothing, kisses him hoping to find precious hidden jewelry in his mouth (Bereshis Rabbah, Vilna Edition 70:13). Each of their actions and attempts to hurt Yaakov reflect their true identities. Esuv aggressively attacks Yaakov, for Esuv, a gangster, is confrontational. Lavan, by contrast, is looking for money, and moreover intends to take it in a sly and sinister manner.

Applying Text to Life: The Hashkafic Message

Lavan has an incredibly self-absorbed perspective viewing his family as extensions of himself. His relationships all revolve around him and how they benefit him.

Beyond Lavan's warped perspective, there is something else that is important to uncover. Being honorable is more than simply avoiding lies or being able to defend one's statements. Honesty is about being upfront, genuine and not misleading. Lavan fails at being upfront and therefore is, correctly, presented by Chazal as manipulative.

However, there is another ideological point to be derived. In Sefer Bereshis, Yaakov encounters and flees two different types of paradigmatic enemies, Esuv and Lavan. One enemy, Esuv, attacks head on. He confronts Yaakov and is not bashful with his hate for Yaakov. The other, more subtle, suave and perhaps more dangerous, camouflages his attack in formalities, rules and laws. Lavan, misleading Yaakov about marriage and salaries, is both more subtle and difficult to detect.

---

[339] The Midrash also presents an alternative approach, that Esuv becomes very merciful and kisses Yaakov with all of his heart. This too reinforces the difference between Lavan and Esuv, for Lavan is unforgiving and would have never done this.

THE COLOSSAL IMPACT
OF THE MERAGLIM'S SIN

MERAGLIM: WHY PUNISH THEM SO SEVERELY?

O f the many transgressions that Bnei Yisrael commit throughout the Torah, astonishingly, the meraglim's sin of speaking negatively about Eretz Yisrael provokes Hashem's strongest response. Hashem initially plans on destroying Bnei Yisrael immediately (Bamidbar 14:12) and ultimately decides to wait forty years for them to all die gradually. Ostensibly, greater sins received lesser punishments; for example, malicious rebellions against Him and Moshe, illicit relations with Midyani women, idolatry, and lashon hara, *evil slander* about Moshe are all severe violations. Yet, the punishments meted out on those occasions do not even approach the severity of Hashem's reaction on this occasion. Hashem completely gives up on this generation. How is ten meraglim's negative assessment and presentation of Eretz Yisrael a sin that prompts such a harsh punishment?

THE COMMAND AND SENDING OF THE MERAGLIM

Let us begin our analysis by looking at the story itself. Strangely, the Torah seems to record Moshe sending the meraglim twice, each time with identical language. First, the Torah presents וַיִּשְׁלַח אֹתָם מֹשֶׁה *And Moshe sent them* (ibid 13:3) before using precisely the exact same language several verses later וַיִּשְׁלַח אֹתָם מֹשֶׁה *And Moshe sent them* (ibid 13:17). Why mention this phrase twice, especially when the meraglim do not actually leave for Eretz Yisrael for another several verses, וַיַּעֲלוּ

וַיַּעֲלוּ אֶת הָאָרֶץ *And they went up and spied the land* (ibid 13:21)? What then does וַיִּשְׁלַח אֹתָם מֹשֶׁה *And Moshe sent them* mean?

THE TWO MISSIONS: UNCOVERING THE CLUES

Clearly Moshe does not actually send the meraglim twice, and yet the Torah presents two distinct "sendings." Seemingly, the intent of this repetition is to convey that the meraglim are sent once with two separate missions.[340] Indeed, after the initial command to send meraglim (Bamidbar 13:1-2), the Torah subsequently outlines two distinct assignments or missions (ibid 13:3-16 and 17 – 20). This raises the question of what these two separate missions are, the difference between them and why both are necessary.

When describing the first mission, the Torah focuses solely on the names of the meraglim. First, the Torah lists only their names along with their tribe (ibid 13:4-16). The Torah further emphasizes the importance of their names by opening the first section with וְאֵלֶּה שְׁמוֹתָם *And these are the names* (ibid 13:4, 13:16) and concluding with the unmistakably corresponding words of אֵלֶּה שְׁמוֹת הָאֲנָשִׁים *these are the names* of the men.[341] Yet, at this point, the goal of their mission is conspicuously absent. There is nothing mentioned for the meraglim to do or look for.

By contrast, the second passage exclusively focuses on the meraglim's assignment. They are commanded to research the geography, topography and fortification of Eretz Yisrael. They are to examine the nations there, determine their population and military strength (ibid 13:18), as well as to look at the land itself (ibid 13:19), and its produce (ibid 13:20).[342]

---

[340] Others answer that the meraglim are sent with extra security accompanying them due to the danger (Ohr HaChaim Bamidbar 13:17) or, alternatively, Hashem is repeating Himself letting them know that they are being sent לתור *to search (for positive things)* and not לרגל *to spy (for negative things)* (Malbim Bamidbar 13:17).

[341] The Ibn Ezra (Bamidbar 13:16) deduces from the phrase אֵלֶּה שְׁמוֹת *these are the names* that none of the other spies undergo name-changes. This is necessary to stress because Yehoshua's name is changed here from Hoshea.

[342] The Rashbam (Bamidbar 13:18-19) understands that all of this is for military preparations. They are sent to investigate Eretz Yisrael in order to develop military strategy. Even the reports about the food are to determine how much food they could rely on from Eretz Yisrael itself.

Subtly, the Torah drives home this message by repeating several key words in the second assignment. The words מַה *what* appears four times (ibid 13:18, 19, 19 and 20), הָאָרֶץ *the land* five times (ibid 13:17, 18, 19, 20 and 20) and אִם *or* on six more occasions (ibid 13:18, 18, 19, 19, 20 and 20). These important words are repeated to capture the central theme, what the meraglim are to look for; *what* (מַה) is in this *land* (הָאָרֶץ), whether is it one thing *or* (אִם) another.

It is clear, then, that the meraglim are sent with two separate missions, but why?

THE TWO MISSIONS: THEIR GOALS AND ORIGINATORS

The first assignment is the primary one. It is mentioned first and is significantly longer. Moreover, it is commanded עַל פִּי ה' *according to the word of Hashem,* (Bamidbar 13:3).

Additional support for the first mission's primacy can be found in how the Torah concludes its description of the first mission. By the Torah stating אֵלֶּה שְׁמוֹת הָאֲנָשִׁים אֲשֶׁר שָׁלַח מֹשֶׁה לָתוּר אֶת הָאָרֶץ *these are the names of the **men** that Moshe **sent** to **spy** out the **land*** (ibid 13:16) and reusing four central words from the opening command (ibid 13:2): אֶרֶץ *land,* אנשים *men,* שלח *send* and ויתרו *and they spied* (ibid 13:16) the Torah clearly is bracketing the first assignment with the entire meraglim story. The implication is that the conclusion of the first mission is really the crux of Hashem's command.

The second assignment directed to the meraglim, to know the demographics and topography, is likely information that would interest a nation just about to embark on conquering that land. We might even suggest that there are two separate missions with two separate goals, even sent by two separate parties.

Hashem is interested in *who* goes, אֲנָשִׁים *men,*[343] and completely silent about what they are to do there. Bnei Yisrael are concerned with *what* they are there to find. Because Bnei Yisrael's interest is intuitive

---

[343] Men of importance (Rashi on Bamidbar 13:3 and Seforno on Bamidbar 13:4) or strength (Ibn Ezra on Bamidbar 13:2) and others.
According to the Kli Yakar (Bamidbar 13:2) Hashem would have preferred Moshe send women, for women have a deeper connection to Eretz Yisrael and would have retuned with a positive report. However, Hashem allows Moshe to send men as he sees fit.

and understandable, what remains to be understood is Hashem's strong interest in sending specific meraglim without a clear, defined mission.

The Torah's presentation of each mission answers a different question. The first answers the question *who* should go. The second, *why*. Hashem, completely aware of Eretz Yisrael's topography, geography and population, does not need meraglim to obtain that information.[344] Instead He wants the leaders to lead; to return optimistically and to inspire the people with confidence and hope.[345] Hashem is not concerned with what the meraglim see or experience; rather He wants them to react properly. On the other hand, Bnei Yisrael, a nation lacking trust in Hashem, need to hear the meraglim's testimony.[346] Bnei Yisrael's additional request is not part of Hashem's original plan. In order to capture these two different missions, the Torah states twice וַיִּשְׁלַח אֹתָם מֹשֶׁה *And Moshe sent them*, once for each mission.

In light of this, Chazal (Bamidbar Rabbah, Vilna Edition 16:7) state,

And so Hashem said to Yisrael "The land is good. You did not believe me and said 'Let us send men ahead of us and investigate for us' (then) Hashem said 'If I prevent them (from going) they will say '(that) it is not good and that is why He is not showing us it' rather they can see it."	וכך הקב"ה אמר לישראל טובה הארץ ולא האמינו אלא אמרו נשלחה אנשים לפנינו ויחפרו לנו אמר הקב"ה אם מעכב אני עליהם הם אומרים על שאינה טובה לא הראה אותה לנו אלא יראו אותה

Hashem criticizes Bnei Yisrael for lacking faith, stating ולא האמינו אלא אמרו נשלחה אנשים לפנינו *You did not believe me and said 'Let us send*

---

[344] The Torah Temimah (Devorim 1:23) adds that the entire notion of sending spies reflects Hashem's flexible attitude with Bnei Yisrael.

[345] The Shadal quoted by the Kesav V'Kabalah (Bamidbar 13:16). He then distinguishes between לתור *to look* which is used when looking for something positive and לרגל *to spy*, looking for something negative. The tragedy is that these men are designed to לתור *to look*, but their negative outlook frames them as meraglim. (Also see the Malbim on Bamidbar 13:1, 3-4, 17, 23, 25, Devorim 1:23 and Netziv Bamidbar 13:2).
Rav Eliyahu Dessler (Michtav M'Eliyahu volume 2 p 262) argues that the battle at Yericho is primarily designed to generate faith in Hashem. Perhaps as Bnei Yisrael enter Eretz Yisrael, another attempt, albeit different, is made to engender the faith needed.

[346] For that reason, the Netziv (Devorim 1:23) adds, Moshe does not outsource hiring foreign assistance to assess Eretz Yisrael.

men ahead of us.' This reinforces our understanding that Bnei Yisrael are behind the second mission of the meraglim.

This is precisely how the Torah Temimah (Devorim 1:23 note 32) understands Reish Lakish's (Sotah 34b) comments, בעיני ולא בעיניו של מקום *'In my eyes' and not the eyes of Hashem.* The Torah Temimah elaborates, יען שהקב"ה בעצמו לא היה צריך לשילוח אנשים שהוא ידע מטיב הארץ ולא הרשה לשלוח אנשים רק להפיס דעתן של ישראל *because Hashem, Himself, does not need to send me for He knows the quality of the land. He only allowed for sending the men to appease (and relate to the) perspective of (Bnei) Yisrael.* Hashem does not need meraglim to investigate Eretz Yisrael. He wants them to inspire the people.

RESOLVING AN OTHERWISE DIFFICULT CONTRADICTION

The Torah begins the meraglim episode with Hashem's command, וַיְדַבֵּר יְקֹוָק אֶל מֹשֶׁה לֵּאמֹר שְׁלַח לְךָ אֲנָשִׁים *And Hashem said to Moshe, send for yourself men* (ibid 13:1-2). This presentation creates a difficulty, for it seems to contradict the one found in Sefer Devorim (1:22-23). There, Moshe, while rebuking Bnei Yisrael, claims that Hashem agreed to Bnei Yisrael's *request* to send meraglim into Eretz Yisrael, וַתִּקְרְבוּן אֵלַי כֻּלְכֶם וַתֹּאמְרוּ נִשְׁלְחָה אֲנָשִׁים לְפָנֵינוּ *And you approached me, all of you, and said 'Let us send men before us.'* In other words, the presentation in Sefer Devorim clearly differs from that in Sefer Bamidbar regarding who initiated sending the meraglim; is it Hashem or Bnei Yisrael?

Based on our analysis, we can offer a resolution to this contradiction.[347] When Moshe holds Bnei Yisrael responsible for sending the meraglim,

---

[347] Alternatively, Rashi (Bamidbar 13:2) reinterprets שְׁלַח לְךָ *Send for yourself* to mean לדעתך *because you want to* because that they had previously requested and the phrase שְׁלַח לְךָ *Send for yourself* is Hashem's consenting.

Sefer Bamidbar does not record Bnei Yisrael's initial request. According to the the Ramban (Bamidbar 13:2) Bnei Yisrael look better this way. Fascinatingly, the Malbim (Devorim 1:22) answers that although the people request meraglim, it is a well-known fact at the time when the Torah is written, and therefore unnecessary to state it explicitly. Accordingly, Sefer Bamidbar omits it. However, Sefer Devorim is written after that entire generation dies. In order to preserve that information, there is a need to record that Bnei Yisrael originally approached Moshe to send them.

Discussing when different books of the Torah are written is beyond our purview, however this Malbim would be an important part in that discussion (for more on this topic, see the Gemara Gitten 60a, Tosfos D"H Torah and Ramban's introduction to Torah). Similarly, discussing whether writing sections of Torah designed for Moshe's generation as a specific

and criticizes their lack of confidence, he is correct. They do initiate the dispatching of the meraglim, as represented in their second mission. In fact, the Torah's presentation in Sefer Devorim (1:22) captures the essence of the second mission, וַיַּחְפְּרוּ לָנוּ אֶת הָאָרֶץ וְיָשִׁבוּ אֹתָנוּ דָּבָר אֶת הַדֶּרֶךְ אֲשֶׁר נַעֲלֶה בָּהּ וְאֵת הֶעָרִים אֲשֶׁר נָבֹא אֲלֵיהֶן *And we will search the land and bring back word, the route we will travel and the cities that we will visit.*[348] The focus is on the demographics and topography. Moshe, in Sefer Devorim, reiterates the people's additional request and criticizes them for their lack of faith.

THE TORAH'S AMBIGUOUS PRESENTATION

Interestingly, the Torah does not explicitly state that the second mission is requested by Bnei Yisrael. Why not? Why present Bnei Yisrael's addition in an apparently vague fashion?

Perhaps the Torah's intent in blending the second mission into the first is to convey that that is precisely Bnei Yisrael's mindset when they request meraglim. Bnei Yisrael do not see their request as independent of Hashem's. It is simply an addition. Because they intend to subtly add to Hashem's command, not independently create their own, the Torah downplays their independent agenda just as they themselves do.

Bnei Yisrael do not see their addition as something independent, but rather the completion of Hashem's mission. Bnei Yisrael are unaware that Hashem intentionally omits details of a particular mission because His goal is for them to return and inspire the nation. This underscores their blindness to the problem in the first place. They do not even realize their own insecurities and cannot imagine Hashem sending meraglim to address that.

---

audience, or not, is also beyond our purview.

[348] That may clarify Chazal's (Sifri, Devorim 20) comment that Bnei Yisrael approach Moshe in a disorganized and hectic manner ילדים דוחפים את הזקנים זקנים דוחפים את הראשים *children were pushing elders and elders were pushing the leaders.* When requesting a second mission, Bnei Yisrael are is a state of disarray and chaos, reflecting a lack of trust in Hashem. It is not surprising that Moshe recalls this in Sefer Devorim, for that is where Moshe critiques the second mission.

FOR WHOM

With the understanding that the meraglim are sent to assuage Bnei Yisrael's lack of confidence, one can offer greater understanding of the phrase שְׁלַח לְךָ *Send for yourself.* Sending meraglim is for each individual, for the word לְךָ *yourself* is singular, not plural. The goal is for each individual person to develop the confidence needed to succeed in entering Eretz Yisrael.[349]

THE GRAVITY OF THEIR SIN

The meraglim are sent to spread confidence, not cast doubt.[350] Sadly the meraglim exacerbate the exact problem they are attempting to solve. They assess the land honestly, and describe it accurately, but only satisfy Bnei Yisrael's request. Their account does not fulfill Hashem's mission, the real reason behind their assignment. Hashem intends for the meraglim to return enthusiastically, dreaming of and yearning for Eretz Yisrael, emboldening the people to conquer and settle it. The goal is not to return with a report, but with hope.

Tragically, the meraglim do not inspire the nation for they, themselves, lack confidence.[351] Their poor self-image is more evident when they state, וַנְּהִי בְעֵינֵינוּ כַּחֲגָבִים וְכֵן הָיִינוּ בְּעֵינֵיהֶם *we were like grasshoppers in our eyes and in their eyes too!* (ibid 13:33). How the giants actually perceive the meraglim is not recorded for it is irrelevant. What

---

[349] The Kli Yakar (Bamidbar 13:2) offers several alternative explanations for לְךָ *for you.* One opinion is that לְךָ *for you* may be directed specifically to Moshe, as he benefits by having his life extended by forty years until Bnei Yisrael are ready to enter Eretz Yisrael. Another, is that it might empower Moshe with complete control over the decision of whom to send. A third, is that לְךָ *for you*, meaning according to your mistaken opinion, the meraglim are good people and likely to succeed. For Hashem, they are not, who He sees the future and knows that they will return with negative reports.
One may wonder why Hashem would have crafted such a plan when He is fully aware of the future and how negatively the meraglim would impact Bnei Yisrael. Perhaps the answer is that although Hashem has the capacity to act based upon His knowledge of the future, He does not. Instead, He interacts with the world as if He is unaware of the future. The philosophical implications are beyond this chapter's purview as well.

[350] Ramban (Bamidbar 13:2)

[351] According to Chazal (Sotah 35a and quoted by Rashi Bamidbar 13:31) the meraglim doubted whether Hashem Himself could be victorious. This illustrates just how deep their lack of faith is.

is important is how the meraglim see themselves, which is how they assume the giants see them.[352]

THE TRAGEDY: FROM TOP TO BOTTOM

The meraglim's sin reveals weak leadership and a complete lack of readiness to lead the people into Eretz Yisrael. And if the leaders sent to instill confidence cannot trust Hashem themselves, how can the people be expected to trust Him?[353] From top to bottom, leader to layman, the people are not ready to enter Eretz Yisrael.[354]

With this perspective, one can better understand Hashem's reaction. The meraglim's sin is not necessarily the most severe, but its impact is most tragically felt. Bnei Yisrael do not wander in the desert for forty years as a punishment, but rather as a natural consequence. Hashem decides to patiently wait for the next generation, one more prepared to enter Eretz Yisrael.[355] This also explains why there is no imminent death, unlike other sins recorded in the Torah.[356] In contrast to other sins where the punishment is immediate, here the deaths occur over the next forty years. The plan to enter Eretz Yisrael is temporary

---

[352] Because the Torah uses the phrase וַיֵּלְכוּ וַיָּבֹאוּ *And they went and they came*, Chazal (Sotah 35b and Rashi Bamidbar 13:26) state that the meraglim leave and return with the same negative mindset. This emphasizes just how bad the situation is. From departure, the meraglim plan to sabotage any optimism.

The Malbim (Bamidbar 13:23) disagrees, offering several proofs that the meraglim only develop their negative plans in Nachal Eshkol as implied throughout different verses in Tanach (Bamidbar 13:23, Devorim 1:24 and Yehoshua 14:12).

[353] Rav Yaakov Kamenetsky (Emes L'Yaakov Shemos 32:1 and Bamidbar 13:3) reiterates that the meraglim's sin is rooted in a lack of faith.

354   According to the Midrash (Midrash Tanchuma, Buber Edition, parshas Shelach 2 and quoted by Rashi Bamidbar 13:30) the only thing that Bnei Yisrael are interested in hearing is Kalev's criticism of Moshe. Kalev, taking advantage of this, begins with וכי זו בלבד עשה לנו בן עמרם *is that all Ben Amram (Moshe) did?* grabbing their attention before listing how wonderful Moshe has been for them.

[355] One may further suggest that this is the straw that breaks the camels back. Throughout the Torah, Bnei Yisrael struggle with developing the attitude needed to successfully enter and conquer Eretz Yisrael. For more on this topic, see the chapter entitled *Yehoshua's First Battle*.

[356] Alternatively, the Tosfos Yom Tov (Sotah 1:9) explains that Hashem's mercy allows this punishment to extend for forty years so those deserving punishment could extend their lives until age sixty.

postponed; allowing the next generation, a more positive and optimistic one, to enter the land.[357]

Hashem's response of עַד אָנָה יְנַאֲצֻנִי הָעָם הַזֶּה וְעַד אָנָה לֹא יַאֲמִינוּ בִי *How long will the nation provoke me? And how long will they not trust me?* (Bamidbar 14:11) reinforces this perspective. Hashem does not criticize them for maliciously disobeying, but for lacking faith in Him.

HOW COULD YEHOSHUA REPEAT THIS MISTAKE?

Surprisingly, immediately after the forty years passed, Yehoshua sends meraglim to Yericho prior to Bnei Yisrael's entrance into the land (Yehoshua 2:1). Would it not have been wiser to avoid repeating mistakes of the previous generation? If anyone should have known better, it would surely have been Yehoshua, for he witnessed first-hand the mistake of the meraglim. What is Yehoshua thinking?

YEHOSHUA'S MERAGLIM

In order to understand why Yehoshua, having seen first-hand the epic failure of the meraglim, still sends his own meraglim, it pays to focus upon the differences between the two episodes, for Yehoshua sends them in an entirely different fashion.

1. In Sefer Bamidbar, the meraglim are sent from Midbar Paran, a considerable distance from Eretz Yisrael, while Yehoshua sends them from Shitim, a location close to their destination.[358]

2. Moshe sends twelve meraglim while Yehoshua sends only two.[359]

---

[357] Presumably the slave mentality cripples them to the point where they can not get past their pessimistic perspective and continuous complaining. Bnei Yisrael having a slave mentality is developed by the Ibn Ezra (Shemos 14:13) who asks why Bnei Yisrael do not defend themselves at the Yam Suf, when they clearly and significantly outnumbered the Egyptians. He answers that since the Egyptians have ruled over the Hebrew slaves for so long, and they are raised from a young age to listen subserviently to them, they are incapable of defending themselves. That is why, the Ibn Ezra continues, the next generation has to be the ones to enter, fight and conquer Eretz Yisrael.

[358] Malbim Yehoshua 2:1

[359] Malbim Bamidbar 13:2

3. The Torah focuses on each of the spies coming from a different tribe.[360] By contrast, the identity of Yehoshua's meraglim's tribes are omitted by the Navi.

4. The Torah emphasizes the names of the meraglim that Moshe sends,[361] while Yehoshua sends his anonymously, as the Navi stresses חֶרֶשׁ *quietly*[362] (Yehoshua 2:1).[363]

5. In Sefer Bamidbar, there is a large public ceremony sending the meraglim off. In contrast, no one besides Yehoshua even knows the meraglim are sent.

6. Sefer Bamidbar (13:2) uses the word לתור *to search* while in Sefer Yehoshua, the word used is לרגל *to spy* (Yehoshua 2:1).

7. Moshe's meraglim investigate all of Eretz Yisrael; Yehoshua's look at Yericho alone.

8. The meraglim in Sefer Bamidbar record the demographics and topography, and bring back food. Yehoshua's meraglim encounter and interact with Rachav.[364]

9. In Sefer Bamidbar, the meraglim return to a public gathering to share their report. In Sefer Yehoshua, the meraglim report directly to Yehoshua and only to Yehoshua, as the Navi stresses וַיָּשֻׁבוּ שְׁנֵי הָאֲנָשִׁים ... **וַיָּבֹאוּ אֶל יְהוֹשֻׁעַ בֶּן נוּן וַיְסַפְּרוּ לוֹ** *And the two men returned ... and they came to Yehoshua Bin Nun and they told him.* Twice the Navi comments that the spies came to Yehoshua alone, וַיֹּאמְרוּ אֶל יְהוֹשֻׁעַ *And they said to Yehoshua* (Yehoshua 2:23-24) and וַיְסַפְּרוּ לוֹ *and they told him.*[365]

As we explained, Hashem's goal in sending meraglim in the Torah is to uplift the morale of Bnei Yisrael. Twelve leaders are designated to return, publicly announce the land's splendor and beauty and that,

---

[360] With the exception of the tribe of Levi where none of the meraglim came from.

[361] As we described. According to the Ramban (Bamidbar 13:4) the Torah orders them according to their importance.

[362] Malbim Bamidbar 13:2

[363] Chazal (Midrash Tanchuma, Parshas Shelach 1) identify them as Pinchas and Kalev.

[364] Abarbanel (Yehoshua 2:1) and Malbim (Yehoshua 2:1)

[365] The Abarbanel (Yehoshua 2:1) and Malbim (Yehoshua 2:1) add that in Sefer Bamidbar, the nation, Bnei Yisrael request the meraglim (as indicated in Devorim 1:22-23) while in Sefer Yehoshua it is the leader, Yehoshua.
Another difference the Radak (Yehoshua 2:1) notes is that these meraglim are significantly greater than the ones sent in the Torah.

with Hashem's help, it could be conquered. Because there is one spy from each tribe, each tribe is properly represented by someone aware of the needs of their tribe and trusted by its members.

Yehoshua does not repeat previous mistakes because his meraglim have a completely different agenda. They have a military agenda, not a religiously uplifting one. Yehoshua's meraglim go to carefully investigate Yericho's people, their attitude and mindset, and report back to Yehoshua alone. In fact, that is exactly how the Navi records their findings וַיְסַפְּרוּ לוֹ אֵת כָּל הַמֹּצְאוֹת אוֹתָם *and they told **him** all of their findings* (Yehoshua 2:2).[366] וַיְסַפְּרוּ לוֹ *and they told him*: him and only him. Military spies report to the general alone.

This is also why Yehoshua sends his spies from an adjacent location. Because they are military spies preparing for an immediate battle, they are sent just before the battle to determine the morale of the enemy. Moshe, by contrast, sends the meraglim from Midbar Paran, a location a great distance away. While still in the desert, there is a need to boost Bnei Yisrael's morale.

Additionally, because the original plan is for the meraglim to return inspired and motivate Bnei Yisrael, Moshe sends twelve important, well-known and trustworthy leaders, אנשים *men*. He sends them off publicly, building towards the great moment of their return. Furthermore, there is an enormous ceremony awaiting their return, anticipating their positive report designed to uplift and inspire the nation. By contrast, Yehoshua sends only two, he sends them off quietly, and they return and report to him alone.

Yehoshua's meraglim succeed and enable Bnei Yisrael to more effectively enter Eretz Yisrael; however, sadly, the meraglim in Torah damage Bnei Yisrael's morale and delay their entry into Eretz Yisrael.

---

[366] Several events that occur in Sefer Yehoshua parallel previous ones mentioned in the Torah. In addition to the meraglim as we developed, Yehoshua's encounter with the Sar Tzava Hashem *military angel of Hashem* (Yehoshua 5:13-15) corresponds with Moshe's encounter with the burning bush (Shemos 3). The war against Ai (Yehoshua 8) recalls the war with Amalek as in both cases, men women and children are to be killed (ibid 22-29). The Karban Pesach brought in Sefer Yehoshua (ibid 5:9-12) clearly recalls the Karban Pesach brought during the Exodus (Shemos 12). The bris milah performed in Sefer Yehoshua (Yehoshua 5) bears resemblance to the bris milah performed after the Exodus (Shemos 12:44, 48), and lastly, the karbanos at Har Eval (Yehoshua 8:30-35) resemble those brought at Har Sinai (Shemos 24:2-5). See "Double Take" chapter *Yehoshua and The Challenges of Following Moshe's Footsteps* for elaboration.

PARALLEL TO THE TWELVE BROTHERS

There is a fascinating parallel to uncover based on similarities between our narrative and the one where Yosef, serving as second-in-command to the king in Egypt, accuses his brothers of being meraglim in Sefer Bereshis.

1. In Sefer Bamidbar, one man represents each tribe (Bamidbar 13:2 and 4-15). And needless to say, in Sefer Bereshis, each brother represents his tribe.

2. On each occasion the central religious leader sends a group identified as spies. Moshe sends the meraglim and Yaakov sends his sons who are accused of being spies.

3. In both situations, Bnei Yisrael are hesitant about entering a new country. Yaakov is clearly reluctant to go to Egypt (Bereshis 45:26). In Sefer Bamidbar, the second half of the meraglim's mission is only necessary because of Bnei Yisrael's apprehensiveness.

4. In both circumstances, Bnei Yisrael's ultimate destination is a fulfillment of a promise made to Avraham at Bris Ben HaBisarim. Avraham is told that his children will suffer in a foreign land (ibid 15:13) and subsequently return to Eretz Yisrael (ibid 15:14-21). The narrative in Bereshis ushers in the suffering of slavery and in Sefer Bamidbar, the return to Eretz Yisrael.

5. In both situations, Bnei Yisrael travel to a country with significantly better food than the one they are currently in. Yaakov, during a famine, sends his sons to return with food for himself and his family (Bereshis 42:2), and the meraglim are sent to return with food to represent the quality of Eretz Yisrael (Bamidbar 13:20).

6. Yaakov sends ten of his twelve sons to Egypt, all besides for Yosef and Binyamin. Essentially the group division is ten and two. Similarly, Yehoshua and Kalev, are separated as a smaller group of two, for only they return speaking positively about Eretz Yisrael. The other ten return with a negative report. In both episodes there are groups of twelve that can be subdivided into smaller groups of ten and two.

7. When the situation seems hopeless, Yehuda, in a powerful and surprising speech challenges Yosef and tries to defend and protect Binyamin. Similarly, Kalev, not coincidentally from Shevet Yehuda,

steps up in an equally unexpected way[367] and speaks out in defense of Eretz Yisrael.[368]

8. Both stories conclude with an unforeseen cry. Yosef unexpectedly loses control of his emotion and weeps (Bereshis 42:24, 43:30, 45:2) and when it is decreed that Bnei Yisrael are to remain in the desert for forty years, they cry as well (Bamidbar 14:1).[369]

The Differences Between the Stories

Although there are similarities between the two episodes, there are several important differences as well which may hint to an important message. After listing them, we will return to understand the Torah's message.

1. In Bereshis, the brothers travel from Eretz Yisrael to Mitzrayim, whereas in Bamidbar they travel in the opposite direction, from Mitzrayim to Eretz Yisrael.

---

[367] Why is it Kalev who quiets the nation? Perhaps his non-central role is precisely what enables him to succeed in quieting the people. In contrast to Yehoshua, who from a young age is groomed to replace Moshe, Kalev does not even previously appear in the Torah. Whereas everyone could have predicted what Yehoshua is going to report, people are genuinely curious as to what Kalev thinks.
According to the Seforno (Bamidbar 13:16), Moshe changes Yehoshua's name immediately before sending the meraglim whereas the Rashbam (Bamidbar 13:16) argues that the name change took place significantly earlier. Either way, Moshe changing only Yehoshua's name supports Yehoshua's role as Moshe's primary student. Alone these lines, Rav Shimshon Rafael Hirsch (Bamidbar 13:16) adds that that Yehoshua's name change is designed to remind him as well as the other meraglim of their mission. Yehoshua's unique role is clear. The Emes L'Yaakov (Bamidbar 13:16) regarding the name change argues that Kalev does not need a name change like Yehoshua. Kalev has a better wife which leads him to have the courage necessary to remain strong.
An alternative reason why Yehoshua does not quiet the people is because Yehoshua is planning on leading Bnei Yisrael into Eretz Yisrael, it would have looked self-promoting for him to publicly encourage them to go to Eretz Yisrael (Meshech Chochoma Bamidbar 13:30).

[368] It is a greater surprise according to Chazal (Sotah 35a and quoted by Rashi Bamidbar 13:30) who explain Kalev's strategy as originally misleading the nation by pretending to slander Moshe in order to grab their attention, וכי זו בלבד עשה לנו בן עמרם סברי בגנותיה קא משתעי אישתיקו אמר להו הוציאנו ממצרים וקרע לנו את הים והאכילנו את המן Is this all Ben *Amram* did? They thought he (Kalev) intended to besmirch him (Moshe), so they were quiet. He said to them 'He took us from Egypt, split the Yam, fed us mann"

[369] Hashem responds, אתם בכיתם בכיה של חנם ואני קובע לכם בכיה לדורות *you cried unnecessarily, I will cause you to cry for generations* (Taanis 29a).

2. Although Yehuda and Kalev both speak out in an unexpected manner, Yehuda's is effective, as his argument is accepted. Kalev, and his argument, are not.

3. In Sefer Bamidbar, the group sent is not caught nor accused of being spies, while in fact, they are. Yaakov's children are apprehended and accused of being spies, when in truth, they are not.

4. In Sefer Bereshis, Yaakov is ambivalent about settling in Mitzrayim. In Sefer Bamidbar, the opposite occurs, as Bnei Yisrael are hesitant about settling in Eretz Yisrael.

5. In Sefer Bamidbar, the meraglim are sent to bring back a story and, instead, they bring back food. In Sefer Bereshis, they are sent to bring back food and instead, they come back with a story.

6. Although food is brought back in each episode, it is for disparate reasons. The food being brought to Eretz Yisrael by Yaakov's sons is for survival, while the food being brought back by the meraglim is for the purposes of examination.[370]

7. When the brothers embark upon a great challenge, they introspect deeply and do teshuva *repentance* (Bereshis 42:21). Sadly, in Sefer Bamidbar, the opposite is true. Instead of introspecting and repenting, the meraglim stray from Hashem, leading the people to distrust Him.

8. Although both stories conclude with crying, it happens for completely different reasons. Whereas Bnei Yisrael, in Sefer Bamidbar, cry selfishly for themselves, Yosef cries selflessly for his brothers.

THE CONTRAST

Why does the Torah weave this comparison and contrast into the narrative of Yaakov's sons? What lesson does each narrative contain that might shed light on the other?

---

[370] Interestingly, the food in Eretz Yisrael is of higher quality but it is not consistently reliable. By contrast, Mitzrayim, due to the Nile, always has water allowing for a greater agricultural stability. This contrast of how each country gets its water is significant. Mitzrayim receives water from the Nile, consistently, without any need to pray to Hashem for it, while Eretz Yisrael's water supply comes from rain, which creates a continuous need for prayer (Devorim 11:10 – 12).

The Yosef affair demonstrates that Hashem orchestrates and intervenes in life. Beyond the overarching theme of the hashgacha pratis *divine intervention*, the details of the story further support this motif. When confronted with trouble, Yosef's brothers look up to Hashem for guidance with complete trust and faith. After being accused of being meraglim, the brothers remark, אֲבָל אֲשֵׁמִים אֲנַחְנוּ עַל אָחִינוּ אֲשֶׁר רָאִינוּ צָרַת נַפְשׁוֹ בְּהִתְחַנְנוֹ אֵלֵינוּ וְלֹא שָׁמָעְנוּ עַל כֵּן בָּאָה אֵלֵינוּ הַצָּרָה הַזֹּאת *but we are guilty on account of our brother when we saw his suffering, when he pleaded with us, we did not listen. Therefore this pain has befallen us* (Bereshis 42:21).

Yaakov's sons travel down to Mitzrayim without the foreknowledge that they are entering a situation that would recall their previous sin, that of selling Yosef. They immediately begin to introspect and reflect on Mechiras Yosef. Yosef, too, consistently sees his experiences of being sold and his journey from there to kingship as part of Hashem's divine plan (Bereshis 45:8, 50:19-21).[371]

The Mechiras Yosef narrative serves as a perfect foil for the meraglim episode in Sefer Bamidbar, for the faith and ability to see Hashem's hashgacha pratis is exactly what the meraglim and Bnei Yisrael lack in the desert. Instead of trusting Hashem, they request that meraglim investigate the quality of Eretz Yisrael. The meraglim report that the obstacles to Eretz Yisrael's conquest are insurmountable, revealing their profound lack of faith that Hashem will take care of them. Instead of calming and reassuring an apprehensive nation, the leaders spread slander, thereby undermining the people's religious confidence and trust in Hashem.

By contrast, in Sefer Bereshis, Yaakov's sons trust Hashem, recognize His providence and turn to Him during times of need. In Sefer Bamidbar, Bnei Yisrael have a significantly greater reason to have that faith in Him. Having seen the extraordinary miracles performed during the Exodus from Mitzrayim, they should have been able to muster up the faith to confidently enter Eretz Yisrael. Unfortunately, because of their distrust and negative attitude, the meraglim doubt Hashem and encourage the nation to do the same. Bnei Yisrael should

---

[371] Additionally, Yosef refuses adultery with Ashes Potifar explaining that he cannot חָטָאתִי לֵאלֹהִים *sin to Hashem* (Bereshis 39:9) and communicates to both the Sar Hamashkim and Sar Haofim that הֲלוֹא לֵאלֹהִים פִּתְרֹנִים *is it not Hashem who interprets dream?* (ibid 40:8) before interpreting their respective dreams. Similarly, Yosef informs Paroh אֲשֶׁר הָאֱלֹהִים עֹשֶׂה הֶרְאָה אֶת פַּרְעֹה *that which Hashem will do, He shows Paroh* (ibid 40:28).

have known that committed religious behavior is rewarded with great success. This lack of faith is why this generation is not ready to enter and conquer Eretz Yisrael, and consequently, Hashem decides to wait for the next.

THE CONNECTION TO MIRIAM

According to Chazal, the meraglim narrative is juxtaposed with Miriam speaking derogatorily about Moshe because they failed to learn from her and proceed to speak slanderously about Eretz Yisrael. Perhaps the connection is deeper than the mere parallel that both spoke negatively.[372]

Just like the meraglim fail to trust Hashem's decision about which land to dwell in, so too Miriam fails to trust Hashem's decision about which Navi to choose. Both Eretz Yisrael and Moshe are special and elevated, yet both the meraglim and Miriam subtly challenge Hashem's decision. Instead of supporting Hashem's selection, the meraglim do not learn from Miriam and undermine His decision. Instead of inspiring the people to trust Hashem, they themselves do not and therefore fail to inspire the nation to do so.

APPLYING TEXT TO LIFE: THE HASHKAFIC MESSAGE

The meraglim's shortcomings underscore how important a good attitude is for leadership. It is the leaders' responsibility to navigate, inspire and direct the people. Positivity is contagious, and good leadership does this with an optimistic vision. Hope is surprisingly powerful. It is hope and optimism that excite people about a brighter future, fuel the fire of dream, and are building blocks for achievement. For Bnei Yisrael to succeed militantly or politically, they require hope.

---

[372] The meraglim's point of departure is Midbar Paran precisely because it is the next stop after Chatziros where Miriam mistakenly speaks lashon hara (Kli Yakar Bamidbar 13:3). Hashem commands the meraglim's departure right after Miriam, hoping they would learn from her mistake. Presumably this is what the Torah emphasizes with וְאַחַר נָסְעוּ הָעָם מֵחֲצֵרוֹת וַיַּחֲנוּ בְּמִדְבַּר פָּארָן *And after the nation traveled from Chatziros and they camped in Midbar Paran* (Bamidbar 12:16).

Nationally, the transition from the lifestyle in the desert to that of living in Eretz Yisrael requires hard work. In the desert, Bnei Yisrael eat *mann*, food that falls from the sky, and drink water from the Baer Miriam or that which emerges miraculously from rocks. Perhaps the Midbar lifestyle, a metaphysical and supernatural existence is designed to imbue Bnei Yisrael with the trust and belief in Hashem they would ultimately need when they began a mundane existence in Eretz Yisrael.[373] Experiencing Hashem in the supernatural is convincing and is designed to inspire one to continue seeing Hashem in the natural.

Additionally, and most importantly, is trust in Hashem. Having faith that Hashem will help is critical, especially for something as central as returning to inhabit Eretz Yisrael.

---

[373] The Netziv (Introduction to Bamidbar) explains that the entire Sefer Bamidbar is designed to capture this transition. This meraglim narrative fits perfectly into Sefer Bamidbar's theme.

Korach's Loud Message Delivered Through the Vehicle of Silence

Korach's Halachik Debate

The Midrash famously records,[374]

And (Korach) said to Moshe, 'a talis which is completely techeles (turquoise), what is the halacha, should it be exempt from tzitzis?' (Moshe) said 'it is obligated.' (Korach) said 'a talis which is completely techeles is not exempt, but four suffice (on a standard garment)!?! (Korach further asked) 'A house of (holy) books, what is the halacha, should it be exempt from mezuzah?' (Moshe) said, 'it is obligated in mezuzah.' (Korach) said 'the entire Torah, 275 parsheyos do not exempt a house, but one mezuzah exempts the entire house!?!' (Korach continued and) said 'these were not commanded to you, (rather) from your heart you created them' (Shemos Rabbah, Vilna Edition, 18:3).

אמר למשה טלית שכולה
תכלת מהו שתהא פטורה מן
הציצית א"ל חייבת בציצית
א"ל קרח טלית שכולה תכלת
אין פוטרת עצמה ארבע חוטין
פוטרות אותה, בית מלא
ספרים מהו שיהא פטור מן
המזוזה אמר לו חייב במזוזה
א"ל כל התורה כולה רע"ה
פרשיות אינה פוטרת את הבית
פרשה אחת שבמזוזה פוטרת
את הבית אמר לו דברים אלו
לא נצטוית עליהן ומלבך אתה
בודאן

The Midrash's narrative presents Korach challenging Moshe regarding two separate halachos. Korach first attacks Moshe concerning the laws of techeles *turquoise* of the tzitzis *strings* that are tied to the

---

[374] This episode is found in several other Midrashim as well, sometimes with additional examples (See Midrash Tanchuma Parshas Korach 2 for example).

corners of garments.[375] Korach reasons that a garment completely made of techeles should not also require a string of the tzitzis to be techeles. After all, the entire garment is turquoise. The second challenge is that a room filled with seferim *holy books* should need no mezuzah.

What is at the core of Korach'a attack? Of all the potential questions to launch at Moshe, why these two? Does this debate between Korach and Moshe revolve around a mere technical halachik issue? The two cases that Korach hounds Moshe with are so strikingly similar to each other that it seems purposeful. We must consider them both to be one overarching debate. What point is Korach driving at? And in addition to uncovering the theological or political point that Korach is making, where do Chazal see it in the text of the Torah itself?

With a deeper understanding of the narrative, we will try to gather clues to develop a theory and then return to answer these questions.

What Does Korach Take?

The Korach narrative begins with the phrase, וַיִּקַּח קֹרַח *And Korach took* (Bamidbar 16:1), yet never records what he took. Even more strange, the verse seems incomplete, for the Torah does not return to finishing the thought. The verse seems incomplete. What is the intent behind this abruptness?

Moshe's Different Conversations

There are several additional elements to the Torah's presentation of Korach's rebellion and Moshe's response that seem to not add up.

The people approach Moshe complaining, רַב לָכֶם כִּי כָל הָעֵדָה כֻּלָּם קְדֹשִׁים וּבְתוֹכָם יְקֹוָק וּמַדּוּעַ תִּתְנַשְּׂאוּ עַל קְהַל יְקֹוָק *Too much! All of the nation is holy and Hashem is among them. Why do you raise yourself above Hashem's nation?* Moshe reacts by falling on his face (ibid 16:4). How does Moshe understand their complaint and why does he react this way?

---

[375] The Baal Haturim (Bamidbar 16:1) explains that the juxtaposition of tzitzis to Korach hints to Korach arguing on the laws of tzitzis.

Moshe's response is a bifurcated one. Moshe first offers the people a test designed to determine who Hashem actually desires, קְחוּ לָכֶם מַחְתּוֹת *take for yourselves pans* (ibid 16:6) and in the morning Hashem will reveal His choice.[376] Moshe accepts their argument completely and responds by suggesting that Hashem should determine who He sees fit. Next, Moshe focuses on Bnei Levi, reprimanding them for requesting religious roles that are not designed or appropriate for them (ibid 16:8-11).

After speaking with those who complain and then the Bnei Levi, Moshe continues by attempting a third conversation with Dasan and Aviram. Seemingly disengaged, they respond לֹא נַעֲלֶה *we will not come up* (ibid 16:12), indicating they have absolutely no interest in dialogue. Still, they add a biting complaint,

Is it not enough that you have taken us up from a land flowing with milk and honey to kill us in the desert, now you rule over us. Also, you did not deliver us to a land flowing with milk and honey, even if you gouge out the eyes of those men, we will not come up (ibid 16:13).	הַמְעַט כִּי הֶעֱלִיתָנוּ מֵאֶרֶץ זָבַת חָלָב וּדְבַשׁ לַהֲמִיתֵנוּ בַּמִּדְבָּר כִּי תִשְׂתָּרֵר עָלֵינוּ גַּם הִשְׂתָּרֵר: אַף לֹא אֶל אֶרֶץ זָבַת חָלָב וּדְבַשׁ הֲבִיאֹתָנוּ וַתִּתֶּן לָנוּ נַחֲלַת שָׂדֶה וָכָרֶם הַעֵינֵי הָאֲנָשִׁים הָהֵם תְּנַקֵּר לֹא נַעֲלֶה

It is noteworthy that this series of objections is presented with a chiastic structure. First, Dasan and Aviram say לֹא נַעֲלֶה *we will not come up* before proceeding to misrepresent how Bnei Yisrael were taken מֵאֶרֶץ זָבַת חָלָב וּדְבַשׁ *from a land flowing with milk and honey* and finally protesting Moshe's תִשְׂתָּרֵר *rule*. They then use the exact same phrases but in the reverse order, saying Moshe's הִשְׂתָּרֵר *rule* is excessive and that they were not brought אֶל אֶרֶץ זָבַת חָלָב וּדְבַשׁ *to a land flowing with milk and honey*, before concluding with the phrase that they opened with: לֹא נַעֲלֶה *we will not come up*, creating a perfect chiasm.

What is the Torah hinting at by recording their response in a chiastic structure? Why present their reply in this manner?

Lastly, and perhaps most interestingly, Moshe's response to Dasan and Aviram differs significantly from his previous reactions. Here, instead of falling on his face, or even rebuking anyone, as he does to

---

[376] However, according to the Malbim (Bamidbar 16:6-7), Aharon is not included in this test. Instead it is to determine which of the two hundred and fifty men or Korach should be selected, even if theoretically Aharon would step down.

Korach, Moshe gets extremely angry and in an uncharacteristic manner, requests from Hashem אַל תֵּפֶן אֶל מִנְחָתָם *do not accept their offerings* (ibid 16:15). Why?

The strength of this reaction is unprecedented in the Torah. What makes this occasion significantly different from previous ones?

WHO SINS?

Later in the story, Hashem instructs both Moshe and Aharon to separate themselves from the rest of the nation. They both fall on their faces and reply, אֵל אֱלֹהֵי הָרוּחֹת לְכָל בָּשָׂר הָאִישׁ אֶחָד יֶחֱטָא וְעַל כָּל הָעֵדָה תִּקְצֹף *God, Lord of all spirits, one man sins and you get angry with the entire nation* (ibid 16:22). How can Moshe and Aharon seriously claim that only one man sinned? Presumably they are referring to Korach, but are Dasan and Aviram innocent? If Moshe gets so frustrated with Dasan and Aviram earlier, how does he forget them now?

UNDERSTANDING KORACH'S REBELLION

The key to understanding Korach's rebellion is realizing that Korach oversees two distinct groups with two opposing agendas. The first group is composed of two hundred and fifty well-intentioned leaders (ibid 16:2) including many Levi'im, sincerely looking for deeper spirituality.[377] The second group is Dasan and Aviram; two troublemakers using this as an opportunity to undermine Moshe's leadership.[378]

The first group has a genuine desire for greater religious opportunity. They honestly seek more spirituality. Innocently, they comment, כִּי כָל הָעֵדָה כֻּלָּם קְדֹשִׁים וּבְתוֹכָם יְקֹוָק *All of the nation is holy*

---

[377] The Midrash Tanchuma (Parshas Korach 1) even identifies the two hundred and fifty men as גדולי ישראל *great (members of) Yisrael*, and members of the Sanhedrin.

[378] Netziv (Bamidbar 16:1). Slightly differently, the Malbim (Bamidbar 16:1) argues that there are many smaller groups with many different agendas. Korach wants to be the Kohen Gadol. Dasan, Aviram and On ben Peles feel that the status of firstborn was wrongfully taken from Reuven. Other firstborns are angry that their firstborn status was given to Kohanim and to make things worse, they mistakenly think that Moshe decided this on his own volition (Malbim ibid 16:2, also see the Ibn Ezra Bamidbar 16:1).

and Hashem is among them. Dasan and Aviram, by contrast, are not interested in conversation. They are troublemakers who simply want to complain.[379] Unwilling to face Moshe, they prefer snubbing him by denying a meeting with him, while communicating all of their negativity through other channels.

Their statements are presented in a chiastic structure, as mentioned above, because talking reason to them is unproductive and useless. One cannot get anywhere with them and the conversation is guaranteed to end the way it began. The Torah symbolically captures this inability to get anywhere with them by presenting their arguments in chiastic structure.

The Torah further displays their inflexibility by quoting their revealing response לֹא נַעֲלֶה *we will not come up;* not לֹא נבוא *we will not come,* or לֹא נלך *we will not go.*[380] This further hints to who they really are, people uninterested in religious elevation.

Upon hearing the first group's sincere question כִּי כָל הָעֵדָה כֻּלָּם קְדֹשִׁים וּבְתוֹכָם יְקֹוָק *All of the nation is holy and Hashem is among them,* Moshe falls on his face. Although the Torah does not explain why, one can assume that he is either surprised, shamed[381] or in prayer.[382] All of these responses reflect a deep respect and care for this group. Nothing like that happens with Dasan and Aviram.

In order to better appreciate the stark contrast the Torah makes in presenting these two groups, it pays to list the differences.

1. The first group of two hundred and fifty men request more spirituality. Dasan and Aviram communicate the opposite, לֹא נַעֲלֶה *we will not come up.* They are disinterested in spiritual elevation.

---

[379] Chazal, and Rashi echoing them, identify Dasan and Aviram as troublemakers throughout the Torah. They are the two slaves fighting who Moshe attempts to break up (Shemos Rabbah, Vilna Edition 1:29, Rashi Shemos 2:13 and 18:4), those who tell Paroh that Moshe killed the Egyptian attempting to have Moshe put to death (Nedarim 64b, Rashi 4:19), and the two who do not trust Moshe and save *mann* after being instructed not to (Rashi Shemos 16:20).

[380] Midrash Tanchuma Korach Parsha 3. The Midrash even reports that Moshe attempts to go to them, but is met with great resistance, as they curse at him upon seeing him. Alternatively, the Netziv (Bamidbar 16:12) explains, the Mishkan is located at a higher location and them stating לֹא נַעֲלֶה *we will not come up* simply means that they are not interested in coming up to Moshe.

[381] Chizkuni (Bamidbar 16:4) and Bechor Shor (Bamidbar 16:4)

[382] Rashbam (Bamidbar 16:4), Netziv (Bamidbar 16:4), one opinion quite by the Avi Ezri (Bamidbar 16:4 note 1)

2. The first group approaches Moshe with an interest in dialogue and Moshe responds by engaging in conversation. By contrast, Moshe reaches out to Dasan and Aviram who are unwilling to even meet him. They tell Moshe that they have no interest in talking.

3. Moshe speaks with the first group face to face. Because Dasan and Aviram refuse to meet Moshe, he can only communicate with them via a messenger.

4. For the first group Moshe falls on his face, reflecting some positive sentiment toward them. He does no such thing for Dasan and Aviram.

5. The two hundred and fifty men, although pursuing the wrong approach, are interested in religious growth, solving problems and improving the future. They envision a future with greater spirituality. Dasan and Aviram focus solely on the past, complaining and offering no constructive suggestions to address and solve the problems they raise.

6. Moshe arranges an opportunity for Hashem to choose one of the two hundred and fifty men. Moshe is genuinely open to having Hashem select one of them if He wants to. Regarding Dasan and Aviram, Moshe does just the opposite. He prays for Hashem not to even give them a chance.

7. Perhaps the clearest distinction is contrasting the two hundred and fifty men who are being consumed by fire and brought *up* to heaven,[383] with Dasan and Aviram (along with some of Korach's family) who are sent *down* as the earth opens its mouth to swallow them (ibid 16:33-34).[384] Whereas one group is elevated, the other descends downwards (ibid 16:35).

Moshe's different reactions clearly highlight his different perspective on these two separate groups with their contrasting agendas. Moshe discourages the Bnei Levi, part of the first group, from misbehaving. Then, he falls on his face and respectfully offers them a genuine

---

[383] This is similar to Nadav and Avihu, who also mistakenly aspire a religious experience in an inappropriate manner. Both groups desire spirituality and look for it in a misguided manner and both are consumed by fire (Netziv Bamidbar 16:35).

[384] According to the Chizkuni (Bamidbar 16:32), Korach's wife, small children and servants are swallowed up, but his sons are not as, the verse attests וּבְנֵי קֹרַח לֹא מֵתוּ *And Korach's sons did not die* (Bamidbar 26:11). Rashi (Bamidbar 26:11) argues that they are swallowed by the earth, but since they repent, they are given an elevated place in hell.

opportunity to be selected by Hashem. Hashem reinforces this group's sincerity by consuming them in fire and bringing them up to heaven. That is very different from Dasan and Aviram. Throughout the entire story, neither Moshe nor Hashem has sympathy for them. Unlike the first group, Dasan and Aviram are not misguided innocent people, they are troublemakers.

Understanding that only One Man Sins

With this new perspective, we can understand how Moshe responds to Hashem saying that only one man sins. The answer may be simple. Dasan and Aviram are physically separate from the larger group at the time, which is not surprising because they are not really part of that group at all. Because Dasan and Aviram are not part of this group, there is only one man from the two hundred and fifty who maliciously sins, Korach.

The Strategy of Silence

Interestingly, throughout the entire episode, the Torah does not record anything that Korach says. Korach simply never speaks to his followers, Dasan and Aviram, to Moshe, or to anyone. Why does the Torah not record anything that Korach says?

Korach's strategy is to skillfully unite everyone who has complaints regardless of what their issue is.[385] He does not preach any message, does not dream or even offer a solution to any problem. He offers no message because he fears preaching could undermine his ability to unite such ideologically disparate groups. It is precisely because Korach collects complaints, and does nothing more, that he is so successful in gathering together these opposing groups.

This ability to assemble different groups without offering any real message may be captured by the Torah's introduction to Korach, וַיִּקַּח קֹרַח *And Korach took*. Korach attracts different groups[386] without

---

[385] Malbim (Bamidbar 16:3)

[386] Ibn Ezra (Bamidbar 16:1), Rashbam (Bamidbar 16:1) Chizkuni (Bamidbar 16:1), one opinion quoted by the Kli Yakar (Bamidbar 16:1) and the Netziv (Bamidbar 16:1).

anything substantive unifying them. By saying וַיִּקַּח קֹרַח *And Korach took,* that he takes them, but intentionally not finishing the sentence, the Torah reinforces that Korach gathers them without a purpose or greater goal. He does take them, but for no cause and to no particular place.

Korach's message is no more profound than this particular leadership, and perhaps leadership in general, is bad. Both groups, albeit for very different reasons, subscribe to Korach's rebellion. Both groups want less leadership so they can do what they please, whether it be to search for more or less spirituality. With no alternative dream, or direction, Korach's rebellion is already seen as divisive.

Once it is clear that Korach preaches no particular ideology, his motives must be reexamined. Because Korach does not lead based on ideals, there is not much else to motivate him besides selfishness desire for his own honor.[387] The Torah's introduction to Korach, וַיִּקַּח קֹרַח *And Korach took* (Bamidbar 16:1), captures something else as well. By not stating ויאסף קרח *And Korach gathers,* or something similar, and instead communicating that he took, the Torah again insinuates Korach's selfishness.

The Midrash (Vilna Edition, Bamidbar Rabbah 18:2) echoes this understanding, accusing Korach of thinking הייתי ראוי להיות נשיא... הריני חולק עליו ומבטל כל מה שנעשה על ידו לכך ויקח קרח *I am entitled to be the prince ... I will rebel and undermine everything he did, therefore 'and Korach took'.* Korach believes that if he cannot be special, then no one should. The Midrash supports its claim from the verse, וַיִּקַּח קֹרַח *And Korach took* reinforcing that Korach does not take anything in any substantive direction.

The Mishneh (Avos 5:17) famously describes Korach's rebellion as paradigmatically not L'Shem Shamayim *for the sake of heaven,* ושאינה לשם שמים? זו מחלוקת קרח וכל עדתו *And which (argument) is not*

However, many other answers are offered. Rashi (Bamidbar 16:1) explains that Korach takes himself away from everyone else in order to undermine the priesthood. Alternatively, the Midrash (Midrash Tanchuma Parshas Korach 3) and Rabaynu Bachaya (Bamidbar 16:1) explain that he takes a talis in his hand to use when arguing with Moshe about its halachos. Another answer presented by the Kli Yakar (ibid 16:1) is that Korach's "taking" here means that he develops complaints. Some (Onkelus Bamidbar 16:1 and one opinion quoted by the Ramban Bamidbar 16:1) translate וַיִּקַּח as *and he divided* or *thought* (one opinion quoted by the Ramban Bamidbar 16:1).

[387] Rabaynu Ovadia M'Bartinura (Avos 5:17)

L'Shem Shamayim? Korach and his followers. This Mishneh conveys two important points. This rebellion is not L'Shem Shamayim because Korach stands for nothing, and offers no constructive goals. Additionally, by the Mishneh omitting who Korach and his followers fight against, the implication is that they fight with each other.[388] This inner squabbling is completely understandable because his followers comprise of two groups with opposing agendas.

KORACH'S NAME

Based on what we have developed so far, one can understand how Korach's name hints to his actions. The name Korach comes from the word קרחה *divide*.[389] Korach is divisive. Without substance or content, he divisively gathers different groups merely to undermine the leadership.

REVIEWING KORACH'S ARGUMENTS

With this new understanding, we can return and explain the initial Midrash that describes the debate between Moshe and Korach about techeles and mezuzah. On a simple level, the Midrash highlights Korach's attitude; instead of offering a solution to a problem, he complains about what exists.

However, the Midrash contains an additional and far more important message. If everyone is special, then no one really is. Consequently, there is no need for anything special. A turquoise garment does not need a special turquoise string and a room with seferim *holy books* does not need a mezuzah. Accordingly, Korach insinuates that a holy nation does not need a Kohen Gadol. This is exactly his attack, one against Aharon's leadership or leadership in general.[390]

---

[388] Alternatively, the Mishneh could not have said Moshe and Aharon for that would incorrectly imply that they did not act L'Shem Shamayim (Tosfos Yom Tov Avos 5:17).

[389] Daas Zekenim M'Baalay HaTosfos (Bamidbar 16:1) and see Devorim 14:1.

[390] Malbim (ibid)

Korach's message is no deeper or more nuanced than saying that the current leadership is bad. Precisely because of the indistinctness of his message, different factions with disparate aims can unite around it.

WHY NOW?

Is there any particular reason that opposing groups join together to challenge Moshe and Aharon's leadership at this particulate point in time?

The Torah records this episode adjacent to the meraglim.[391] Assuming that the juxtaposition is meaningful and the meraglim episode is connected to ours, the subtle message may be that, on some level, the meraglim episode triggers this rebellion. After the meraglim are rebuked, Bnei Yisrael are told they cannot enter into Eretz Yisrael now and it will only be the next generation who can.

Many, knowing their generation's fate, completely loose hope. Even at the best of times, optimism is a struggle for this generation.[392] Hopeless, they become interested in a different plan. A regime change is plainly more attractive than waiting in the desert to die.[393]

THE MATTAH TEST

After the earth opens its mouth and swallows Dasan and Aviram, Moshe conducts one more test. Moshe labels twelve staffs, each one with a different tribe's name, with the exception of the tribe of Levi, which instead has Aharon's name written on it (ibid 17:18). He places them in the Ohel Moed and the next morning flowers and almonds appear on Aharon's staff (ibid 17:23).

---

[391] Interestingly, several commentaries believe that this episode does not actually occur at this point. For example, the Ibn Ezra (Bamidbar 16:1) argues that it takes place at Har Sinai. According to the Baal HaTurim (Bamidbar 16:1), this story is told here, adjacent to that of tzitzis, because it is the subject of Korach's first halachik attack. The implication is that the story's location is based on theme and not chronology.

[392] For a greater understanding of how the meraglim episode reflects Bnei Yisrael's hopelessness, see *The Colossal Impact of the Meraglim's Sin*.

[393] Bechor Shor (Bamidbar 16:1)

Two major questions arise. Why does Moshe replace the tribe's name, Levi, with Aharon's, an individual's? Additionally, why does the staff grow flowers and almonds?

Moshe writes Aharon's name on the staff to further emphasize Hashem's decision to both select not just the tribe of Levi, but specifically Aharon. One should not mistakenly think that Korach's rebellion is quashed because Korach fails to act L'Shem Shamayim or that teaming up with Dasan and Aviram causes their failure. Rather, Hashem wants Aharon as Kohen Gadol and that becomes abundantly clear.

The flowers and almonds that grow from the staff reinforce a second idea. Although the generation in the desert is going to die before entering into Eretz Yisrael, and that can be depressing, one should never give up, for there is great hope for the next generation. This generation's children will have a better life and that should inspire them with optimism. The almonds growing from a dead stick symbolize optimism for the next generation, and the flowers are the aesthetics that accompany the almonds, creating a profound symbolism. Life is both promising and beautiful and the next generation should see it that way. Instead of giving up, Bnei Yisrael should work for a better life for their children in Eretz Yisrael.[394]

APPLYING TEXT TO LIFE: THE HASHKAFIC MESSAGE

This story's religious message exists on several fronts. Most prominent is the underlying lesson about leadership. Uniting people to undermine good leadership for selfish purposes is not a virtue. Torah leadership mandates leaders to motivate and navigate people in the right direction, not simply to run to the front of groups already moving in a particular direction. Moshe and Aharon strive to lead Bnei Yisrael in the path Hashem desires. Korach, caught up in his own self-glorification, attempts to amalgamate people of opposing ideologies by telling them what they want to hear, not what they need to hear.

There is an important lesson about leadership to learn as well. Korach selfishly and arrogantly desires leadership, which is clearly a

---

[394] Rabbi Ari Berman

mistake. Leadership is about inspiring people. It is a responsibility, not a path to receive honor.

These two hundred and fifty men, although altruistic and sincerely seeking spirituality, do not understand that religious observance is heartfelt dedication to what Hashem wants and not a man-made creation of it. Their desire for religious growth distinguishes them from Dasan and Aviram but does not justify their actions. In addition to wanting the right things, one should want them the right way.

Lastly, hope is a critical element in religious ambition which facilitates religious commitment. Here we see the damage of hopelessness and, by contrast, how important hope is. When people lose hope, they become desperate and can easily make bad decisions. Serenity only returns when they have something to dream of; in this situation, a better life for their children.

RECREATION OF THE WORLD: DIFFERENT APPROACHES TO THE POST-FLOOD WORLD

AN UNEXPECTED INSIGHT INTO NOACH'S VINEYARD

After departing from the ark, Noach plants a vineyard. The Targum Yonason Ben Uziel (Bereshis 9:20), who both translates and homiletically interprets the Torah, writes, ואשכח גופנא דמושכיה נהרא מן גינוניתא דעדן ונצביה לכרמא וביה ביומא אניצת ובשילת ענבין ועצרינון *And he found a grapevine connected to the river from Gan Eden and established it as a vineyard, and cooked his wine and got drunk.*[395] Noach finds a small grapevine which is sustained by a river that flows from Gan Eden, and with that he grows his vineyard.[396]

How does one understand the Targum Yonason? What prompts the Targum Yonason to add this element to an otherwise simple story? At first glance, there is no hint to this in the verse at all. Moreover, there is no glaring conceptual problem that he seems to be solving either. Why add this seemingly odd comment?

---

[395] Similarly, Pirkei D'Rebbi Eliezar (23) writes that מצא נח גפן שגרשה ויצאה מגן עדן ואשכלותיה עמה, נטל מפרותיה ואכל *Noach found a vine from Gan Eden and connected it, and took the fruit and ate.* This idea is echoed by the Baal HaTurim (Bereshis 9:20).

[396] The Gemara (Sanhedrin 70a) critiques Adam saying אמר לו הקדוש ברוך הוא לנח: נח, לא היה לך ללמוד מאדם הראשון שלא גרם לו אלא יין כמאן דאמר אותו אילן שאכל ממנו אדם הראשון גפן היה *The Holy Blessed be He said to him, 'Noach, did you not learn from Adam HaRishon, whose cause of sin was wine,' according to the opinion that the tree he (Adam) ate from was a grapevine.* This opinion of Chazal also connects Noach to Gan Eden and Adam, but at as a criticism.

SEVERAL ODDITIES ABOUT NOACH BECOMING INTOXICATED

In order to explain the Targum Yonason's addition, and really his perspective on the entire episode, we must first look at the relevant narrative where Noach gets drunk.

The most basic questions that need to be addressed are twofold. What spurs Noach to drink? What is he trying to accomplish? It is tough to imagine that he gets drunk for no reason, for the Torah presents Noach's planting a vineyard, and getting drunk, as one of the first things he does after leaving the ark. Surprisingly, he plants this vineyard before planting anything that would produce food or necessary sustenance. It seems as if getting drunk is his goal.

The second critical question is why Noach undresses himself (Bereshis 9:21)? Most drunken people do not remove their clothing. What prompts Noach to act this way? What is he trying to achieve?

There are some other interesting details included in the story worth noting. Noach chooses to get drunk inside his tent (ibid 9:21). Why specifically engage in this behavior inside a tent?

The Torah introduces this episode with the departure of Noach's three sons from the ark, וַיִּהְיוּ בְנֵי־נֹחַ הַיֹּצְאִים מִן־הַתֵּבָה שֵׁם וְחָם וָיָפֶת *And the sons of Noach, who are leaving the ark, are Shem, Cham and Yefes* (ibid 9:18). Notably, this is repetitive for they have already left the ark (ibid 8:18) long enough to have brought karbanos (8:20)! Why repeat this now? There is also the more basic conundrum of why the Torah introduces the story with this seemingly irrelevant fact. Moreover, how is this connected to Noach subsequently getting drunk? Additionally, it is noteworthy that Noach, himself, is omitted. Only Noach's sons are recorded leaving the ark now. Does he not also exit the ark with them?

Lastly, the Torah notes שְׁלֹשָׁה אֵלֶּה בְּנֵי־נֹחַ וּמֵאֵלֶּה נָפְצָה כָל־הָאָרֶץ *These three are Noach's sons, and they inhabit the land* (ibid 9:19). This verse is both obvious and irrelevant. It is obvious that they repopulate and inhabit the earth after the flood, for there is no one else to do so.[397] This

---

[397] Interestingly, the Netziv (Bereshis 9:19) argues that Noach has many more children than these three listed. These three sons are listed because they each represent something. We will develop each personality in this chapter.

Methodologically, the Netziv assumes that when the Torah lists people, the list may be incomplete. The people included in a list are included to make a point, after all, the Torah is not a history book. Another example of this phenomenon is when the Torah describes

verse is also ostensibly irrelevant. It has nothing to do with Noach's drunkenness or his subsequently cursing Canaan.

We will return and address these questions.

Uncovering the Structure of the Flood

Hashem's decision to destroy the world with a flood is fascinating for it seems to directly parallel the story of creation. During the flood, water continues to rain down from above while it gathers below. This is strikingly reminiscent of the second day of creation where water too is both above and below. After the flood water recedes, the land resurfaces (Bereshis 8:3,5), which vividly recalls the third day of creation. Then, when the earth's surface can be seen, Noach sends out birds (ibid 8:7, 8, 10). Now there are birds and fish[398] out in the world which unmistakably reminds us of the fifth day of creation where Hashem creates birds and fish. When the animals and Noach return to the dry land, man is created בְּצֶלֶם אֱלֹהִים *in the image of God* (ibid 9:6) and Noach is commanded פְּרוּ וּרְבוּ *Be fruitful and multiply* (ibid 8:17, 9:7), which unquestionably recalls the sixth day of creation where Hashem creates animals (ibid 1:25) and mankind and commands them with identical phrases (ibid 1:27, 28).

The flood appears to model four of the seven days of Creation – two, three, five and six – in an uncanny fashion. Perhaps, the flood is a medium through which Hashem resets Creation. Hashem, disappointed with man's iniquities, decides to refresh the world and start it anew (ibid 6:5-7). What better way to do that than by repeating the exact steps of creation? The way Hashem chooses to destroy and restart the world is designed to reinforce the theological message. It pays for Him to go back and start again.

Interestingly, days one, four and seven of creation are not repeated in the flood. These days do not need to be refreshed for a simple reason; they are not parts of the world with which Hashem is disappointed. Hashem finds fault with mankind and the earth. By contrast, on days

---

seventy members of Yaakov's family who go to Egypt where the Netziv (Bereshis 46:5) again argues that it is incomplete as there are many females that Yaakov and his sons must have had who are not included in the list.

[398] The fish did not die in the flood (Zevachim 113b, Sanhedrin 108a, Rashi Bereshis 7:22).

one and four, He created light and darkness as well as the celestial beings, all of which do not sin, and therefore do not need to be refreshed. The same is true of day seven, Shabbos. Shabbos, the day where Hashem rested, does not need to be destroyed or recreated.

NOACH HARISHON

Having witnessed the destruction and recreation of the world via the flood, Noach finds himself alone in a new world, in an almost identical position to Adam HaRishon. Noach sees himself as the first man created after the flood, after Hashem's recreation. In addition to seeing himself alone in a new world, he is reminded that man is created בְּצֶלֶם אֱלֹהִים *in the image of God.* Then, he too, like Adam, is commanded פְּרוּ וּרְבוּ *Be fruitful and multiply.*

Noach identifies as the replacement for Adam HaRishon, seeing himself as Noach HaRishon. Intending to further mimic Adam HaRishon, who was unknowingly naked in Gan Eden, Noach gets drunk and undressed attempting to copy Adam's unawareness of his own nakedness.[399]

Noach desires to achieve the same innocence and naivety that Adam had before he sinned, as described by the Torah, וַיִּהְיוּ שְׁנֵיהֶם עֲרוּמִּים הָאָדָם וְאִשְׁתּוֹ וְלֹא יִתְבֹּשָׁשׁוּ *And they were both naked (Adam and Chava) and they were not embarrassed* (ibid 2:25). The Torah's word selection, וַיִּתְגַּל *And he undressed* (ibid 9:21), may even capture Noach's attempt to recapture simplicity and purity, for this word is never used in a sexual context. Furthermore, in searching for his Gan Eden, Noach enters into his tent. Being inside his tent is the closest thing to replicating the isolation of Gan Eden.[400]

There are additional literary hints that reference this parallel. The Torah describes Noach's intoxication as בְּתוֹךְ אָהֳלֹה *in the **center** of his tent* (ibid 9:20) which clearly recalls, וְעֵץ הַחַיִּים בְּתוֹךְ הַגָּן *the tree of life in the **center** of the garden* (ibid 2:9).[401]

---

399 However, others (Malbim Bereshis 9:20) argue that Noach plants the vineyard with no intention of getting drunk.

400 Tzror Hamaor (Parshas Lech Lecha)

401 Netziv (Bereshis 9:21)

The Torah recounts Noach planting the vineyard with the phrase וַיִּטַּע כָּרֶם *and he **planted** the vineyard* (ibid 9:20), using the same word that describes Hashem's creation of Gan Eden וַיִּטַּע יְקֹוָק אֱלֹהִים גַּן בְּעֵדֶן *and Hashem, the God, **planted** Gan Eden* (ibid 2:8).

Additionally, the Noach narrative opens with אֵלֶּה תּוֹלְדֹת נֹחַ *these are the **generations** of Noach*, using the same words as in Gad Eden אֵלֶּה תוֹלְדוֹת הַשָּׁמַיִם וְהָאָרֶץ *these are the **generations** of the heaven and the earth* (ibid 2:4) further emphasizing the parallel between these two narratives.[402]

However, the clearest and most powerful hint is the Torah referring to Noach as אִישׁ הָאֲדָמָה *man of the land* (ibid 9:20). In addition to being man of the field,[403] Noach is אִישׁ הָאֲדָמָה *man of (Adama), a man of Adam*, namely, Adam HaRishon.[404] [405]

UNDERSTANDING THE TARGUM YONASON

In light of this theory, we can now return to the Targum Yonason. There is a clear connection between Adam in Gan Eden and Noach's intoxication. Now that we have established that Noach is mimicking Adam HaRishon, specifically by planting a vineyard, intoxicating himself and removing his clothes to search for the innocence that Adam had, we can better understand that this response is triggered by Noach finding a river flowing from Gan Eden. This is another reason for Noach to see this as an opportunity to recreate Gan Eden.

WHY NOACH DOES THIS

While Noach's attempt to repeat Adam's experience is fascinating, it is worthwhile to ask why Noach wants to relive Adam's situation.

---

[402] Rav Shimshon Rafael Hirsch (Bereshis 6:9)

[403] Rashi (Sanhedrin 70a). The Meshech Chochma adds (Bereshis 9:20) that Noach spiritually retreats from being an אִישׁ צַדִּיק *righteous man* (ibid 6:9) to an אִישׁ הָאֲדָמָה *man of the land.*

[404] Kli Yakar (Bereshis 9:20)

[405] The Malbim (Bereshis 9:24) adds that Noach realizing what has happened to him mirrors Adam realizing that he was unclothed.

Throughout his life, Noach valued an insular existence. Before the flood, Noach does not reach out to inspire, educate or even pray for those bound to be punished by the flood. Now, after the flood, when it is time to spread out, repopulate and inhabit the land, Noach, again, mistakenly chooses an insular lifestyle.[406] When it is time to move forward, Noach attempts to retreat.

In order to stress Noach's flawed attitude, the Torah begins this narrative by informing us that Noach's three sons leave the ark וַיִּהְיוּ בְנֵי נֹחַ הַיֹּצְאִים מִן הַתֵּבָה *And it was that the sons of Noach, who are leaving the ark* (ibid 9:18). Only Noach's sons leave to spread out throughout the earth, but Noach does not. This contrast between Noach and his three sons is reinforced in the next verse שְׁלֹשָׁה אֵלֶּה בְּנֵי נֹחַ וּמֵאֵלֶּה נָפְצָה כָל הָאָרֶץ *These three are Noach's sons, and they inhabit the land* (ibid 9:19).

Additionally, this theory explains why the Torah repeats their departure from the ark after previously mentioning it. The Torah is not describing the physical exiting of the ark, for that has already taken place. Rather, the Torah here is offering a description as to who the three sons of Noach are; people looking to leave, inhabit the world and move forward. Moreover, the Torah does not state that ויצאו בני נח *And Noach's sons leave*, merely to describe the action of leaving; rather וַיִּהְיוּ בְנֵי נֹחַ הַיֹּצְאִים *And it was that the sons of Noach, who are leaving*, reflects not just what they do but who they are. That may also explain why the Torah says הַיֹּצְאִים *who are leaving* in the present form as opposed to the past, *who left*. The Torah is not technically describing their actions, but their nature. The Torah captures the nature of Noach's sons as people interested in leaving and developing the world.

In order to reinforce this point, the Torah, after listing Noach's lineage, repeats וּמֵאֵלֶּה נִפְרְדוּ הַגּוֹיִם בָּאָרֶץ אַחַר הַמַּבּוּל, *from these, the nations of the world spread out after the flood* (ibid 10:32). The point is clear: it is Noach's descendants who redevelop the planet, not Noach.

Noach is mistakenly insular and introverted when it is time to rebuild the world.

---

[406] According to Rav Shimshon Rafael Hirsch (19 Letters, letter 6), separating communities minimizes the chance of them all sinning and deserving destruction. Alternatively, Hashem values mankind to inhabit and develop His earth.

MIGDAL BAVEL

This idea can help shed light on the Migdal Bavel account as well. The most glaring problem with the Migdal Bavel narrative is that Hashem punishes the people for an unknown crime. The Torah does not explicitly delineate what the people do wrong. Seemingly building a large tower is not a crime and there is no other overt disobedience or sinful behavior. Yet, Hashem is surprisingly angered by their behavior. What do they do wrong? And moreover, why are they punished by being scattered throughout the world (ibid 11:8-9)? How is that punishment commensurate with the crime?

Once Noach has erroneously attempted to recreate Adam's insular life, as opposed to resettling Hashem's world, it should be self-evident that such attempts are wrong. And yet, the people building the Migdal Bavel also display disinterest in settling Hashem's world. Instead of spreading out to inhabit the globe, the people move into a valley,[407] a place which physically blinds them from seeing anything outside of their own society.

Accordingly, it is understandable why the narrative opens with the preamble that וַיְהִי כָל הָאָרֶץ שָׂפָה אֶחָת וּדְבָרִים אֲחָדִים *And all the earth spoke one language and had one ideology* (ibid 11:1). This is more than a description, it is a critique. Because the people are aware that at this time in history Hashem desires diversity and inhabiting of the earth, it is sinful to disobey and build an insular community in a valley.

We can also, now, understand how perfect Hashem's punishment for these people is: וַיָּפֶץ יְקֹוָק אֹתָם מִשָּׁם עַל פְּנֵי כָל הָאָרֶץ וַיַּחְדְּלוּ לִבְנֹת הָעִיר *And Hashem scattered them from the face of the earth and they stopped building their city* (ibid 11:8). Hashem is ensuring that His will is brought to fruition. The subsequent verse's description reinforces that as well, עַל כֵּן קָרָא שְׁמָהּ בָּבֶל כִּי שָׁם בָּלַל יְקֹוָק שְׂפַת כָּל הָאָרֶץ וּמִשָּׁם הֱפִיצָם יְקֹוָק עַל פְּנֵי כָּל הָאָרֶץ *therefore it is called Bavel, because, Hashem had confused the languages of the all of earth, and from there Hashem has scattered them from the face of the earth* (ibid 11:9).

---

[407] They chose to relocate into a valley (ibid 11:2), long before they develop plans to build a large tower (ibid 11:4), otherwise, that decision would be self-defeating. Alternatively, the valley is a small part of the larger area (Ibn Ezra ibid 11:2) or there is no other place to settle (Rashi Shabbos 10b)

There is an important hint that the Torah shares while shedding light on this perspective. The reason that this group chooses to build a tower is, וְנַעֲשֶׂה לָּנוּ שֵׁם פֶּן נָפוּץ עַל פְּנֵי כָל הָאָרֶץ *And let us make for ourselves a name, lest we be scattered throughout the world* (ibid 11:4). Their mistake is their selfish interest and desire to remain in one area. Instead of developing the world for Hashem, they develop an insular culture for themselves.[408]

The Torah itself alludes to the builders of the Migdal Bavel as mistaken followers of Adam HaRishon as well. When Hashem looks down at the iniquitous people, the Torah specifically calls them בְּנֵי הָאָדָם *sons of man (Adam)* (ibid 11:5). They are interested in an insular life like that of Adam HaRishon.[409]

In order to emphasize the mistake the builders of Migdal Bavel make focusing on נַעֲשֶׂה לָּנוּ שֵׁם *And let us make for ourselves a **name***, the Torah contrasts it with Avraham's journey to teach and inspire the world with monotheism, וַיִּקְרָא בְּשֵׁם יְקֹוָק *And he called in the **name** of God* (ibid 12:8).[410] Avraham makes a name for Hashem, not himself.

CHAM AND CANAAN

This incident is not just a story of Noach getting drunk and attempting to return to the lost innocent lifestyle that Adam had. In this episode, Cham sees his father naked and calls his brothers to join him in mocking Noach, yet they respond very differently. Shem and Yefes cover their helpless father with a cloak (ibid 9:23). Once Noach sobers, he realizes what has occurred and curses Cham's son, Canaan.

---

[408] Rashbam (ibid 11:4). Others provide different explanation for why Hashem punishes these people differently. Some (quoted by Rashi ibid 11:1) answer that they plan on waging war on Hashem. Others (quoted by Rashi ibid 11:1), that they are building the tower to save themselves from another potential flood. Others (Seforno ibid 11:4), still, argue this is an attempt to (appoint Nimrod as king and) rule over humanity. Yet, others say they build it for idolatrously purposes (Rashi Iyov 1:1). The Kli Yakar (Bereshis 11:1) argues that their mistake is their attitude, וְנַעֲשֶׂה לָּנוּ שֵׁם פֶּן *And let us make for ourselves a name* and otherwise, simply building the tower would have been fine.

[409] The Midrash (Bereshis Rabbah, Vilna Edition 38:9) accuses the builders of the Migdal Bavel of being selfish and not learning from the flood. Moreover, it explains that the Torah hints at that criticism with the phrase בְּנֵי הָאָדָם *sons of man (Adam)*.

[410] Ibn Ezra ibid 12:8, Ramban Bereshis 12:8

While this narrative contains several questions that need to be addressed, the most outstanding and difficult one is why Noach curses Canaan if he does nothing wrong. It is understandable that Noach blesses Shem and Yefes because they respectfully cover him. However, why curse Canaan? It is Cham, בְּנוֹ הַקָּטָן *the youngest son* (ibid 9:24), who misbehaves. Why, then, curse Canaan?[411]

Additionally, Cham is addressed twice in this episode as אֲבִי כְנַעַן *Canaan's father* (ibid 9:18, 22), with one of those references in the story's introduction, before Noach becomes intoxicated. Why does the Torah stress this fact?

Understanding Cham's True Nature

The Torah omits Cham's specific actions but unquestionably communicates that he does something sexually inappropriate as the verse states, וַיַּרְא חָם אֲבִי כְנַעַן אֵת עֶרְוַת אָבִיו *And Cham, the father of Canaan, saw his father's nakedness* (ibid 9:22). Cham's inappropriate sexual behavior is certainly inexcusable, yet, because the Torah does not communicate specifically what Cham does, we can conclude that what he does is less important than the fact that he does something sexually inappropriate. Although the Torah's message about Cham may be better delivered without that detail, we are not told explicitly what that message is.

Cham's inability to control himself here is pathetic. Even in a situation where he should have been able to act responsibly, where his

---

[411] Because of this powerful question, some (Ibn Ezra Bereshis 9:24, Seforno 9:22) answer that Cham passively watches his son, Canaan, mistreat Noach. Accordingly, Cham, equally bad (Ibn Ezra Bereshis 9:18), even watches happily (Seforno ibid 9:22). They explain בְּנוֹ הַקָּטָן *the youngest son*, the one who mistreats Noach, is Canaan, not Cham (Seforno 9:24).

Most assume that the Torah refers to Cham with the phrase בְּנוֹ הַקָּטָן *the youngest son* (Bereshis 9:24), because he is biologically the youngest son (Ramban ibid 9:10, 10:21), or called הַקָּטָן because he is disgraced and small (Rashi ibid 9:24).

Interestingly, the Bechor Shor (ibid 9:24) argues that Shem is בְּנוֹ הַקָּטָן *the youngest son*, and what Noach hears about him are positive things rather than negative.

Regarding what actually happens, the Torah itself is ambiguous (Bereshis Rabbah, Vilna Edition 38:6, Ibn Ezra 9:24), yet two opinions of Chazal (Sanhedrin 70a) debate whether Noach is raped or castrated.

Alternatively, and fascinatingly, Rav Yaakov Medan is quoted to argue cleverly that Cham is intimate with Noach's wife which is what the language עֶרְוַת אָבִיו *father's nakedness* usually means (Vayikra 18). This illicit relationship actually leads to Canaan, which explains why Noach curses him.

old, helpless, naked and intoxicated father needs assistance, he cannot offer that assistance. Instead, Cham sees this as an opportunity to sexually exploit his father.

Based on this, we can understand why the Torah, in our narrative, describes Cham as Canaan's father. Noach enters the ark with his three sons, who each have no children, and exits with Cham as a father. Noach, Shem and Yefes, sensitive to the devastating tragedy outside, practice celibacy while in the ark. According to Chazal (Bereshis Rabbah, Vilna Edition, 34:8), they are even commanded to refrain from intimacy with their wives as the world is destroyed.[412] Noach, Shem and Yefes obey; Cham does not.[413] The Torah alludes to this by stating, וְחָם הוּא אֲבִי כְנָעַן *and Cham is the father of Canaan* hinting to Cham's fathering a child in the ark.

THE NAME CHAM

The Torah cleverly hints to Cham's inability to control his sexuality with his name, Cham, *heat*, implying that Cham's sexuality burns uncontrollably.[414] While the rest of the family can control themselves, Cham demonstrates in the ark and when Noach is naked and helpless, that he cannot.

CURING CANAAN

Noach wants to curse Cham's inability to control his sexual urges and the best way of doing so is cursing the result of those desires, Canaan.[415] Noach does not curse Canaan for his misdoings. He curses Chan for being a personification of Cham's unrestrained sexual drive.

---

[412] Rashi (Bereshis 7:7, 8:16). This is hinted to by the Torah itself, which describes their entry to the ark in an unusual order; Noach, his sons, his wife and then his sons' wives (Bereshis 7:7). The Torah separates the males from females which clearly contrasts with the order of this grouping upon their exit; Noach, his wife, his sons and then his sons' wives (ibid 8:16). The subtle implication is that they should be together again from that point.

[413] Sanhedrin 108b, Chizkuni (Bereshis 9:18) and Malbim (9:18)

[414] Rav Shimshon Rafael Hirsch (Bereshis 6:10)

[415] Ramban (9:18). However, others (Rashi Bereshis 9:25, Ibn Ezra ibid 9:24) argue that Canaan is the fourth son and add that he is cursed because Noach is prevented from having

In fact, the curse comes true.[416] The Canaanim are notorious throughout Tanach for inappropriate sexual behavior.[417]

CHAM AND NOACH

Just as Cham's personality is reflected by his name, Noach's is as well, but his name captures his opposing nature. Noach is passive, controlled and relaxed, which naturally fits with his desire for Adam's insular lifestyle. While Noach can unclothe himself independent of any sexual thoughts, Cham cannot even see his intoxicated father's attempt to imitate Adam HaRishon innocently.

In order to highlight the different perspectives that Noach and Cham each have, the Torah uses distinct words to describe how they view Noach's nakedness. The Torah uses וַיִּתְגַּל *and he undressed* in describing Noach's pure and naive perspective, yet refers to עֶרְוַת אָבִיו *father's nakedness*, the vile language used in Vayikra (Chapter 18) regarding elicit relationships to reflect Cham's frame of mind.

SHEM AND YEFES

The difference between Cham's untamed sexuality and Noach's opposing passivity is illustrated most vividly in our episode. However, there are two more characters in the episode, Shem and Yefes. What are their perspectives?

Shem and Yefes certainly see things differently from Cham, as clearly indicated by their actions. Entering backwards, they both respectfully cover Noach while looking away from his nakedness (ibid 9:23). However, they also view things distinctly from Noach. Noach sees it as appropriate to undress in search of Adam's innocence, yet Shem and Yefes are aware that it is time to move forward. They therefore cover their father, underscoring that Noach is supposed to be clothed because he unable to return to Adam's original state. Shem and

---

a fourth son.

[416] According to the Ibn Ezra (Bereshis 9:18), the episode is recorded to foreshadow to the Canaanite people being cursed and promiscuous.

[417] Vayikra 18:24-25, Devorim 9:5

Yefes subscribe to a middle approach; one that is respectful to Noach reflecting a controlled sexuality, and simultaneously progressive in aiming to spread out and settle the world, rather than return to Gan Eden.

By turning their faces away, they show both extreme sensitivity for him as well a commitment to pursuing an opposite ideological direction. They both understand that it is time to move forward and develop the world.

The Difference Between Shem and Yefes

Shem and Yefes both act correctly, yet, according to Chazal, they do so for different reasons. Shem is apparently the more noble of the two. Some midrashim (Bereshis Rabbah, Vilna Edition 36:6, Yalkut Shimoni Parshas Noach) argue that Shem initiates, whereas others claim that Shem is motivated religiously, whereas Yefes is motivated by external appearances.

Several phrases in the text hint to this distinction. The Torah writes וַיִּקַּח שֵׁם וָיֶפֶת *And he took, Shem and Yefes* (ibid 9:23). By using the singular language וַיִּקַּח *And he took* to describe both Shem and Yefes, the Torah creates some textual tension. While they both act, there is something that one of them, presumably Shem because he is mentioned first, does.

Additionally, Shem's blessing בָּרוּךְ יְקֹוָק אֱלֹהֵי שֵׁם *Blessed Hashem the God of Shem* (ibid 9:26) seems more religious in its nature than Yefes', whose implies an attachment to materialism and beauty, stating יַפְתְּ אֱלֹהִים לְיֶפֶת וְיִשְׁכֹּן בְּאָהֳלֵי שֵׁם *May Hashem make Yefes nice*,[418] *in the tents of Shem* (ibid 9:27). These differences in character are hinted to by their different names: שם, *Shem*, acts לשמה *for Hashem's sake* whereas יפת *Yefes* acts for the sake of beauty or appearances.[419]

From an outside perspective, both Shem and Yefes appear to act correctly. The difference in their motives cannot be detected on a peripheral level. Only by getting to know them and noticing

---

[418] Alternatively, extend Yefes (Rashi Bereshis 9:27)

[419] Rav Shimshon Rafael Hirsch (Bereshis 6:9). However, the Malbim (Bereshis 9:19) and Netziv (Bereshis 9:26) argue that Yefes acted for moral and humanistic reasons.

subtle nuances can one determine the difference. Accordingly, the Torah does not overtly communicate this distinction, but chooses to hint to it. The Torah conceals the differences in attitude to reflect how an onlooker sees them, both acting correctly, but subtly hints at the difference in religious level that one can uncover with greater investigation.

In summary, this short episode captures four different post-flood approaches. While Noach is regressive his three sons act progressively, but in different ways. Cham is controlled by his fiery sexuality. Yefes, superficially, cares about how things look and is blessed accordingly. Shem acts לשמה *for Hashem's sake,* and is also blessed accordingly. The forward moving desire shared by all three sons is captured by the Torah opening with the description of them leaving the ark, while omitting any mention of Noach acting in a similar fashion.

APPLYING TEXT TO LIFE: THE HASHKAFIC MESSAGE

Many religious values remain stagnant and unchanged throughout the generations, yet simultaneously, changes in life often invite different approaches, strategies and goals. Adapting to a new context and new set of rules is not always easy and clearly something with which Noach struggles. Before the flood, remaining insular is at least defensible,[420] earning Noach the title, אִישׁ צַדִּיק *righteous man.* Yet, after the flood, Hashem expects Noach to rebuild, repopulate and redevelop the world. The ultimate goal of serving Hashem and maintaining a commitment to His will is perpetual, yet how it is implemented has changed greatly and Noach's shortcoming is in not adjusting accordingly.

Cham's mistake is allowing his sexuality to control his life. It begins with his insensitivity while in the ark, and climaxes with Cham's inability to see his helpless father as anything but sexual. Sexuality can pervert people's perspective and control people, as it does to Cham.

---

[420] For a greater discussion on Noach's shortcoming, see Double Take, the chapter entitled, *Noach, Yonah, Lot and Avraham — "What it Takes to Start up a Nation"*

Additionally, by contrasting Shem to Yefes, the Torah reinforces the value of attitude. The Torah strongly supports people acting correctly and for the right reasons. Worshiping Hashem with the correct motivation is significantly greater than simply worshiping Hashem.

Achsah: A Prize to be Won

The Odd Location and Other Strange Details

Much of Sefer Yehoshua is dedicated to the division and settling of Eretz Yisrael (chapters 13-19). The Navi describes in great detail the geographical boundaries that each tribe receives. Curiously, there are several small stories couched in these sections that primarily describe the land allocation. The first one is about Achsah's marriage and subsequent request for better land (Yehoshua 15:13-19).

This story seems to be misplaced on two levels. First, it deals with individuals in a section of Tanach designed to focus on the nation; but most obviously, it is located in the midst of a passage whose subject is the allocation of land. In order to answer why the author[421] places this short narrative where he does, one must answer a more central question. What is the purpose of this story? Once that is clarified, we should be able to explain the placement.

There are a host of additional questions regarding the details of this short narrative which will help us unpack and understand the central theme of this episode. Foremost among them is that the story itself seems to be a collection of random events. In this short episode, Kalev drives three giants out Keryas Arba (ibid 15:14), and then offers his daughter, Achsah, to whomever can conquer Keryas Sefer (ibid

---

[421] Usually assumed to be Yehoshua, himself, (Bava Basra 14b), however, surprisingly, the Abarbanel (Introduction to Sefer Yehoshua, page 7) argues that the author of Sefer Yehoshua is Shmuel.

15:16).[422] Interestingly, Osniel, Kalev's brother,[423] successfully does so and is rewarded with Achsah as a wife (ibid 15:17). Achsah then induces Osniel to ask her father for extra land, before she dismounts a camel and Kalev asks her what she wants (ibid 15:18). She responds with a request for land with springs of water and is given them (ibid 15:19). What point do these details come together to illustrate?

Several additional questions should be raised as well. Why does Kalev leave his daughter's future open to anyone who might conquer the city? Is this not risky and irresponsible? Furthermore, is it merely a coincidence that Kalev's own brother, Osniel, is the military hero who conquers Keryas Sefer? This is unlikely to be pure chance. The episode concludes with Achsah's plan for Osniel to ask for more land. He asks and even successfully receives extra land. Why is this significant? This narrative is extremely short with no clear point. What is the story's message and how is it supported by these, otherwise, random details?

Interestingly, this story is retold in Sefer Shoftim (chapter 1). Why it is repeated there? In addition to wanting to know the point of this story and how it contributes to Sefer Yehoshua and, specifically, the section about dividing land, we also have to understand how it contributes to Sefer Shoftim as well.[424]

---

[422] The Alshich (Yehoshua 15:1-17) raises the possibility that Achsah is given to Osniel as a reward for reminding Bnei Yisrael of the three hundred Halachos lost when Moshe died.

[423] The Navi clearly records Osniel as אֲחִי כָלֵב Kalev's *brother* (ibid 15:17), yet it is strange that different father's names are mentioned. Kalev's father is recorded as Yifuneh whereas Osniel's is Kenaz.
Rashi (Yehoshua 15:17) answers that Kalev and Osniel have the same mother but different fathers. The Radak (Yehoshua 15:17) quotes those who argue that Yifuneh and Kenaz are the same person. Alternatively, he answers that Yifuneh is their father's name and Kenaz is a title given to leaders in their family.

[424] This story does appear in Sefer Shoftim, however it is a repetition because it is identical to ours.
Rashi (Yehoshua 15:14) and the Ralbag (Shoftim 1:13), place the chronology of this story in Sefer Shoftim after Yehoshua dies. Although the story of conquering Chevron occurs later, it is mentioned in Sefer Yehoshua along with the other land conquering done by Shevet Yehuda. By contrast, according to the Abarbanel (Shoftim 1:8) and Malbim (Yehoshua 15:14) the story really belongs in Sefer Yehoshua and is repeated in Shoftim.

YEHUDA'S PROMINENCE

In a departure from convention, the Achsah narrative is introduced without a new pesecha *indentation,* suggesting that it is part of the previous section and not an independent one. Assuming that the Achsah account is linked to the previous portion of the Navi, the one describing the tribe of Yehuda's inheritance, looking at Yehuda's inheritance should be helpful in understanding the Achsah narrative.

The tribe of Yehuda clearly has a special role in settling Eretz Yisrael. Of all the tribes described, the Navi chooses to list Yehuda first. Moreover, more importantly, there is a uniquely detailed description of Yehuda's topography. There is far more coverage on Yehuda's land-division than that of other tribes.

Beyond being the first tribe listed and having extra detailed coverage, Yehuda's land mass is significantly larger than others'. They inherit the width of the entire country from East[425] to West.[426] Their Southern border is the Southern border of Eretz Yisrael (ibid 15:1-12),[427] and the Northern boundary cuts horizontally across the mid-point of Eretz Yisrael. Beyond inheriting half of Eretz Yisrael, they receive half of Yerushalayim as well.[428] One can safely conclude that the tribe of Yehuda receives a prime inheritance.

This presentation expressing Yehuda's central role may be due to Yehuda's great success at settling the land. Because of their remarkable dedication and success the Navi depicts them as such.[429] Being mentioned first, having their inheritance mentioned with such great detail, and the sizable amount of land that they receive are all designed

---

[425] Yehoshua 1:5

[426] Yehoshua 1:12

[427] Malbim (Yehoshua 1:1)

[428] Yehoshua 1:8

[429] After all, Shevet Yehuda conquers everything they are responsible for besides Yerushalayim (ibid 15:63). That remains under Yevusi control until it is captured later by Dovid (Shmuel II 5:5-6). According to Rashi (Devorim 12:17 and Yehoshua 15:63), not conquering it is more than excusable, for they are unable to break Avraham's promise to Avimelech. Alternatively, the Malbim (Yehoshua 15:63) argues that the Yevusim are simply too powerful to conquer. Bnei Yisrael successfully conquer everything that is militarily possible. Moreover, according to Rashi (Yehoshua 15:14) the Achsah episode belongs in Sefer Shoftim. Presumably it is additionally placed here to reinforce this point. Bnei Yehuda are passionate about and successful at settling Eretz Yisrael.

to reward Yehuda's relentless commitment and enthusiastic attitude towards properly settling the land.[430]

A FAMILY OF HEROES

Shevet Yehuda's exceptional success may be reflected by the Achsah story as well. After all, everyone involved in the story comes from Shevet Yehuda. Kalev, a patriarch from Yehuda, serves as a religious role model due to his dedication and love for the land. He passionately wants his daughter to marry someone equally dedicated. He therefore offers her hand in marriage to anyone willing and able to fight for and conquer Eretz Yisrael.

The fact that they come from the same family is not coincidental either. This is a story about commitment to settling Eretz Yisrael. It is a story about the most dedicated family, within the most dedicated tribe. This also explains why the Navi, specifically here, emphasizes that Kalev and Osniel are brothers (ibid 15:17).

This enthusiasm and resolve is equally well illustrated by Achsah. She does not sit passively accepting her inferior dry land. Instead she voices her passion and successfully receives additional higher-quality land.

This narrative fits completely into the larger theme of Shevet Yehuda's success. Both narratives are included to emphasize how Shevet Yehuda heroically stands out in their willing to work extraordinarily hard to accomplish the national mission.

Not only does this story fit perfectly into the chapter and the theme of Shevet Yehuda receiving their land, it connects two integral components. Directly before this episode is an account of Yehuda's boundaries (ibid 15:1-12) and immediately after it is a list of its cities (ibid 15:20-63). Placed directly in between is our story linking the boundaries of Shevet Yehuda with the cities. Our story is precisely what links the boundaries to the cities. It is the people who live in those cities and it is the dedication of those people which make inhabiting the boundaries with cities meaningful.

---

[430] Abarbanel (Shoftim 1:8)

YEHUDA AND YOSEF'S LAND DIVISION

Interestingly, in the middle of the Bnei Yosef's[431] land divisions, just like Shevet Yehuda's, a small story is placed. There, the Navi records the Bnos Tzlafchad *daughters of Tzlafchad* (ibid 17:3) requesting land which is promised to them by Moshe (Bamidbar 27:7). The placement of this story is striking for its location seems equally misplaced. Why is the Bnos Tzlafchad's request placed here?

Similar to the Achsah episode, the recounting of the Bnos Tzlafchad story seemingly interrupts the flow with a story of individuals, in a section designed to deal with the national issue of land distribution. In addition to the similar manner in which this episode is presented, there are many other thematic elements found reinforcing the parallels between how Shevet Yehuda and Bnei Yosef's land distribution works. Let us list them before trying to uncover their meaning.

1. The Navi describes Yehuda's land allocation (chapter 15) with extraordinary detail, as we previously noted. Bnei Yosef (chapter 16-17) are covered by the Navi in equally great detail. Far more verses are dedicated to these two tribes' land division than any of the other tribes.[432]

2. Both tribes, Yehuda and the Bnei Yosef, receive a uniquely large geographical inheritance spanning across the entire country, East to West, with each reaching from the Mediterranean Sea to the Dead Sea.

3. Only the tribes of Yehuda and the Bnei Yosef are directly given land divinely, as the Navi emphasizes, אֶל פִּי יְקֹוָק *according to the word of Hashem* (ibid 14:13 and 17:4).[433]

4. Kalev, a member of Shevet Yehuda, makes a request of Yehoshua for land previously promised to him by Moshe (ibid 14:6-8). In a similar fashion, the Bnos Tzlafchad do the same, reminding Yehoshua of land that Moshe has promised them (ibid 17:4-8).

---

[431] More specifically, Menashe's

[432] Later in Sefer Yehoshua (chapter 18), when dealing with the other tribes, far fewer verses are dedicated to describing their land division.

[433] These are the only two times the word אֶל is spelled with an א and not an ע. The Malbim (Yehoshua 15:13) explains that these two are repeated commands.

5. The Navi presents the conclusion of Yehuda's division with the sections of his inheritance still not conquered, וְאֶת הַיְבוּסִי יוֹשְׁבֵי יְרוּשָׁלַם לֹא יָכְלוּ בְנֵי יְהוּדָה לְהוֹרִישָׁם וַיֵּשֶׁב הַיְבוּסִי אֶת בְּנֵי יְהוּדָה בִּירוּשָׁלַם עַד הַיּוֹם הַזֶּה *And the Bnei Yehuda could not settle the (land that the) Yevusi, settlers of Yerushalayim (were inhabiting). And the Yevusi dwelt in Bnei Yehuda's (land), until today* (ibid 15:63). In an identical fashion, the Navi concludes each of the Bnei Yosef, Menashe and Efrayim, with the same statement, highlighting that their's too is incomplete. For Efrayim the Navi records, וְלֹא הוֹרִישׁוּ אֶת הַכְּנַעֲנִי הַיּוֹשֵׁב בְּגָזֶר וַיֵּשֶׁב הַכְּנַעֲנִי בְּקֶרֶב אֶפְרַיִם עַד הַיּוֹם הַזֶּה וַיְהִי *And they did not settle the Canaanites, who are dwelling there. And they dwelt in Gezer, and the Canaanites dwelt in the midst of Efrayim until today* (ibid 16:10), and for Menashe, וְלֹא יָכְלוּ בְּנֵי מְנַשֶּׁה לְהוֹרִישׁ אֶת הֶעָרִים הָאֵלֶּה וַיּוֹאֶל הַכְּנַעֲנִי לָשֶׁבֶת בָּאָרֶץ הַזֹּאת *And Bnei Menashe could not conquer these cities, and the Canaanim are dwelling in the land* (ibid 17:13).

6. Each tribe's landscape is interrupted with a short story about women, Achsah and the Bnos Tzlafchad displaying a tremendous amount of love and passion for the dividing and settling of Eretz Yisrael.[434] This, as noted, is very uncommon for Sefer Yehoshua.

Before explaining the underlying message of this parallel, it pays to add another connection between Shevet Yehuda and the Bnei Yosef. Whereas most of the tribes receive their land after relocating the Mishkan from Gilgal to Shiloh (Yehoshua 18), only Shevet Yehuda and the Bnei Yosef are given theirs beforehand. This further links them together and separates them from the others.

This connection may be designed to underscore the extraordinary success of tribes of Yehuda and the Bnei Yosef. Their exceptional passion to settle and develop Eretz Yisrael is illustrated by the aforementioned parallel. The Navi presents Yehuda's land division first, and the Bnei Yosef immediately after. Furthermore, he spends much time describing the typography of each inheritance. And most notably, the Navi records a short vignette about women who passionately and eagerly desire and receive land. All of these ingredients together reflect the enthusiasm and zeal they have for Eretz Yisrael.

---

[434] The Bnos Tzlafchad episode in Sefer Bamidbar is placed adjacent to the Torah's testifying that Yehoshua and Kalev will enter into Eretz Yisrael in order to highlight their passion and love of Eretz Yisrael (Rashi Bamidbar 27:1).

Their love and commitment is highlighted specifically because women, who are not traditionally involved in war and do not typically receive an inheritance, are deeply committed and motivated to conquering and inhabiting Eretz Yisrael.

THE OTHER TRIBES

Unlike Shevet Yehuda and Bnei Yosef, many of the other tribes seem at least to be passive or perhaps even lazy and uninterested in dividing and receiving inheritance. Yehoshua has to rebuke them to motivate them, אָנָה אַתֶּם מִתְרַפִּים לָבוֹא לָרֶשֶׁת אֶת הָאָרֶץ *How long will you slack in inhabiting the land* (ibid 18:3). Yehoshua's criticism, even more than their location, suggests that the other tribes are less motivated. Yehuda and Bnei Yosef, by contrast, jump eagerly to inhabit their inheritance first.

TRACING THESE TWO TRIBES BACK TO THE CHUMASH

It may be more than a coincidence that the two meraglim Kalev and Yehoshua, who speak positively about Eretz Yisrael, come from Shevet Yehuda and Efrayim (Bamidbar 13:8), one of the Bnei Yosef. These two tribes have always had a positive perspective towards Eretz Yisrael. This positive attitude simply manifests itself on both occasions.

However, maybe we can trace these two tribes back even further. Out of all of Yaakov's sons, it seems that Yosef and Yehuda are the two with the most potential for leadership. That potential is inherited by their descendants, best personified by Kalev and Yehoshua, and ultimately the tribes who, in Sefer Yehoshua, settle and inhabit Eretz Yisrael successfully.

ANOTHER APPEARANCE

The Achsah narrative is found again in the beginning of Sefer Shoftim as well. The beginning of Sefer Shoftim (chapter 1) summarizes how the tribe of Yehuda succeeds in settling and inhabiting Eretz Yisrael. What better story to include than this one to reinforce their commitment.

A Parallel to Rivka

In addition to the similarities between Shevet Yehuda's and Bnei Yosef's land division, there is a more striking and fascinating parallel to uncover as well. The Achsah narrative shares many details with incidents from Rivka's lifetime.

1. Both Achsah and Rivka marry someone without having previously met them based upon one singular event. For Rivka it is her encounter with Avraham's servant at the well and for Achsah it is Osniel's military success.

2. Each marriage is left open to anyone, meaning that anyone could have been at the well and offered to give water to the camels. Similarly, anyone could have conquered Keryas Sefer. Yet in both episodes, it is specifically a family member who does so.[435]

3. Achsah persuades Osniel to make a request for her (ibid 15:18). She subtly manages to have her husband do what she wants.[436] Rivka too, manipulates Yitzhak, arranging for him to bless Yaakov.

4. Both Rivka and Achsah are born outside of Eretz Yisrael and both immigrate to it.

5. The Navi records how Achsah rides and dismounts the donkey (Yehoshua 15:18).[437] This clearly recalls how Rivka falls from a camel (Bereshis 24:64).

---

[435] Chazal (Vayikra Rabbah, Vilna Edition, 4:37, Midrash Agada, Buber Edition 24:15) reinforce this parallel, by stating that in both situations, leaving marriage open to anyone, is irresponsible and a mistake.

[436] According to the Ralbag (Shoftim 3:30), she has Osniel ask for something small to feel out the situation. Then, once she feels out her father's attitude, she follows up with the real request. Accordingly, she is seen and an operator as well, more similar to Rivka.

[437] The Abarbanel (Yehoshua 15:18) offers two answers as to why Achsah descending from the donkey is mentioned. Perhaps, he suggests, it is so she can fall at her father's feet while requesting more land. Alternatively, in order to illustrate how deeply she is thinking, the Navi records Achsah's falling off the donkey.

6. Achsah receives the springs of water as an extra blessing (Yehoshua 15:19). Rivka too facilitates an extra blessing for her son, but what makes it more remarkable, is that she arranges for him to receive, dew and water, just like Achsah, for a plentiful crop (Bereshis 27:28).

This parallel is particularly strong when taking into account the paucity of information the Navi presents about Achsah. Because of the few details mentioned in the Achsah account, and how many of them recall Rivka's story, it is difficult to imagine that the parallel is unintended. This raises the question of what motivated the Navi to include details that recall the Rivka narrative?

Rivka and Achsah, are powerful women who arrange and operate from behind the scenes. Each may appear non assuming at first, but they both know how to accomplish great things. However, there might be more to this parallel.

THE CONTRAST

In addition to similarities between these episodes, there are significant differences. The contrast between the two stories may help provide a deeper understanding as to why the parallel is drawn in the first place. But before speculating with a theory, it pays to list the differences.

1. Rivka leaves her home and family to join a new one. By contrast, Achsah brings someone new into her family.

2. In the Achsah account, the woman, Achsah, is the prize to be won. Osniel wins, and therefore receives Achsah. By contrast, Rivka, the woman, passes her test by drawing water for the camels, and she merits to marry Yitzhak.

3. Kalev clearly offers his daughter as a prize to be won. This is illustrated by him publicly offering Achsah to anyone who can defeat Keryas Sefer. Although, Rivka, because of her care and selflessness, marries Yitzhak, there is no contest, and nothing is made public.

4. Achsah attempts to persuade her husband but it never comes to fruition. Instead Achsah, herself, requests extra land from Kalev

(ibid 15:19).[438] By contrast, Yitzhak is tricked. The original plan in implemented.

5. Although both Rivka and Achsah descend from the animals that they are riding, Rivka comes off a camel (Bereshis 24:64), whereas Achsah dismounts a donkey (Yehoshua 15:18).

6. In contrast to Rivka who falls off a camel, Achsah descends of her own volition.

7. Although they both agree to marry someone they do not know, Rivka agrees to marry a spiritual leader, and Achsah, a military one.

COMING FULL CIRCLE

Recording the Achsah narrative displays the passion and leadership of Shevet Yehuda in Bnei Yisrael's return to Eretz Yisrael. Returning home is the final significant step in establishing nationhood. Perhaps contrasting returning to Eretz Yisrael now to the beginning of Bnei Yisrael's creation highlights how things have come full circle. The first real step to transforming Avraham's monotheistic dreams and beliefs into a stable and concretized religion is Yitzhak marrying Rivka. Bnei Yisrael fighting to establish their home in Eretz Yisrael is the final one. In Sefer Bereshis there are traces of potential for a great nation and that potential is actualized here, for now a great nation is settling in its great land.

This message is hinted at by contrasting the stories. Neither Yitzhak, nor Rivka know who they are to marry, symbolic of the unknown and insecure future. Rivka falls from her camel, reinforcing the impression that this is an unstable time.[439] Osniel knows that he is fighting for Achsah. There is more clarity symbolizing a more stable time in Jewish History. Furthermore, Achsah descends from her donkey with complete control, hinting to a greater level of national stability that exists during these days. For Osniel to win Achsah's hand in marriage it requires military victory. This too symbolizes Bnei

---

[438] Radak (Yehoshua 15:18) and implied by the Metzudas Dovid (Yehoshua 15:19). Alternatively, first Osniel asks and then she asks for more (Ralbag Shoftim 3:30).

[439] See Double Take *A Blind Date Perhaps, But a Blind Marriage* for an additional angle on Rivka's falling off of the camel.

Yisrael's current stage in history. In contrast to Rivka's time period, the beginning of a nation, where the future was unknown, things are now visibly stable. Bnei Yisrael have transformed from a family into a nation and are now ready to settle the land.

THE NAME ACHSAH

The name Achsah means *princess*.[440] On a simple level, Achsah serves the role of a princess, as she is the prize to be won by a chivalrous military hero. However, there is another level as well. She represents the women of Bnei Yisrael and now, at home, the women of Bnei Yisrael are princesses.

APPLYING TEXT TO LIFE: THE HASHKAFIC MESSAGE

Both Achsah and the Bnos Tzlafchad demonstrate deep commitment and love for Eretz Yisrael. Women's special love for, and role in developing Eretz Yisrael should not be overlooked.[441]

Another significant religious conclusion to draw from our analysis is the remarkable influence that one's family and tribe has. Values are passed down from parents to children and develop in societies. The eagerness of Kalev, Osniel, Achsah and the Bnos Tzlafchad reflect that entire tribe's zeal. However, it may not be by chance that the stories are about women and most characters presented are women. In addition to demonstrating that women, who traditionally do not go to war and inherit land, are equally passionate, as previously mentioned, there may be another element. Perhaps family cultures are more influenced by women than men. The Navi chooses stories of Achsah and the Bnos Tzlafchad in order to reveal an important ingredient in successfully passing these values from generation to generation: women who care.[442]

---

[440] See Yeshayahu (3:18). Alternatively, the Gemara (Temurah 16a) traces the name Achsah to the root כעס *anger* explaining that any man would be mad as his wife once he has seen Achsah's beauty.

[441] According to the Kli Yakar (Bamidbar 13:2) Moshe should have sent female spies for they would have certainly returned with a positive report about Eretz Yisrael.

[442] Ibn Ezra (Mishlei 1:8)

On a simple level, we should learn from Yehuda and Yosef, who serve as religious role models exemplifying impeccable dedication and passion to settling the land. Settling Eretz Yisrael, like all religious behavior, should be taken seriously and done eagerly. The Navi rewards Yehuda and Yosef for their devotion.

Lastly, there is another significant conclusion. In light of comparing and contrasting Achsah to Rivka, and the Navi's message that things come around in a full circle, the religious point is clear. First Am Yisrael is built and then it can conquer and inhabit Eretz Yisrael.